TESTAMENT

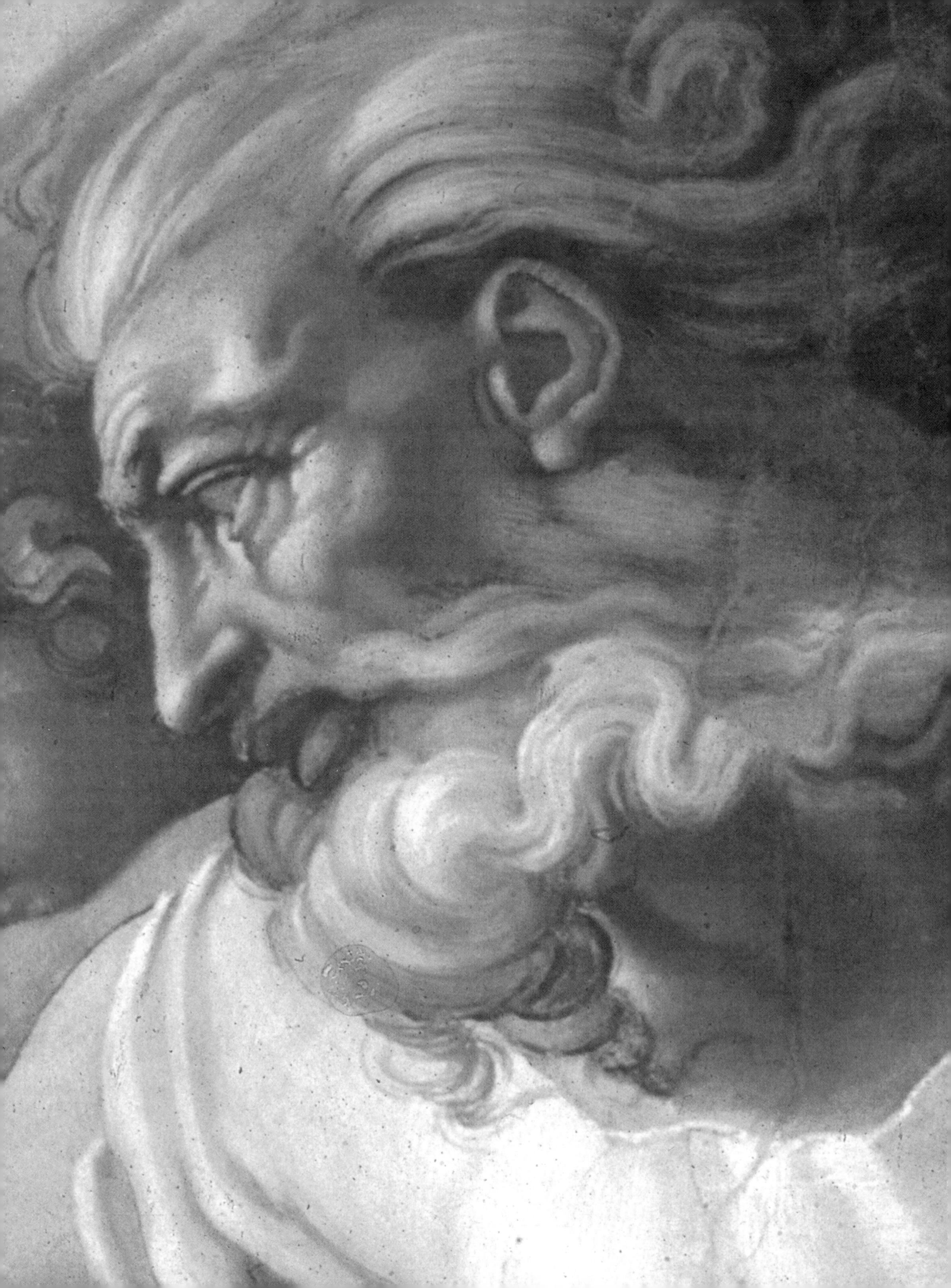

TESTAMENT

METRON
PRESS™

TESTAMENT

ISBN 1-58516 - 765 - 7

Printed & Bound in Canada
Eng. Comic - Testament - 112933
ABS - 7/03 - 25,000 —Amerkml
Metron Press is an imprint of the American Bible Society New York.

CONTENTS

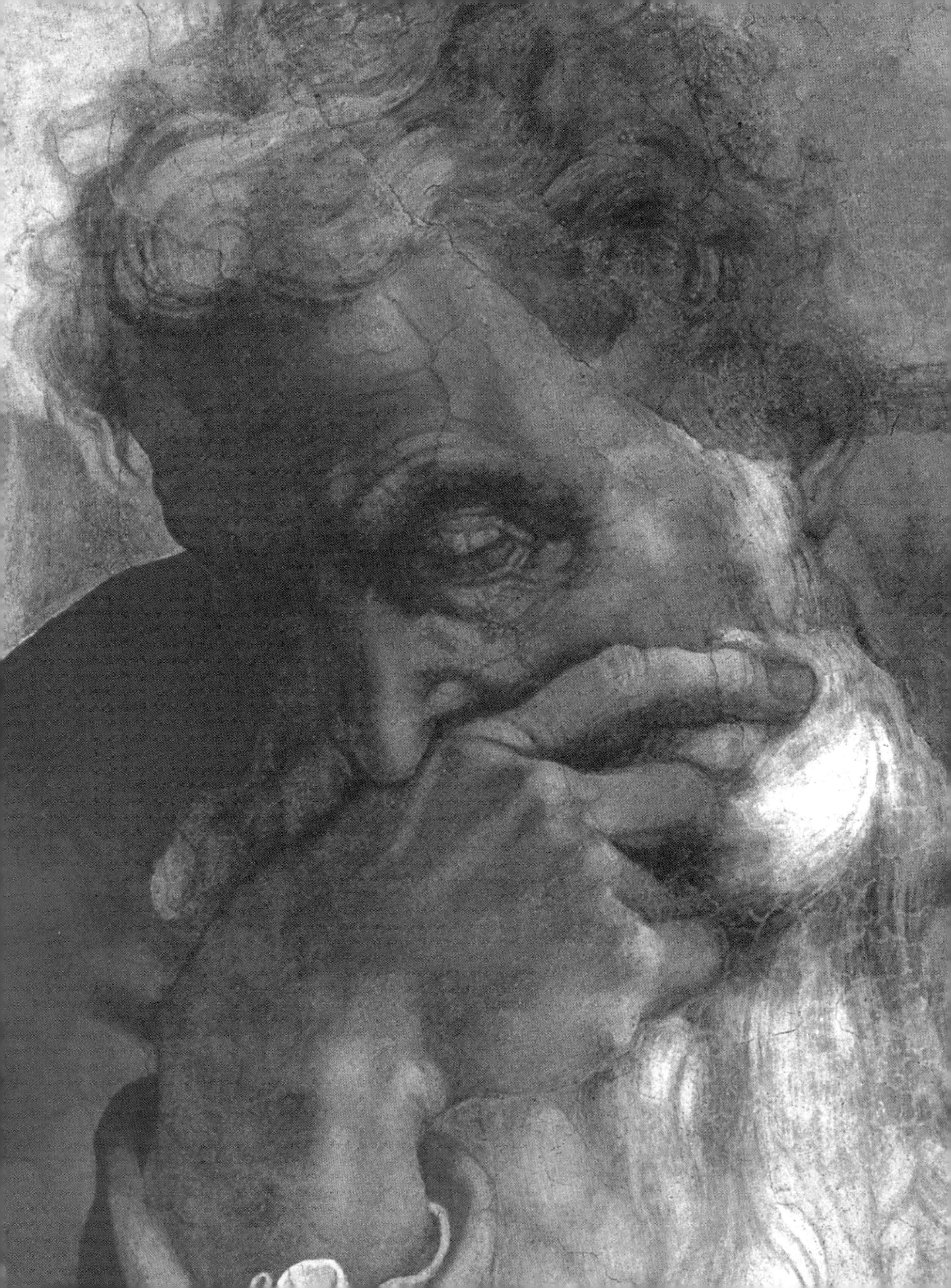

INTRODUCTION

I love comics, I always have. They combine the real and the ideal in wonderful ways that fire our imagination and link us to a world transformed in which decency, goodness, and humanity are affirmed, even if they do not always win. So When Mario Ruiz came to me with the first example of what would become Testament, I was immediately excited. Now that I have had the privilege of seeing the completed work, I am deeply moved.

The book that you hold in your hands is a timely version of the world's most timeless stories. Whenever they were first written, by whomever they were first told, they speak directly to us, right here, right now. In fact, they are about us and the world in which we live, told with the words and images that we really use. In that way, the authors and artists of Testament have kept alive the ancient tradition of telling these tales in ways that could be easily understood by all who wanted to listen. Interest, not a particular dogma, has always been the best door through which to enter these stories. By locating the telling in a bar, a place where people really do come together, they demonstrate their understanding that these stories were always meant to reach us where we really live.

The words and pictures in this book will help you find the best parts of yourself and those around you. In it you will meet good guys and bad guys, heroes and heroines. And even though they are characters from a time long past, they are very much like us. They want a safe place to hang out, the love of their family and friends, and to leave the world a little bit better than they found it. In fact, that is why these stories still work so well after all these years.

The authors of Testament have pulled off a major achievement in returning these stories to their rightful audience, you and me. In fact, one of the most beautiful things about this book, is that it has so much love for both the ancient author and the current audience, that it puts neither on a pedestal. There is no distance here, between the stories and the audience, just a wonderful opportunity to hear for ourselves what these stories say to us. After all, they belong, not to any one group or faith, but to all of us who are looking for everything from a better read, to a better life. Testament offers us both.

Rabbi Bradley Hirschfield
Vice President
CLAL–The National Jewish
Center for Learning and Leadership

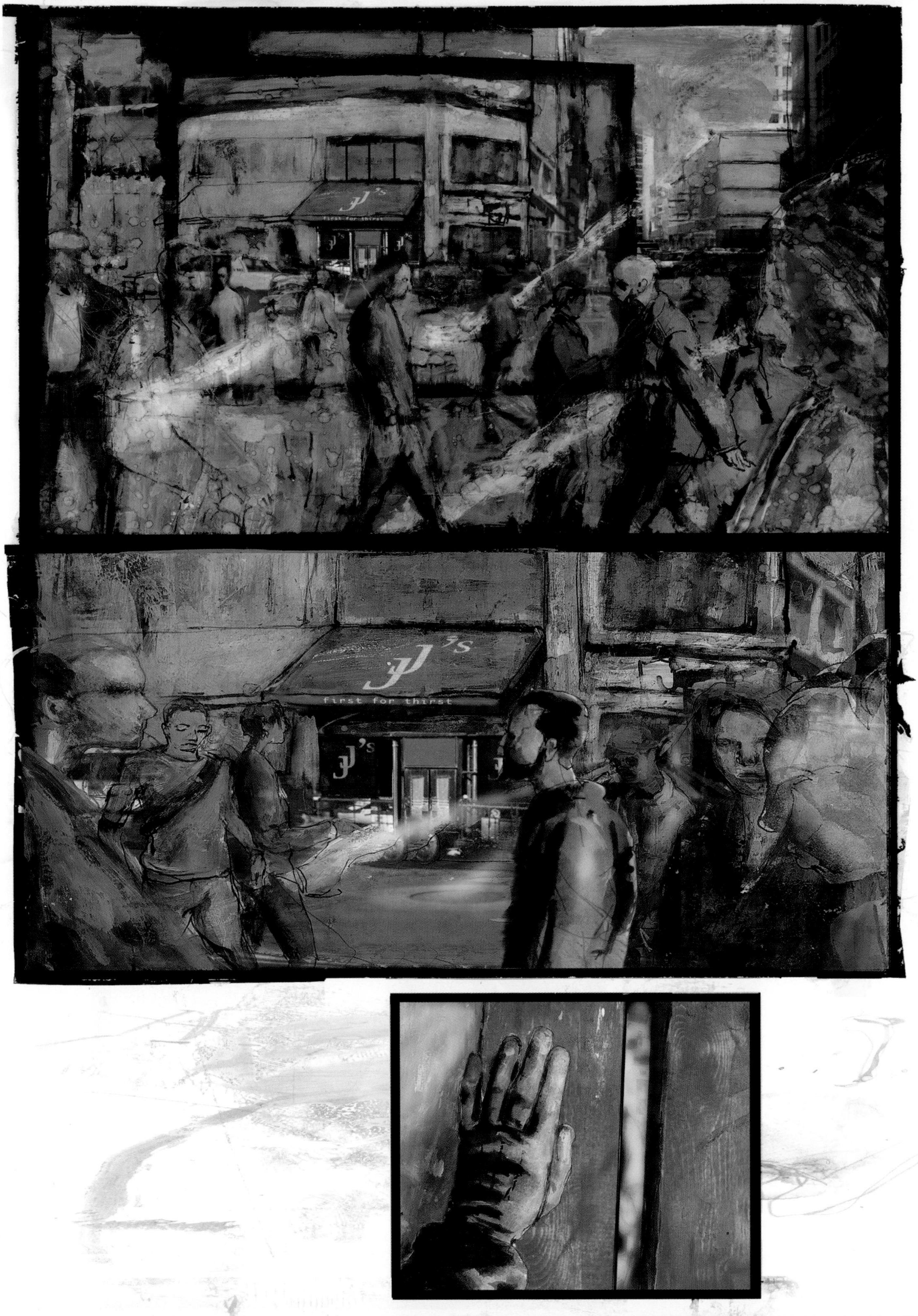
first for thirst
first for thirst

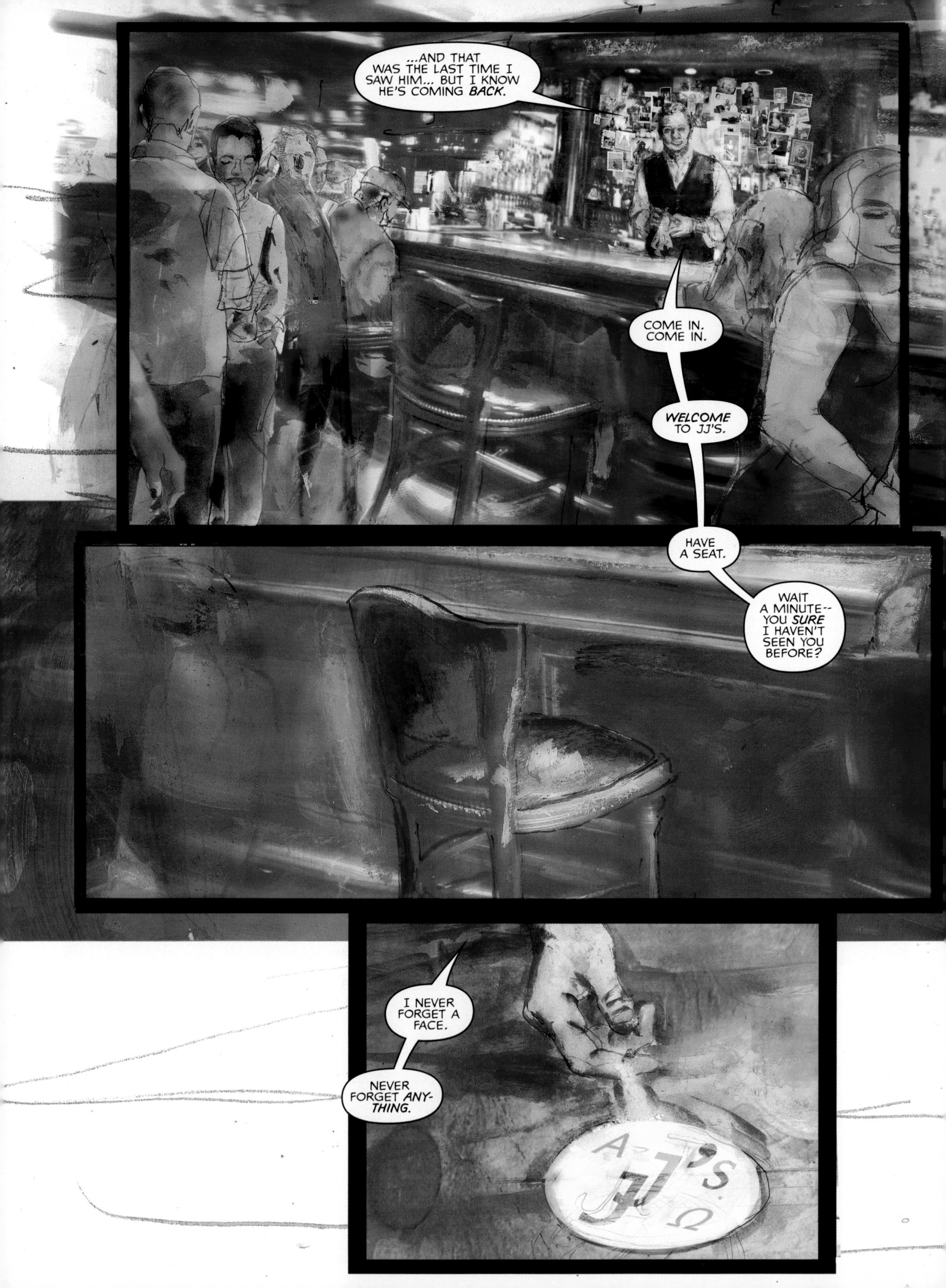
...AND THAT WAS THE LAST TIME I SAW HIM... BUT I KNOW HE'S COMING *BACK*.
COME IN. COME IN.
WELCOME TO JJ'S.
HAVE A SEAT.
WAIT A MINUTE-- YOU *SURE* I HAVEN'T SEEN YOU BEFORE?
I NEVER FORGET A FACE.
NEVER FORGET *ANY-THING*.
JJ'S

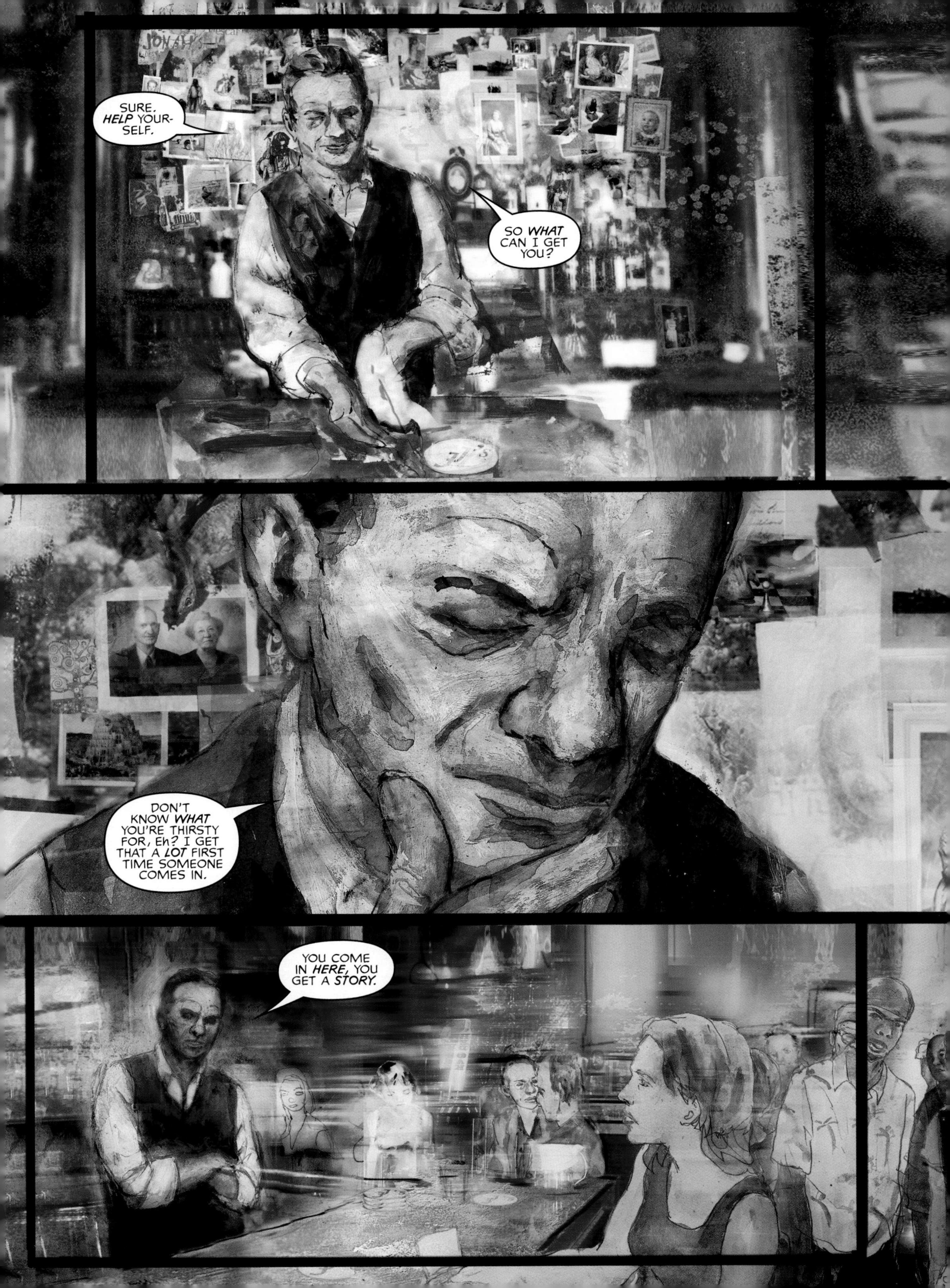
SURE. HELP YOURSELF.
SO WHAT CAN I GET YOU?
DON'T KNOW WHAT YOU'RE THIRSTY FOR, Eh? I GET THAT A LOT FIRST TIME SOMEONE COMES IN.
YOU COME IN HERE, YOU GET A STORY.

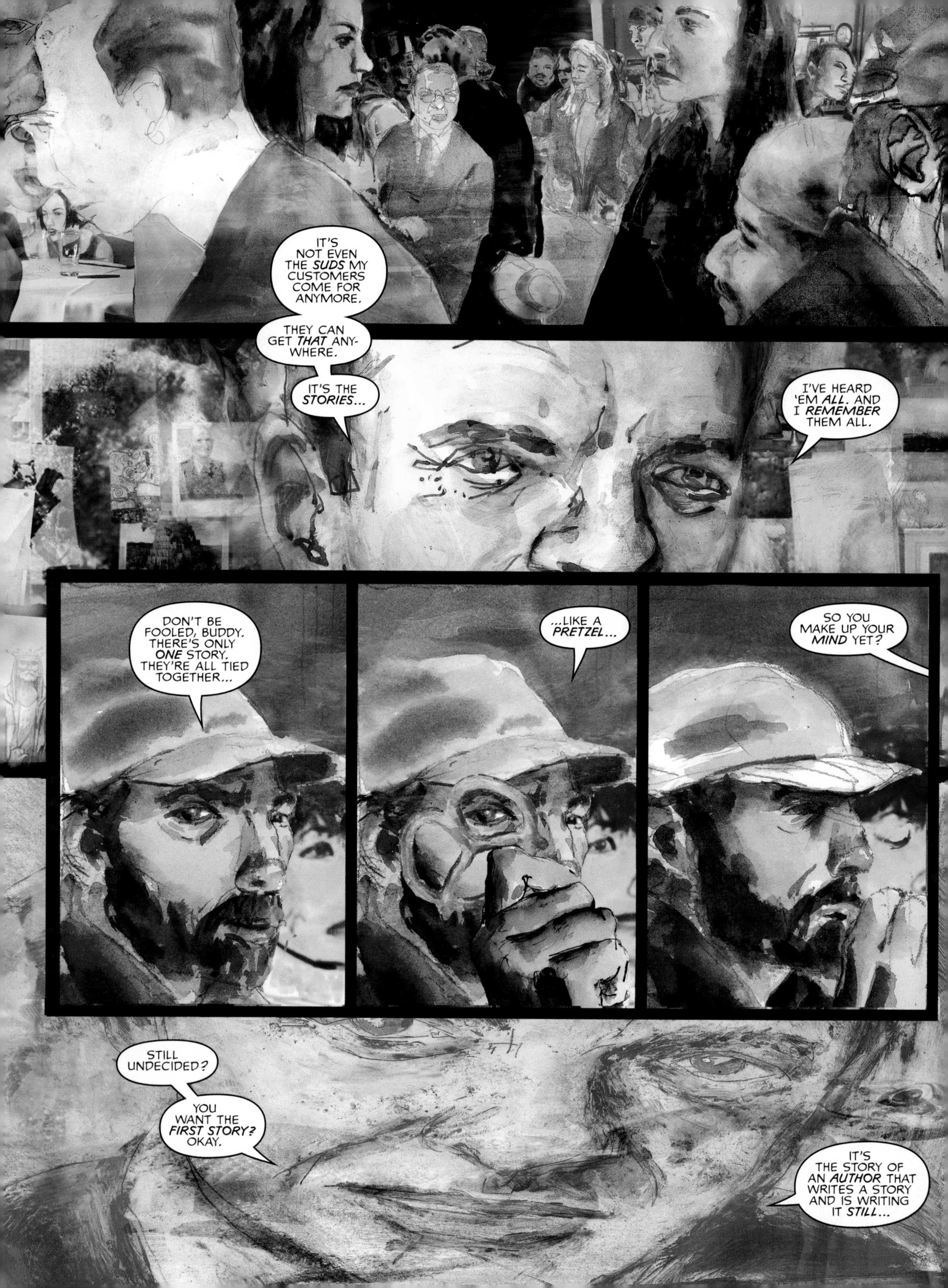
IT'S NOT EVEN THE SUDS MY CUSTOMERS COME FOR ANYMORE.
THEY CAN GET THAT ANY-WHERE.
IT'S THE STORIES...
I'VE HEARD 'EM ALL. AND I REMEMBER THEM ALL.
DON'T BE FOOLED, BUDDY. THERE'S ONLY ONE STORY. THEY'RE ALL TIED TOGETHER...
...LIKE A PRETZEL...
SO YOU MAKE UP YOUR MIND YET?
STILL UNDECIDED?
YOU WANT THE FIRST STORY? OKAY.
IT'S THE STORY OF AN AUTHOR THAT WRITES A STORY AND IS WRITING IT STILL...

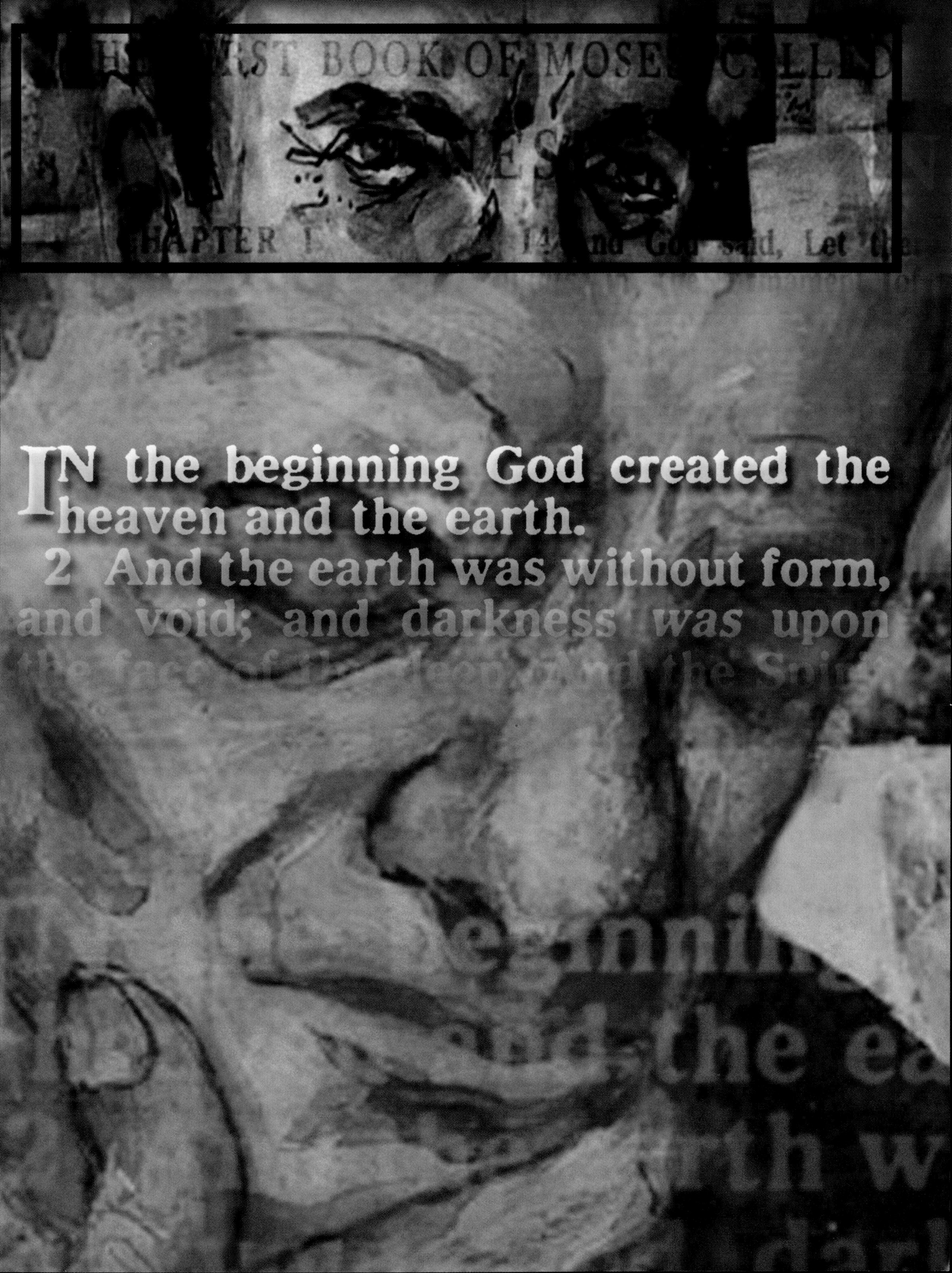

IN the beginning God created the heaven and the earth.

2 And the earth was without form, and void; and darkness was upon the face of the deep. And the Spirit

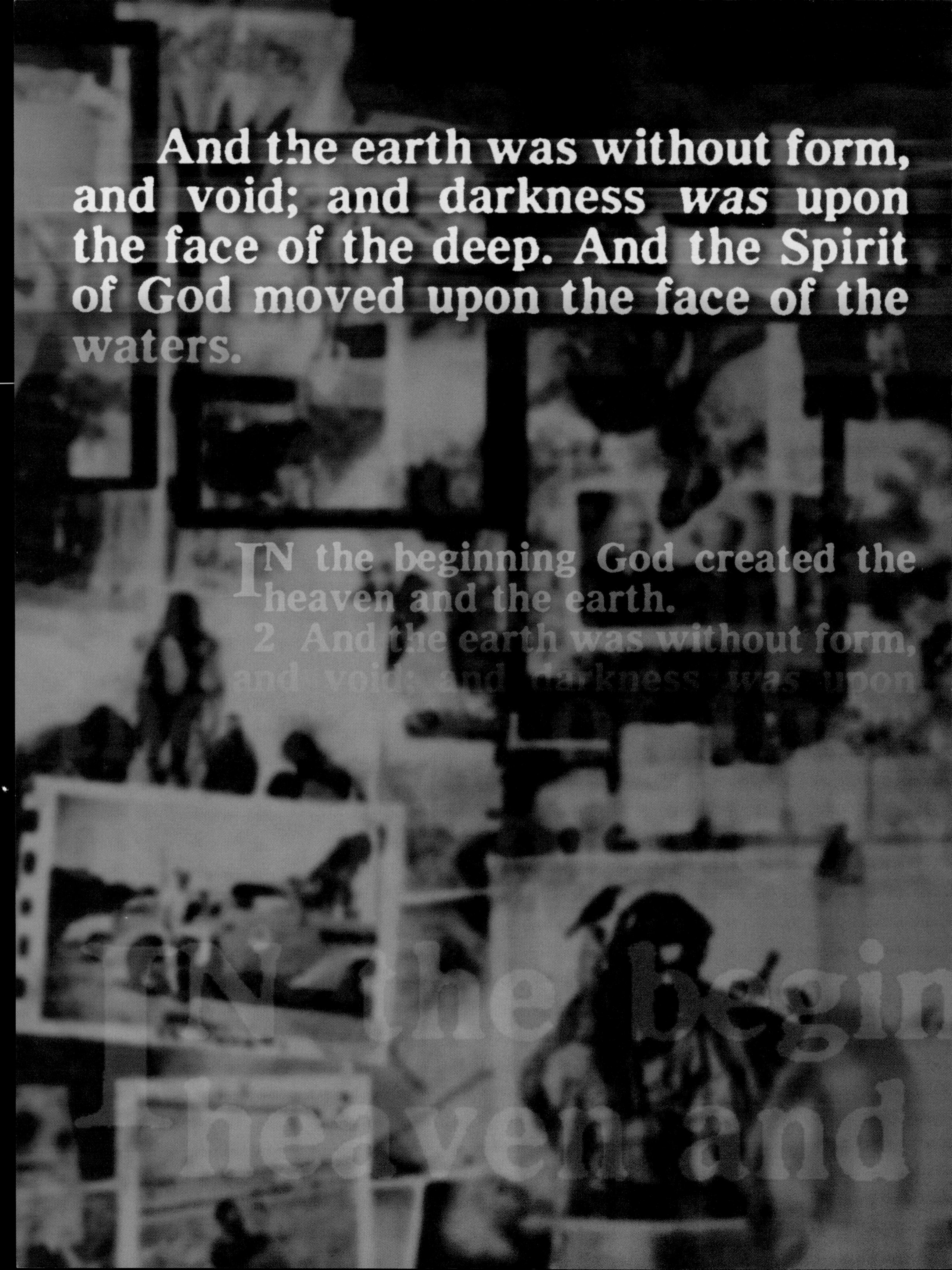
And the earth was without form, and void; and darkness *was* upon the face of the deep. And the Spirit of God moved upon the face of the waters.
IN the beginning God created the heaven and the earth.
2 And the earth was without form, and void; and darkness *was* upon
IN the begin
heaven and

And the Spirit of God moved upon the face of the waters.

3 And God said, Let there be light: and there was light.

4 And God saw the light, that *it was* good: and God divided the light from the darkness.

It begins...

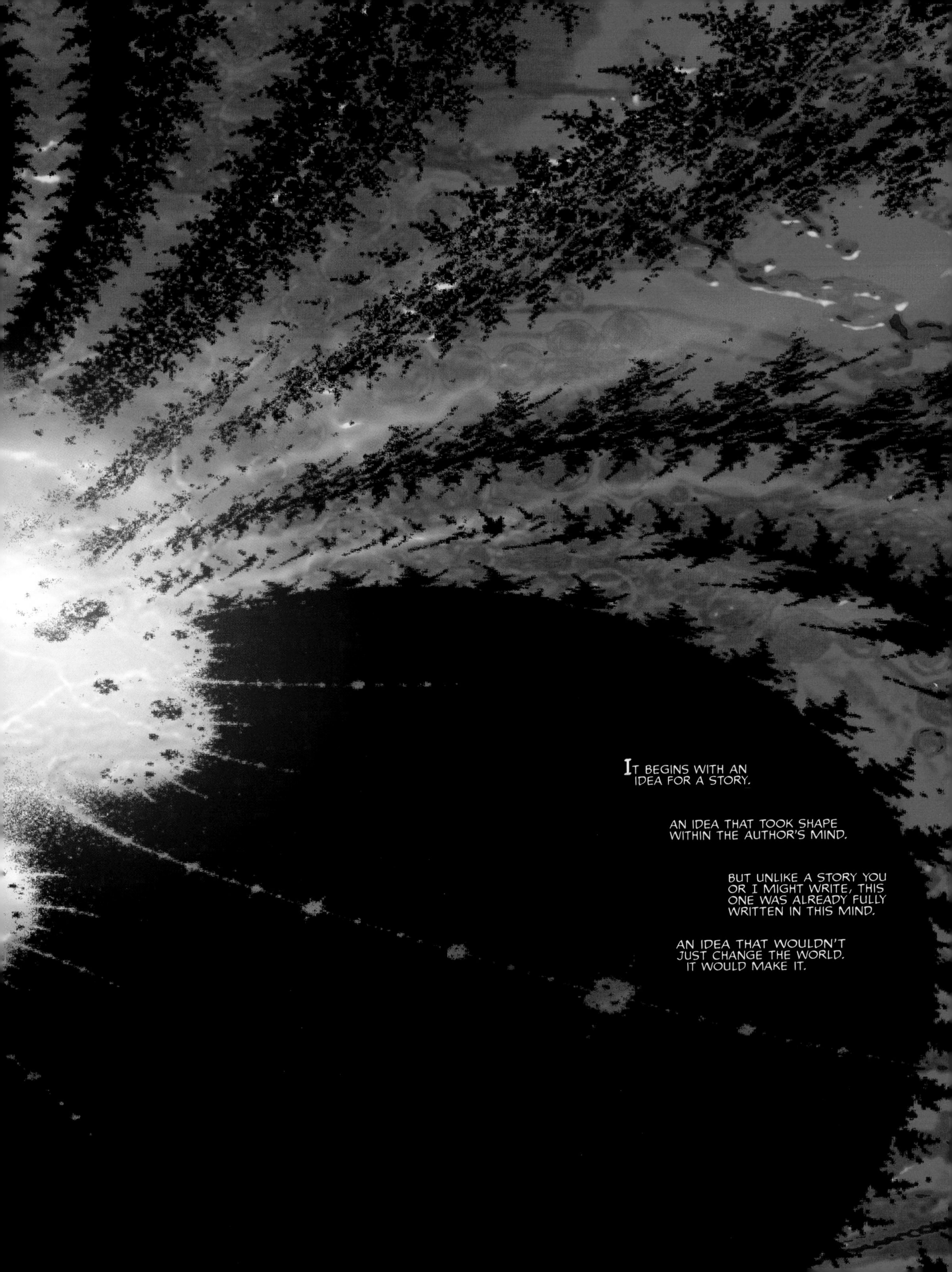
IT BEGINS WITH AN IDEA FOR A STORY.
AN IDEA THAT TOOK SHAPE WITHIN THE AUTHOR'S MIND.
BUT UNLIKE A STORY YOU OR I MIGHT WRITE, THIS ONE WAS ALREADY FULLY WRITTEN IN THIS MIND.
AN IDEA THAT WOULDN'T JUST CHANGE THE WORLD. IT WOULD MAKE IT.

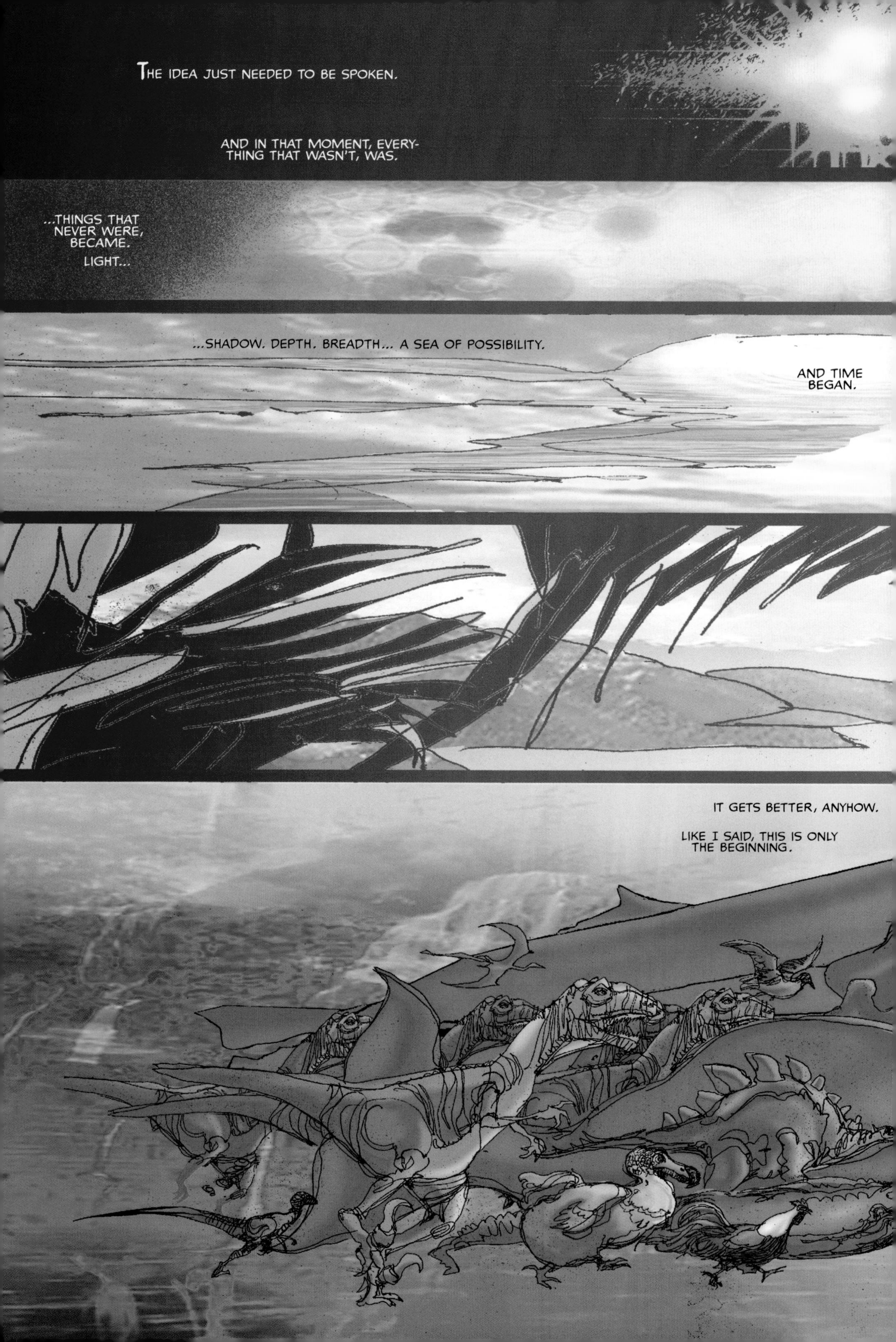
THE IDEA JUST NEEDED TO BE SPOKEN.
AND IN THAT MOMENT, EVERYTHING THAT WASN'T, WAS.
...THINGS THAT NEVER WERE, BECAME.
LIGHT...
...SHADOW. DEPTH. BREADTH... A SEA OF POSSIBILITY.
AND TIME BEGAN.
IT GETS BETTER, ANYHOW.
LIKE I SAID, THIS IS ONLY THE BEGINNING.

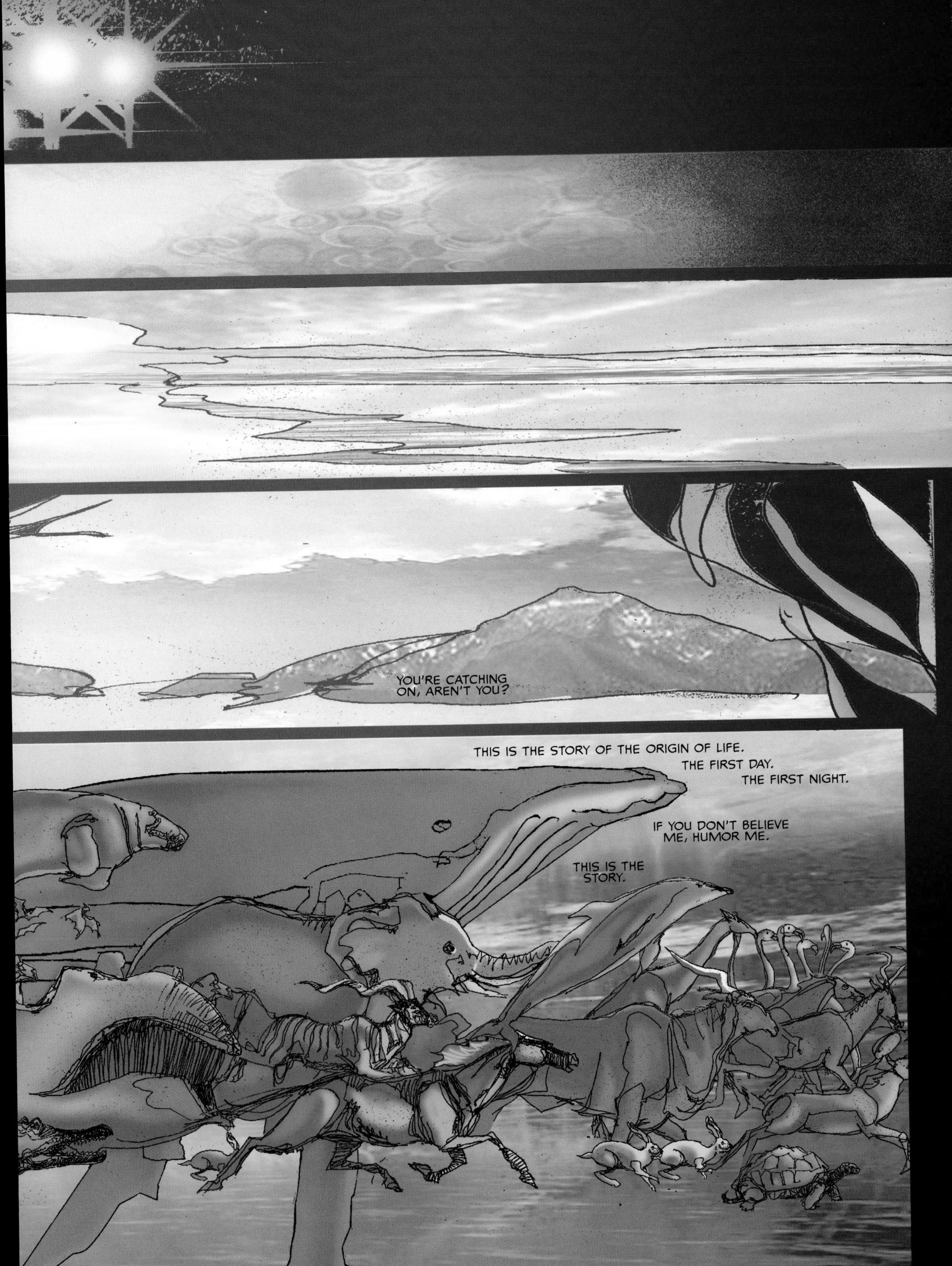
YOU'RE CATCHING ON, AREN'T YOU?
THIS IS THE STORY OF THE ORIGIN OF LIFE.
THE FIRST DAY.
THE FIRST NIGHT.
IF YOU DON'T BELIEVE ME, HUMOR ME.
THIS IS THE STORY.

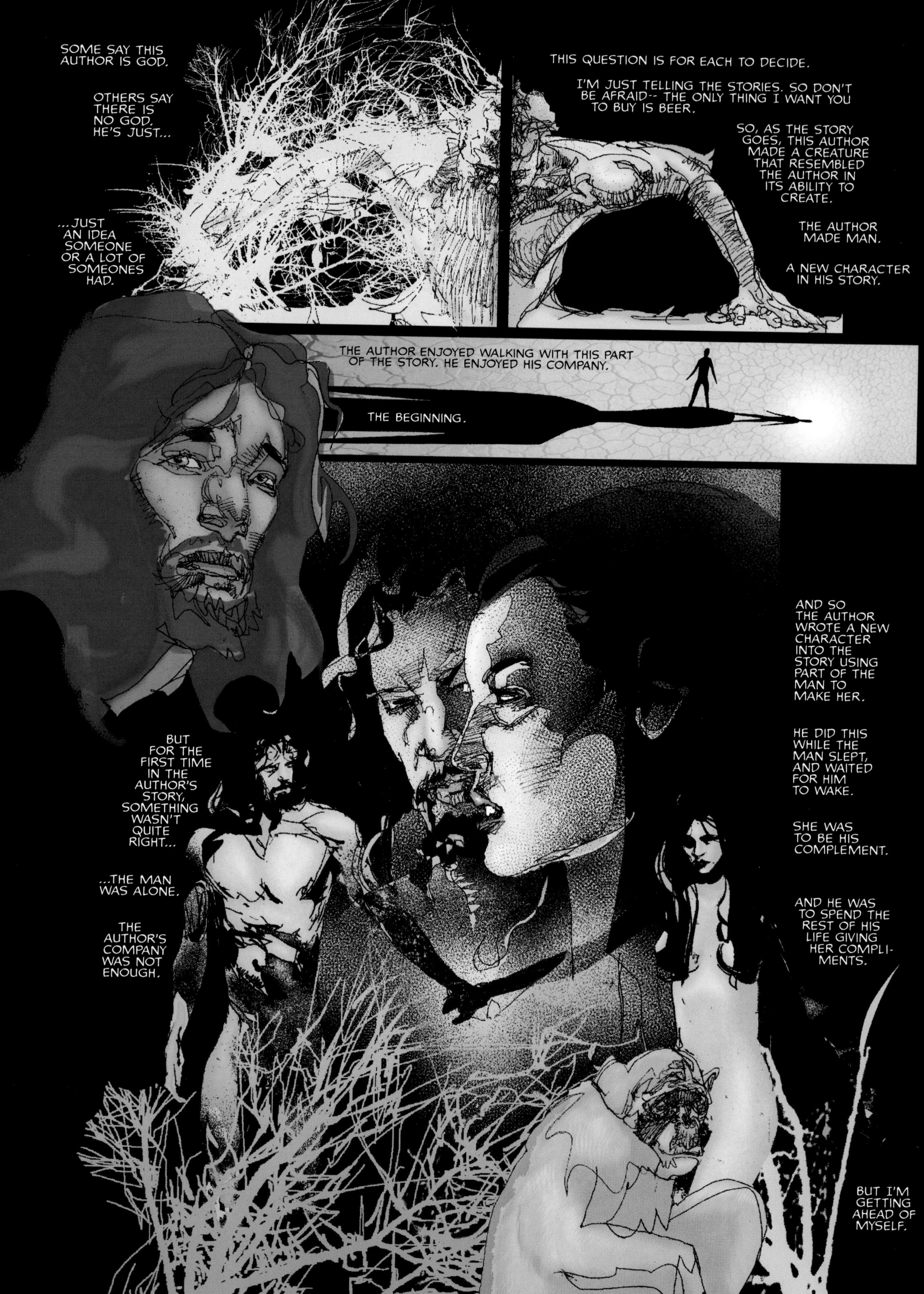
SOME SAY THIS AUTHOR IS GOD.
OTHERS SAY THERE IS NO GOD. HE'S JUST...
...JUST AN IDEA SOMEONE OR A LOT OF SOMEONES HAD.
THIS QUESTION IS FOR EACH TO DECIDE.
I'M JUST TELLING THE STORIES. SO DON'T BE AFRAID-- THE ONLY THING I WANT YOU TO BUY IS BEER.
SO, AS THE STORY GOES, THIS AUTHOR MADE A CREATURE THAT RESEMBLED THE AUTHOR IN ITS ABILITY TO CREATE.
THE AUTHOR MADE MAN.
A NEW CHARACTER IN HIS STORY.
THE AUTHOR ENJOYED WALKING WITH THIS PART OF THE STORY. HE ENJOYED HIS COMPANY.
THE BEGINNING.
BUT FOR THE FIRST TIME IN THE AUTHOR'S STORY, SOMETHING WASN'T QUITE RIGHT...
...THE MAN WAS ALONE.
THE AUTHOR'S COMPANY WAS NOT ENOUGH.
AND SO THE AUTHOR WROTE A NEW CHARACTER INTO THE STORY USING PART OF THE MAN TO MAKE HER.
HE DID THIS WHILE THE MAN SLEPT, AND WAITED FOR HIM TO WAKE.
SHE WAS TO BE HIS COMPLEMENT.
AND HE WAS TO SPEND THE REST OF HIS LIFE GIVING HER COMPLI- MENTS.
BUT I'M GETTING AHEAD OF MYSELF.

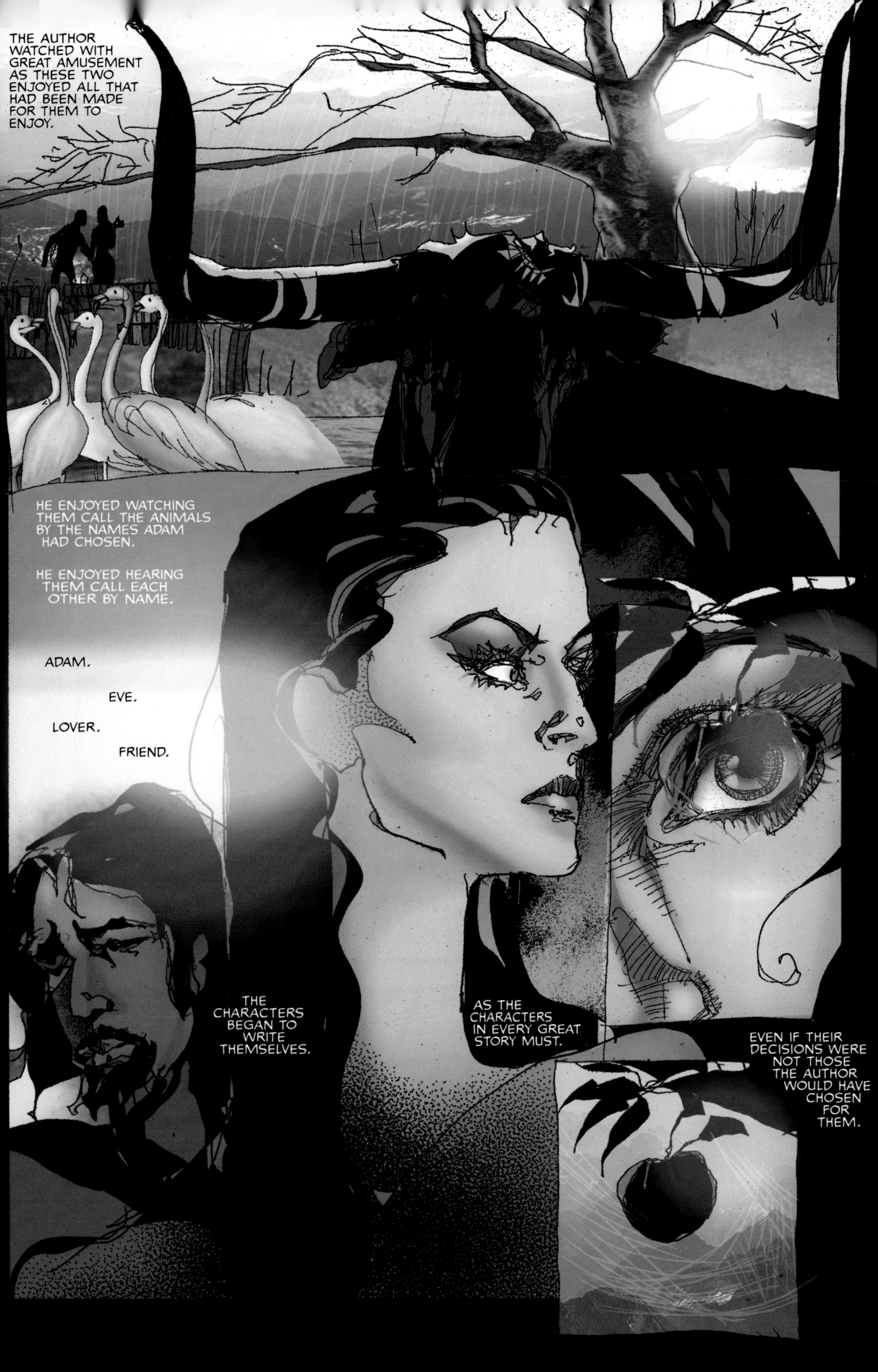
THE AUTHOR WATCHED WITH GREAT AMUSEMENT AS THESE TWO ENJOYED ALL THAT HAD BEEN MADE FOR THEM TO ENJOY.
HE ENJOYED WATCHING THEM CALL THE ANIMALS BY THE NAMES ADAM HAD CHOSEN.
HE ENJOYED HEARING THEM CALL EACH OTHER BY NAME.
ADAM.
EVE.
LOVER.
FRIEND.
THE CHARACTERS BEGAN TO WRITE THEMSELVES.
AS THE CHARACTERS IN EVERY GREAT STORY MUST.
EVEN IF THEIR DECISIONS WERE NOT THOSE THE AUTHOR WOULD HAVE CHOSEN FOR THEM.

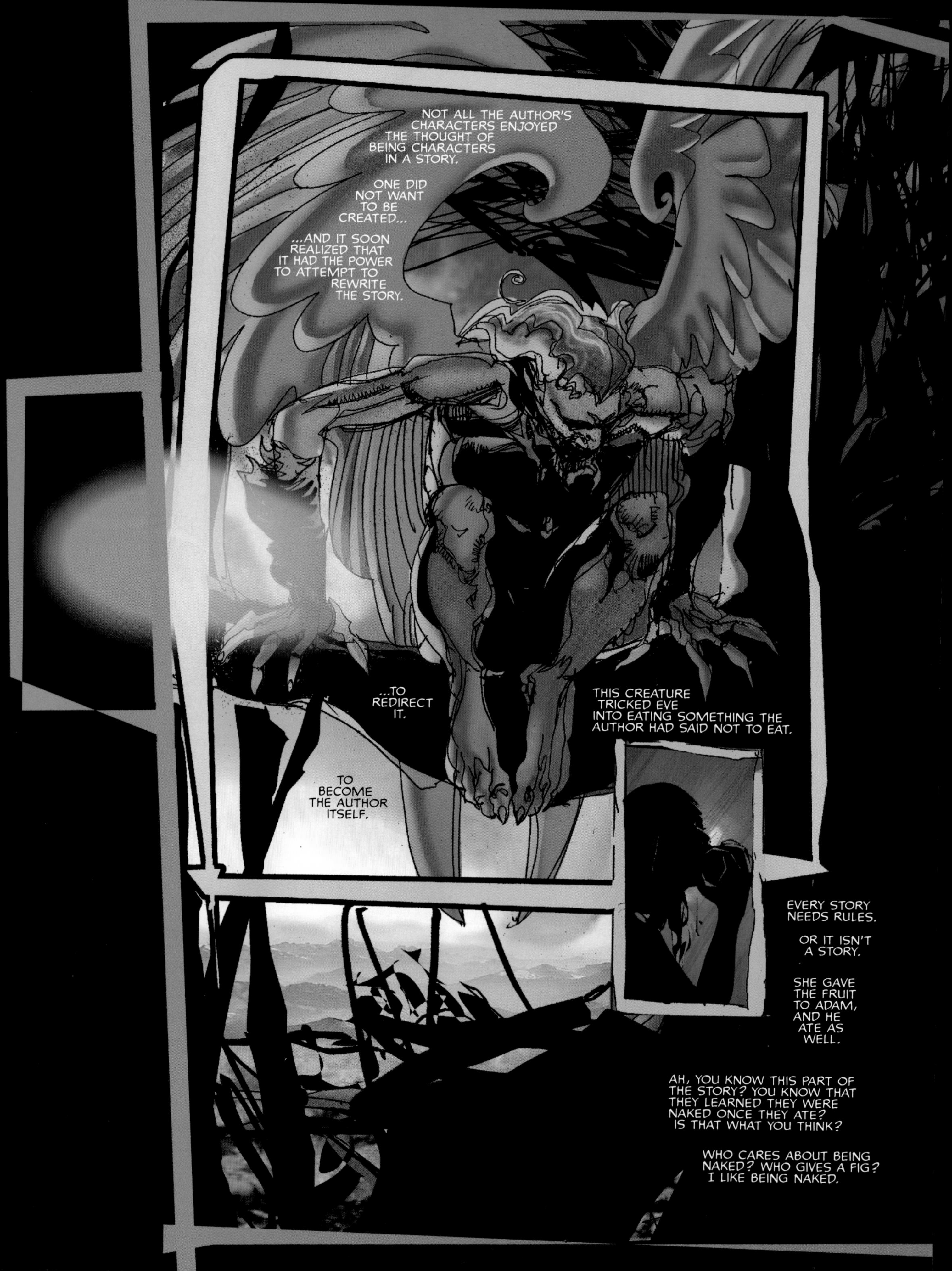
NOT ALL THE AUTHOR'S CHARACTERS ENJOYED THE THOUGHT OF BEING CHARACTERS IN A STORY.
ONE DID NOT WANT TO BE CREATED...
...AND IT SOON REALIZED THAT IT HAD THE POWER TO ATTEMPT TO REWRITE THE STORY.
...TO REDIRECT IT.
TO BECOME THE AUTHOR ITSELF.
THIS CREATURE TRICKED EVE INTO EATING SOMETHING THE AUTHOR HAD SAID NOT TO EAT.
EVERY STORY NEEDS RULES.
OR IT ISN'T A STORY.
SHE GAVE THE FRUIT TO ADAM, AND HE ATE AS WELL.
AH, YOU KNOW THIS PART OF THE STORY? YOU KNOW THAT THEY LEARNED THEY WERE NAKED ONCE THEY ATE? IS THAT WHAT YOU THINK?
WHO CARES ABOUT BEING NAKED? WHO GIVES A FIG? I LIKE BEING NAKED.

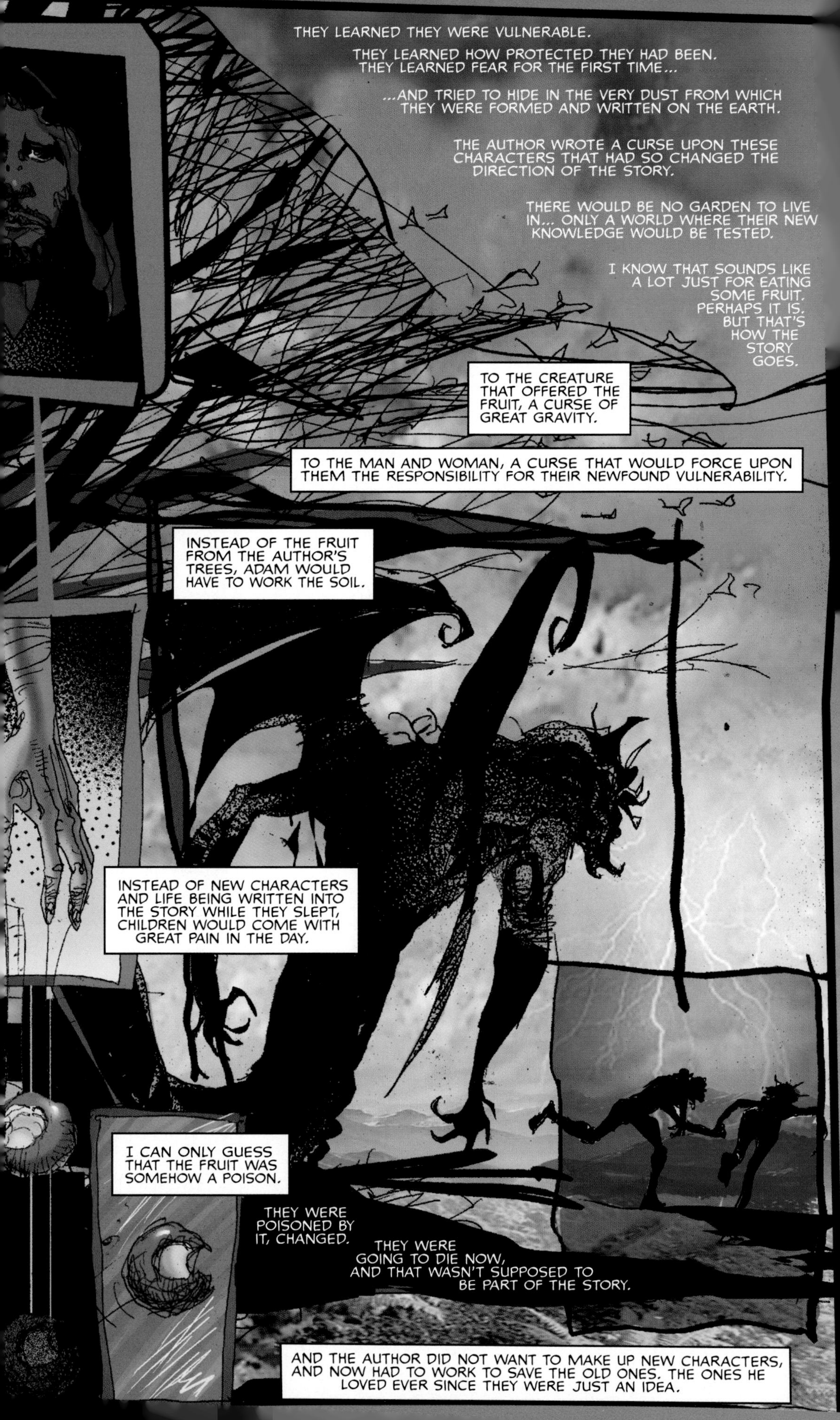

THEY LEARNED THEY WERE VULNERABLE.
THEY LEARNED HOW PROTECTED THEY HAD BEEN. THEY LEARNED FEAR FOR THE FIRST TIME...
...AND TRIED TO HIDE IN THE VERY DUST FROM WHICH THEY WERE FORMED AND WRITTEN ON THE EARTH.
THE AUTHOR WROTE A CURSE UPON THESE CHARACTERS THAT HAD SO CHANGED THE DIRECTION OF THE STORY.
THERE WOULD BE NO GARDEN TO LIVE IN... ONLY A WORLD WHERE THEIR NEW KNOWLEDGE WOULD BE TESTED.
I KNOW THAT SOUNDS LIKE A LOT JUST FOR EATING SOME FRUIT. PERHAPS IT IS. BUT THAT'S HOW THE STORY GOES.
TO THE CREATURE THAT OFFERED THE FRUIT, A CURSE OF GREAT GRAVITY.
TO THE MAN AND WOMAN, A CURSE THAT WOULD FORCE UPON THEM THE RESPONSIBILITY FOR THEIR NEWFOUND VULNERABILITY.
INSTEAD OF THE FRUIT FROM THE AUTHOR'S TREES, ADAM WOULD HAVE TO WORK THE SOIL.
INSTEAD OF NEW CHARACTERS AND LIFE BEING WRITTEN INTO THE STORY WHILE THEY SLEPT, CHILDREN WOULD COME WITH GREAT PAIN IN THE DAY.
I CAN ONLY GUESS THAT THE FRUIT WAS SOMEHOW A POISON.
THEY WERE POISONED BY IT, CHANGED.
THEY WERE GOING TO DIE NOW, AND THAT WASN'T SUPPOSED TO BE PART OF THE STORY.
AND THE AUTHOR DID NOT WANT TO MAKE UP NEW CHARACTERS, AND NOW HAD TO WORK TO SAVE THE OLD ONES. THE ONES HE LOVED EVER SINCE THEY WERE JUST AN IDEA.

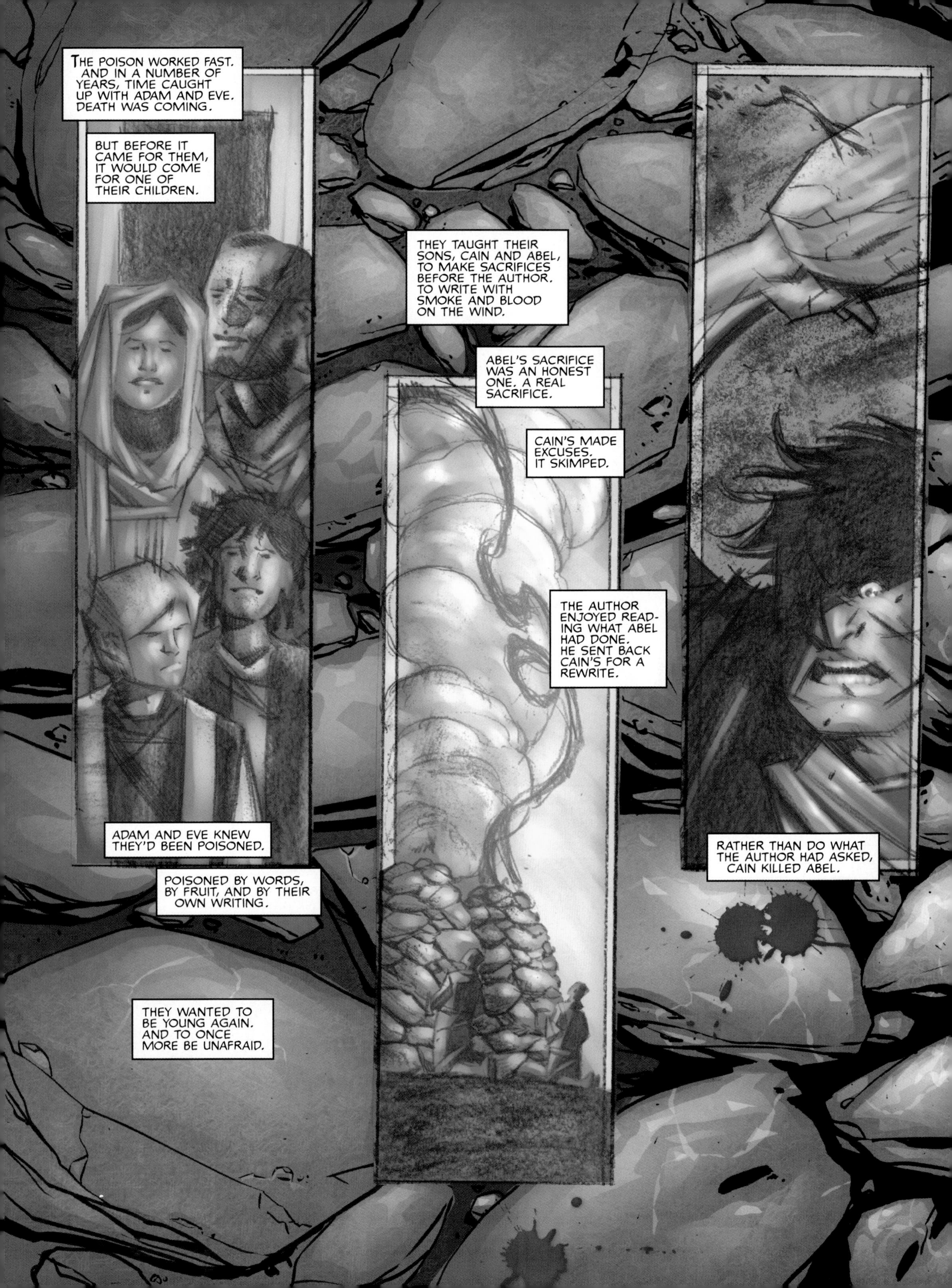

THE POISON WORKED FAST. AND IN A NUMBER OF YEARS, TIME CAUGHT UP WITH ADAM AND EVE. DEATH WAS COMING.
BUT BEFORE IT CAME FOR THEM, IT WOULD COME FOR ONE OF THEIR CHILDREN.
ADAM AND EVE KNEW THEY'D BEEN POISONED.
POISONED BY WORDS, BY FRUIT, AND BY THEIR OWN WRITING.
THEY WANTED TO BE YOUNG AGAIN. AND TO ONCE MORE BE UNAFRAID.
THEY TAUGHT THEIR SONS, CAIN AND ABEL, TO MAKE SACRIFICES BEFORE THE AUTHOR. TO WRITE WITH SMOKE AND BLOOD ON THE WIND.
ABEL'S SACRIFICE WAS AN HONEST ONE. A REAL SACRIFICE.
CAIN'S MADE EXCUSES. IT SKIMPED.
THE AUTHOR ENJOYED READING WHAT ABEL HAD DONE. HE SENT BACK CAIN'S FOR A REWRITE.
RATHER THAN DO WHAT THE AUTHOR HAD ASKED, CAIN KILLED ABEL.

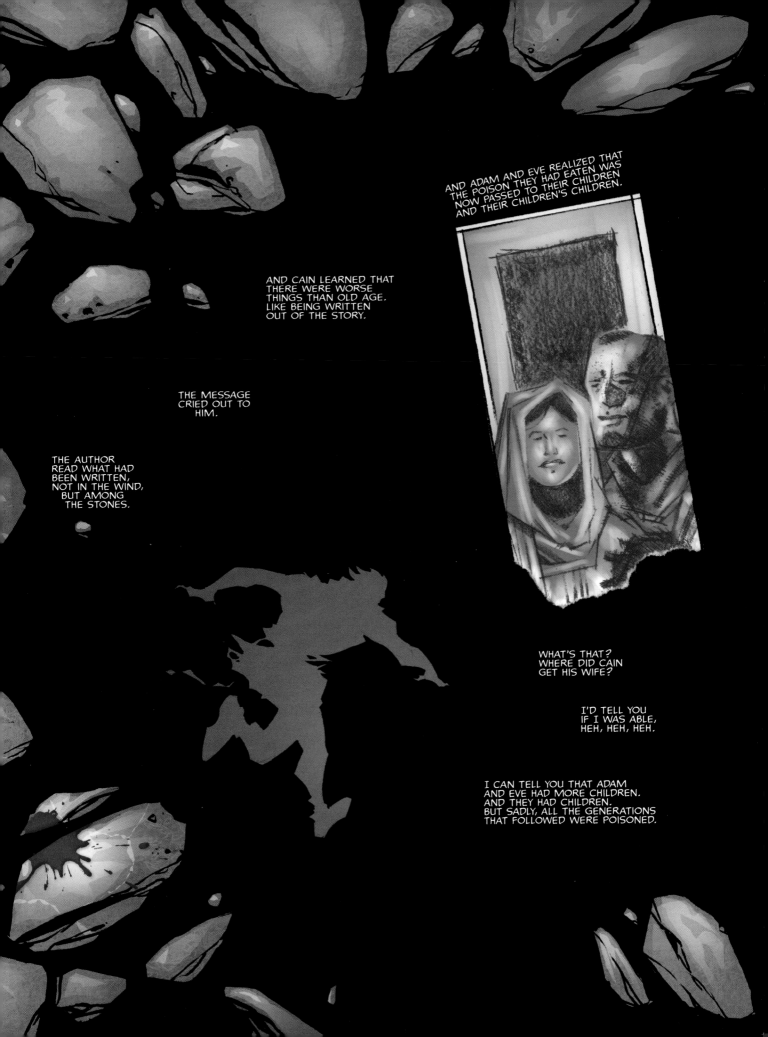

AND ADAM AND EVE REALIZED THAT
THE POISON THEY HAD EATEN WAS
NOW PASSED TO THEIR CHILDREN
AND THEIR CHILDREN'S CHILDREN.

AND CAIN LEARNED THAT
THERE WERE WORSE
THINGS THAN OLD AGE.
LIKE BEING WRITTEN
OUT OF THE STORY.

THE MESSAGE
CRIED OUT TO
HIM.

THE AUTHOR
READ WHAT HAD
BEEN WRITTEN,
NOT IN THE WIND,
BUT AMONG
THE STONES.

WHAT'S THAT?
WHERE DID CAIN
GET HIS WIFE?

I'D TELL YOU
IF I WAS ABLE,
HEH, HEH, HEH.

I CAN TELL YOU THAT ADAM
AND EVE HAD MORE CHILDREN.
AND THEY HAD CHILDREN.
BUT SADLY, ALL THE GENERATIONS
THAT FOLLOWED WERE POISONED.

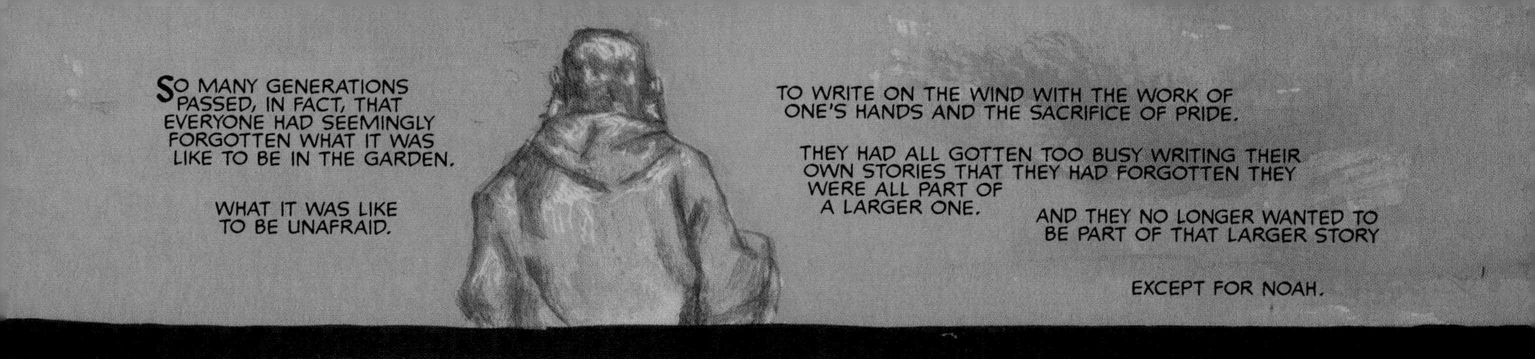
SO MANY GENERATIONS PASSED, IN FACT, THAT EVERYONE HAD SEEMINGLY FORGOTTEN WHAT IT WAS LIKE TO BE IN THE GARDEN.
WHAT IT WAS LIKE TO BE UNAFRAID.
TO WRITE ON THE WIND WITH THE WORK OF ONE'S HANDS AND THE SACRIFICE OF PRIDE.
THEY HAD ALL GOTTEN TOO BUSY WRITING THEIR OWN STORIES THAT THEY HAD FORGOTTEN THEY WERE ALL PART OF A LARGER ONE.
AND THEY NO LONGER WANTED TO BE PART OF THAT LARGER STORY
EXCEPT FOR NOAH.

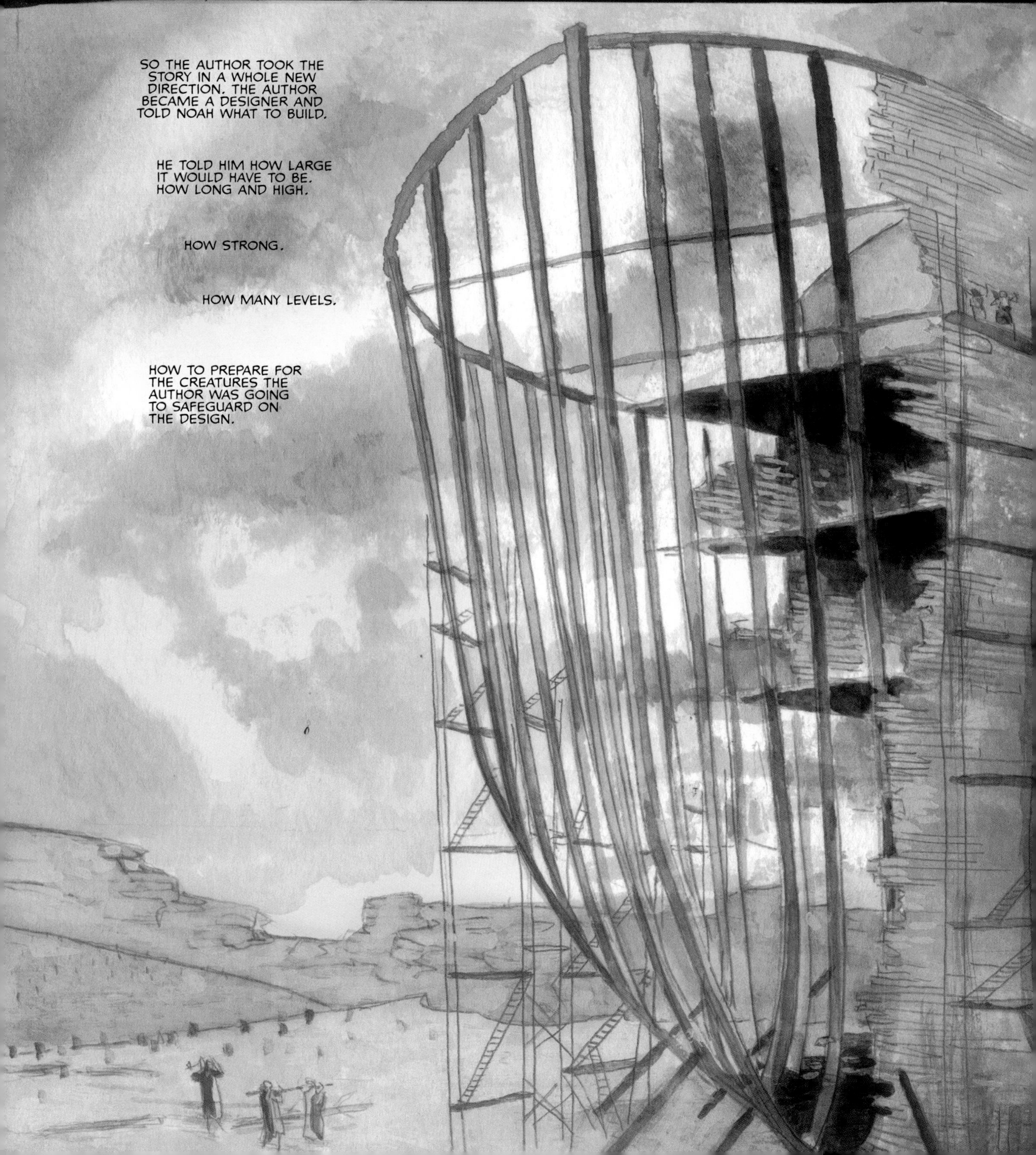
SO THE AUTHOR TOOK THE STORY IN A WHOLE NEW DIRECTION. THE AUTHOR BECAME A DESIGNER AND TOLD NOAH WHAT TO BUILD.
HE TOLD HIM HOW LARGE IT WOULD HAVE TO BE. HOW LONG AND HIGH.
HOW STRONG.
HOW MANY LEVELS.
HOW TO PREPARE FOR THE CREATURES THE AUTHOR WAS GOING TO SAFEGUARD ON THE DESIGN.

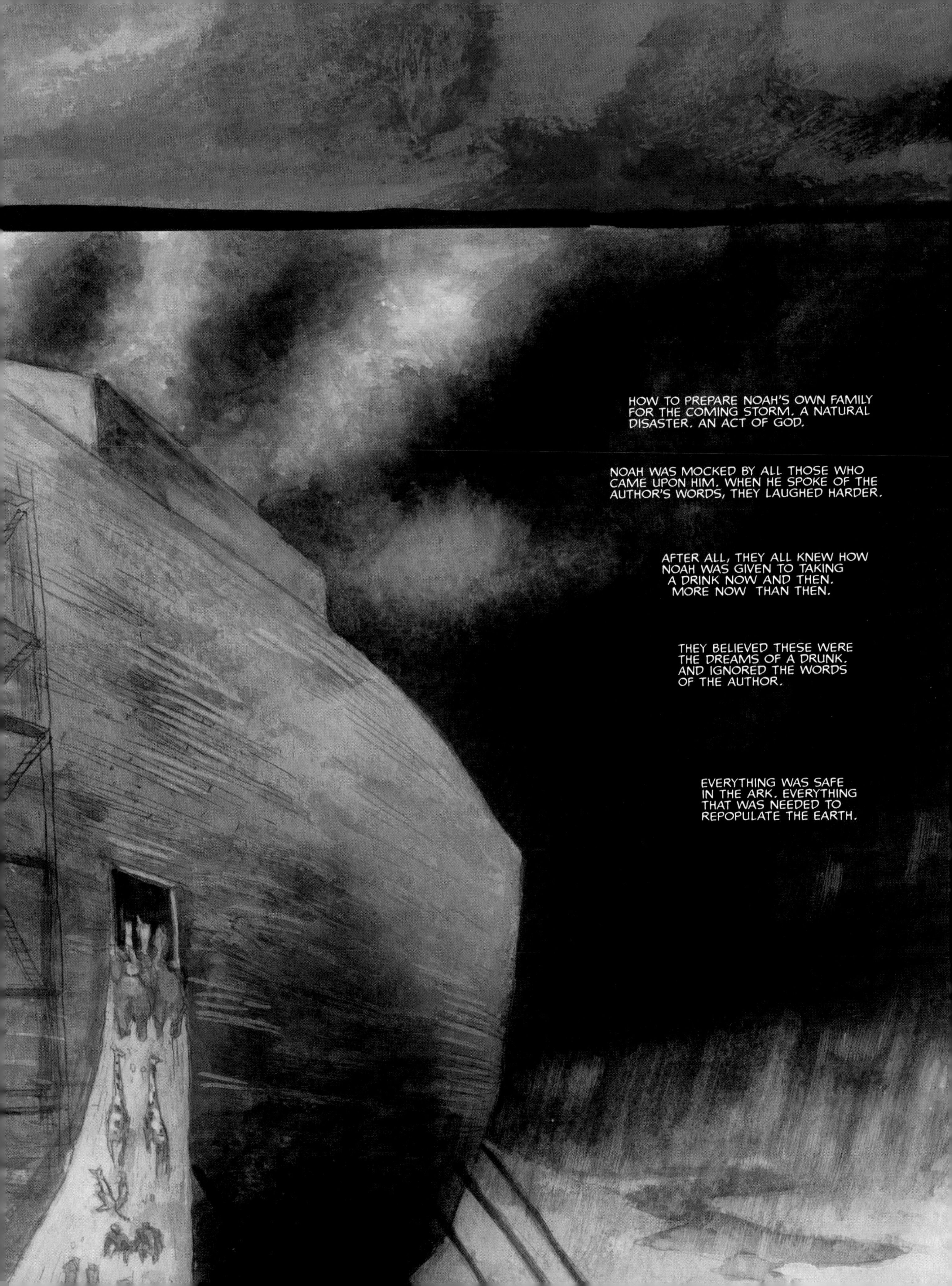
HOW TO PREPARE NOAH'S OWN FAMILY FOR THE COMING STORM. A NATURAL DISASTER. AN ACT OF GOD.
NOAH WAS MOCKED BY ALL THOSE WHO CAME UPON HIM. WHEN HE SPOKE OF THE AUTHOR'S WORDS, THEY LAUGHED HARDER.
AFTER ALL, THEY ALL KNEW HOW NOAH WAS GIVEN TO TAKING A DRINK NOW AND THEN. MORE NOW THAN THEN.
THEY BELIEVED THESE WERE THE DREAMS OF A DRUNK. AND IGNORED THE WORDS OF THE AUTHOR.
EVERYTHING WAS SAFE IN THE ARK. EVERYTHING THAT WAS NEEDED TO REPOPULATE THE EARTH.

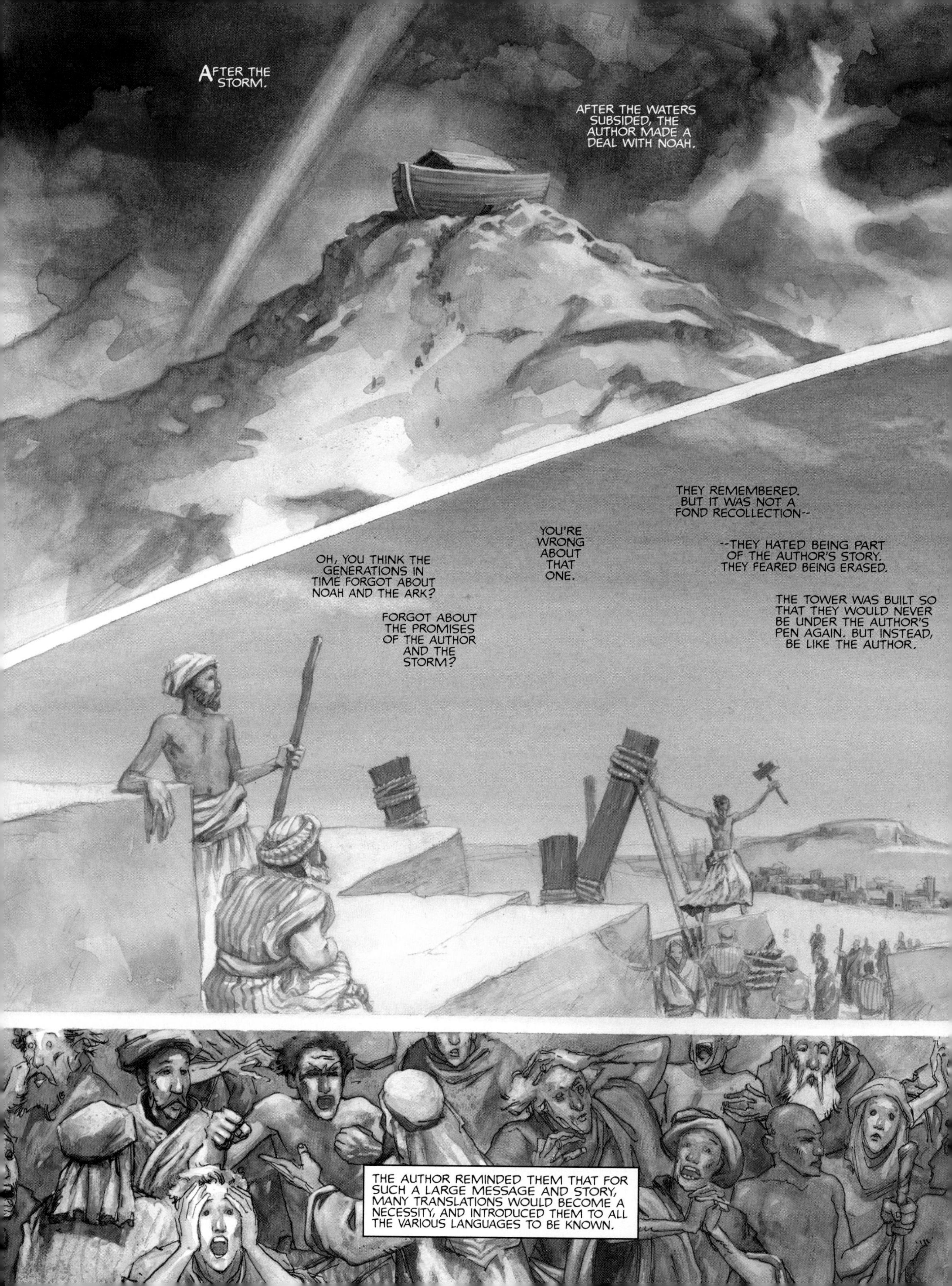
AFTER THE STORM.
AFTER THE WATERS SUBSIDED, THE AUTHOR MADE A DEAL WITH NOAH.
OH, YOU THINK THE GENERATIONS IN TIME FORGOT ABOUT NOAH AND THE ARK?
FORGOT ABOUT THE PROMISES OF THE AUTHOR AND THE STORM?
YOU'RE WRONG ABOUT THAT ONE.
THEY REMEMBERED. BUT IT WAS NOT A FOND RECOLLECTION--
--THEY HATED BEING PART OF THE AUTHOR'S STORY. THEY FEARED BEING ERASED.
THE TOWER WAS BUILT SO THAT THEY WOULD NEVER BE UNDER THE AUTHOR'S PEN AGAIN. BUT INSTEAD, BE LIKE THE AUTHOR.
THE AUTHOR REMINDED THEM THAT FOR SUCH A LARGE MESSAGE AND STORY, MANY TRANSLATIONS WOULD BECOME A NECESSITY, AND INTRODUCED THEM TO ALL THE VARIOUS LANGUAGES TO BE KNOWN.

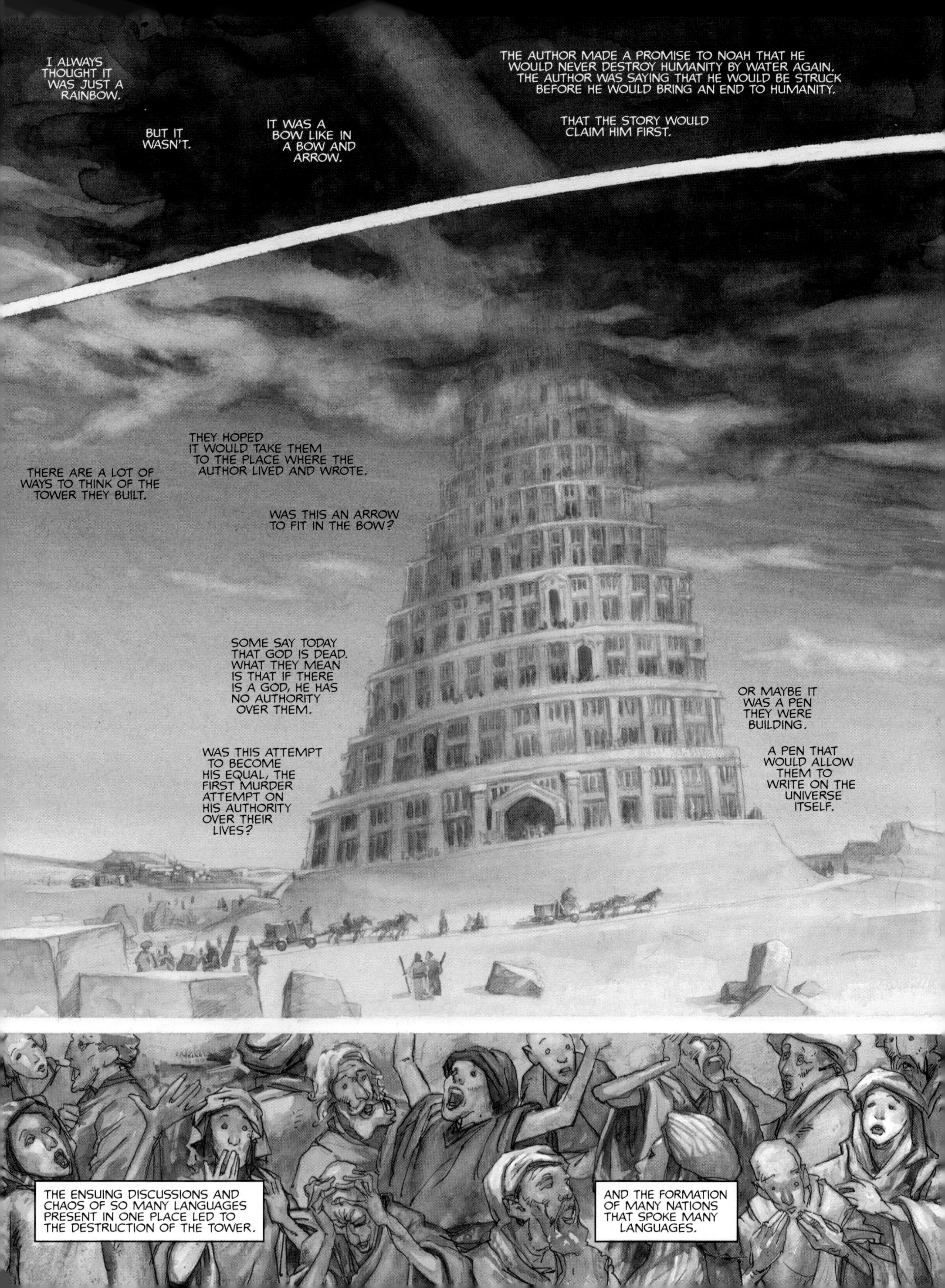
I ALWAYS THOUGHT IT WAS JUST A RAINBOW.
BUT IT WASN'T.
IT WAS A BOW LIKE IN A BOW AND ARROW.
THE AUTHOR MADE A PROMISE TO NOAH THAT HE WOULD NEVER DESTROY HUMANITY BY WATER AGAIN. THE AUTHOR WAS SAYING THAT HE WOULD BE STRUCK BEFORE HE WOULD BRING AN END TO HUMANITY.
THAT THE STORY WOULD CLAIM HIM FIRST.
THERE ARE A LOT OF WAYS TO THINK OF THE TOWER THEY BUILT.
THEY HOPED IT WOULD TAKE THEM TO THE PLACE WHERE THE AUTHOR LIVED AND WROTE.
WAS THIS AN ARROW TO FIT IN THE BOW?
SOME SAY TODAY THAT GOD IS DEAD. WHAT THEY MEAN IS THAT IF THERE IS A GOD, HE HAS NO AUTHORITY OVER THEM.
WAS THIS ATTEMPT TO BECOME HIS EQUAL, THE FIRST MURDER ATTEMPT ON HIS AUTHORITY OVER THEIR LIVES?
OR MAYBE IT WAS A PEN THEY WERE BUILDING.
A PEN THAT WOULD ALLOW THEM TO WRITE ON THE UNIVERSE ITSELF.
THE ENSUING DISCUSSIONS AND CHAOS OF SO MANY LANGUAGES PRESENT IN ONE PLACE LED TO THE DESTRUCTION OF THE TOWER.
AND THE FORMATION OF MANY NATIONS THAT SPOKE MANY LANGUAGES.

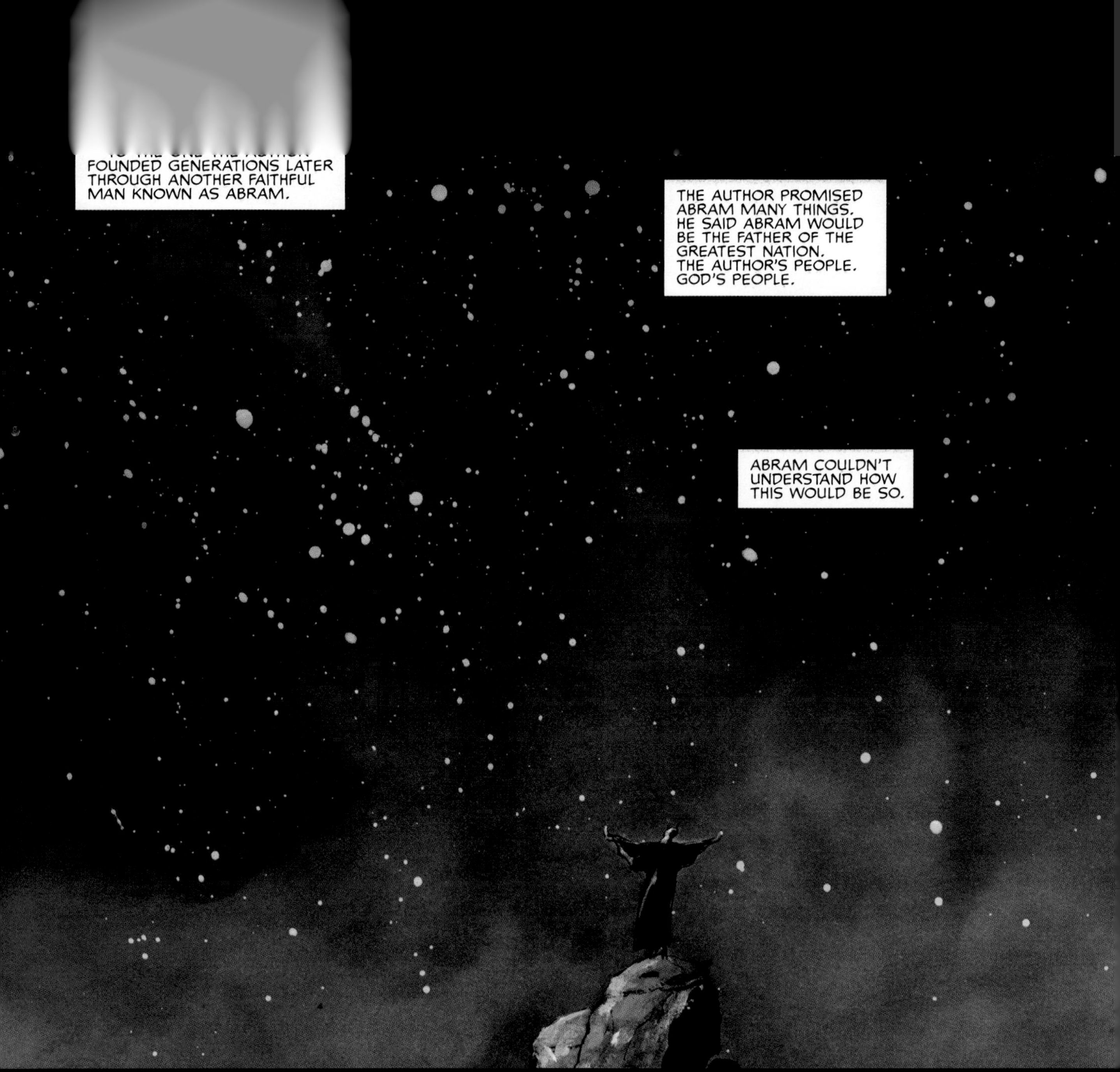
FOUNDED GENERATIONS LATER THROUGH ANOTHER FAITHFUL MAN KNOWN AS ABRAM.
THE AUTHOR PROMISED ABRAM MANY THINGS. HE SAID ABRAM WOULD BE THE FATHER OF THE GREATEST NATION. THE AUTHOR'S PEOPLE. GOD'S PEOPLE.
ABRAM COULDN'T UNDERSTAND HOW THIS WOULD BE SO.

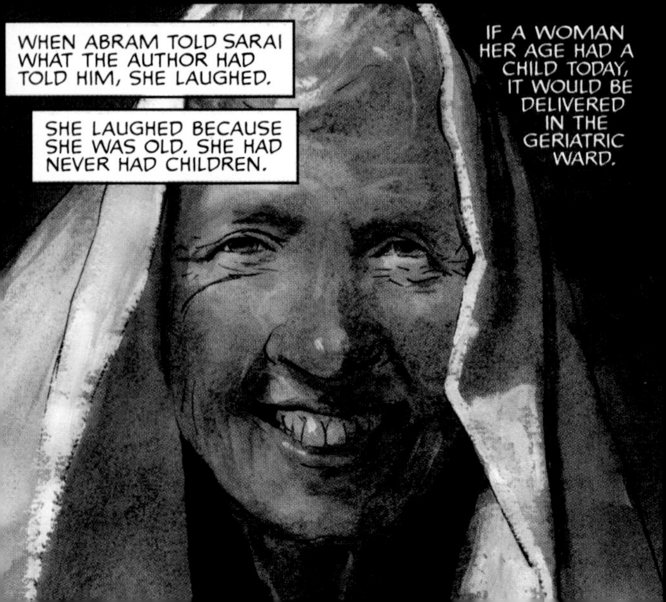
WHEN ABRAM TOLD SARAI WHAT THE AUTHOR HAD TOLD HIM, SHE LAUGHED.
SHE LAUGHED BECAUSE SHE WAS OLD. SHE HAD NEVER HAD CHILDREN.
IF A WOMAN HER AGE HAD A CHILD TODAY, IT WOULD BE DELIVERED IN THE GERIATRIC WARD.

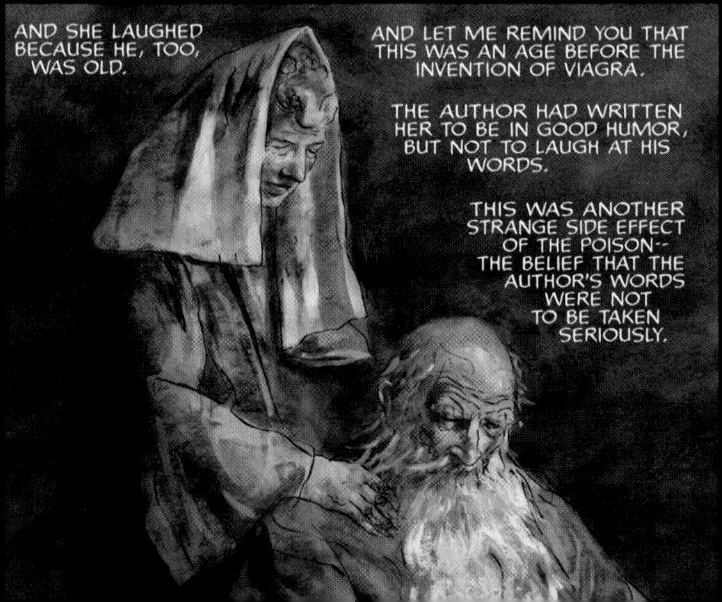
AND SHE LAUGHED BECAUSE HE, TOO, WAS OLD.
AND LET ME REMIND YOU THAT THIS WAS AN AGE BEFORE THE INVENTION OF VIAGRA.
THE AUTHOR HAD WRITTEN HER TO BE IN GOOD HUMOR, BUT NOT TO LAUGH AT HIS WORDS.
THIS WAS ANOTHER STRANGE SIDE EFFECT OF THE POISON-- THE BELIEF THAT THE AUTHOR'S WORDS WERE NOT TO BE TAKEN SERIOUSLY.

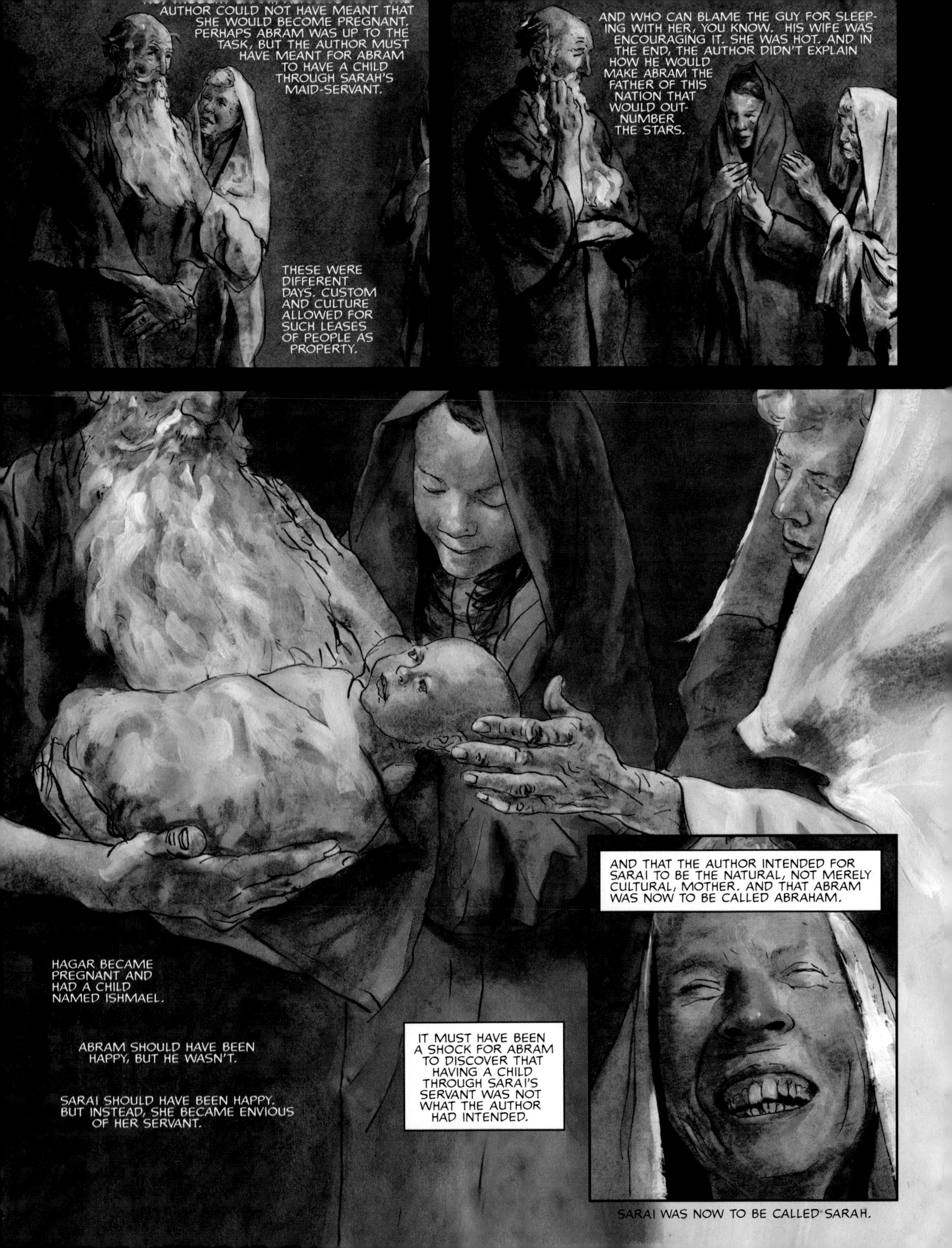

AUTHOR COULD NOT HAVE MEANT THAT SHE WOULD BECOME PREGNANT. PERHAPS ABRAM WAS UP TO THE TASK, BUT THE AUTHOR MUST HAVE MEANT FOR ABRAM TO HAVE A CHILD THROUGH SARAH'S MAID-SERVANT.
THESE WERE DIFFERENT DAYS. CUSTOM AND CULTURE ALLOWED FOR SUCH LEASES OF PEOPLE AS PROPERTY.
AND WHO CAN BLAME THE GUY FOR SLEEPING WITH HER, YOU KNOW. HIS WIFE WAS ENCOURAGING IT. SHE WAS HOT. AND IN THE END, THE AUTHOR DIDN'T EXPLAIN HOW HE WOULD MAKE ABRAM THE FATHER OF THIS NATION THAT WOULD OUTNUMBER THE STARS.
HAGAR BECAME PREGNANT AND HAD A CHILD NAMED ISHMAEL.
ABRAM SHOULD HAVE BEEN HAPPY, BUT HE WASN'T.
SARAI SHOULD HAVE BEEN HAPPY. BUT INSTEAD, SHE BECAME ENVIOUS OF HER SERVANT.
IT MUST HAVE BEEN A SHOCK FOR ABRAM TO DISCOVER THAT HAVING A CHILD THROUGH SARAI'S SERVANT WAS NOT WHAT THE AUTHOR HAD INTENDED.
AND THAT THE AUTHOR INTENDED FOR SARAI TO BE THE NATURAL, NOT MERELY CULTURAL, MOTHER. AND THAT ABRAM WAS NOW TO BE CALLED ABRAHAM.
SARAI WAS NOW TO BE CALLED SARAH.

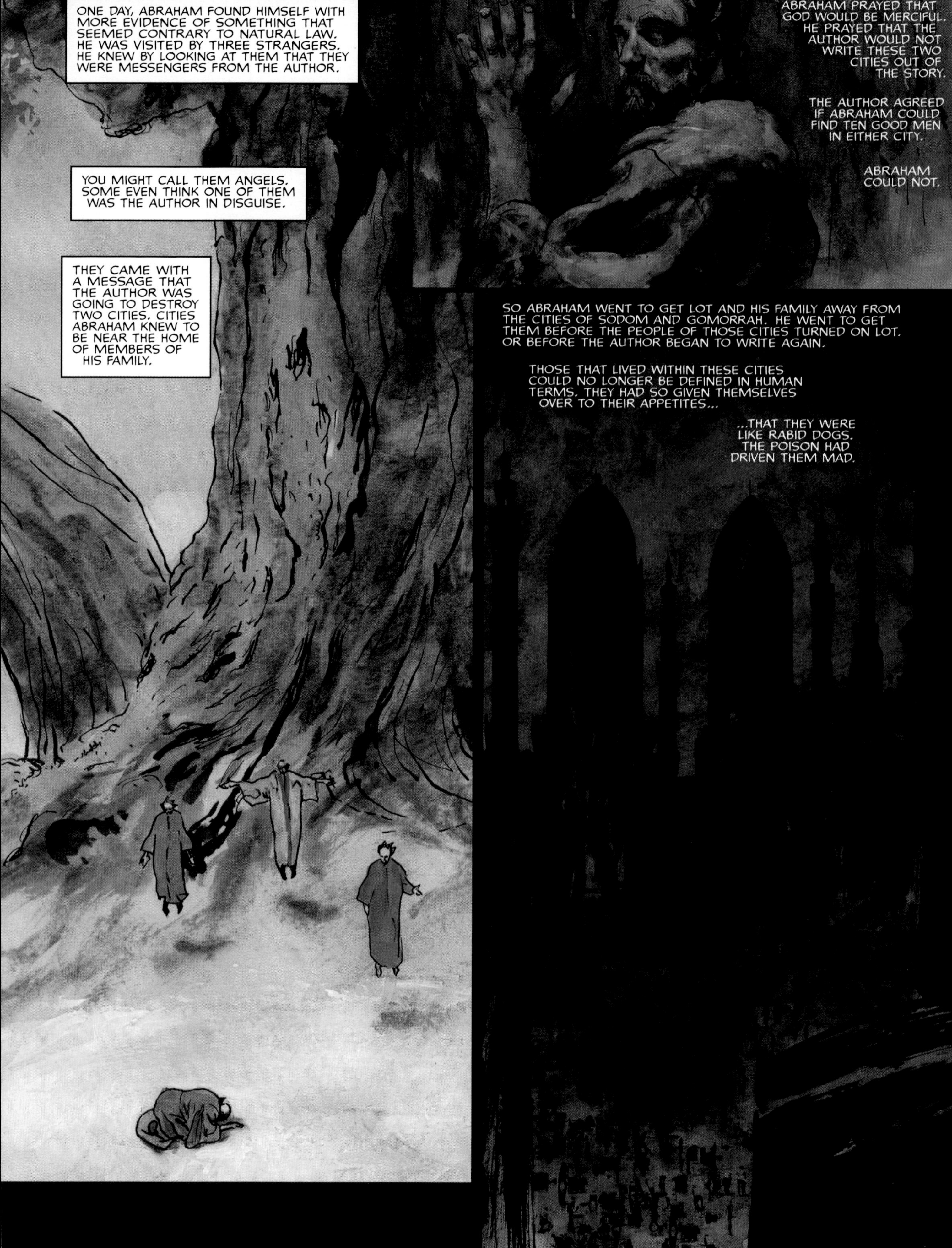
ONE DAY, ABRAHAM FOUND HIMSELF WITH MORE EVIDENCE OF SOMETHING THAT SEEMED CONTRARY TO NATURAL LAW. HE WAS VISITED BY THREE STRANGERS. HE KNEW BY LOOKING AT THEM THAT THEY WERE MESSENGERS FROM THE AUTHOR.
YOU MIGHT CALL THEM ANGELS. SOME EVEN THINK ONE OF THEM WAS THE AUTHOR IN DISGUISE.
THEY CAME WITH A MESSAGE THAT THE AUTHOR WAS GOING TO DESTROY TWO CITIES. CITIES ABRAHAM KNEW TO BE NEAR THE HOME OF MEMBERS OF HIS FAMILY.
ABRAHAM PRAYED THAT GOD WOULD BE MERCIFUL. HE PRAYED THAT THE AUTHOR WOULD NOT WRITE THESE TWO CITIES OUT OF THE STORY.
THE AUTHOR AGREED IF ABRAHAM COULD FIND TEN GOOD MEN IN EITHER CITY.
ABRAHAM COULD NOT.
SO ABRAHAM WENT TO GET LOT AND HIS FAMILY AWAY FROM THE CITIES OF SODOM AND GOMORRAH. HE WENT TO GET THEM BEFORE THE PEOPLE OF THOSE CITIES TURNED ON LOT, OR BEFORE THE AUTHOR BEGAN TO WRITE AGAIN.
THOSE THAT LIVED WITHIN THESE CITIES COULD NO LONGER BE DEFINED IN HUMAN TERMS. THEY HAD SO GIVEN THEMSELVES OVER TO THEIR APPETITES...
...THAT THEY WERE LIKE RABID DOGS. THE POISON HAD DRIVEN THEM MAD.

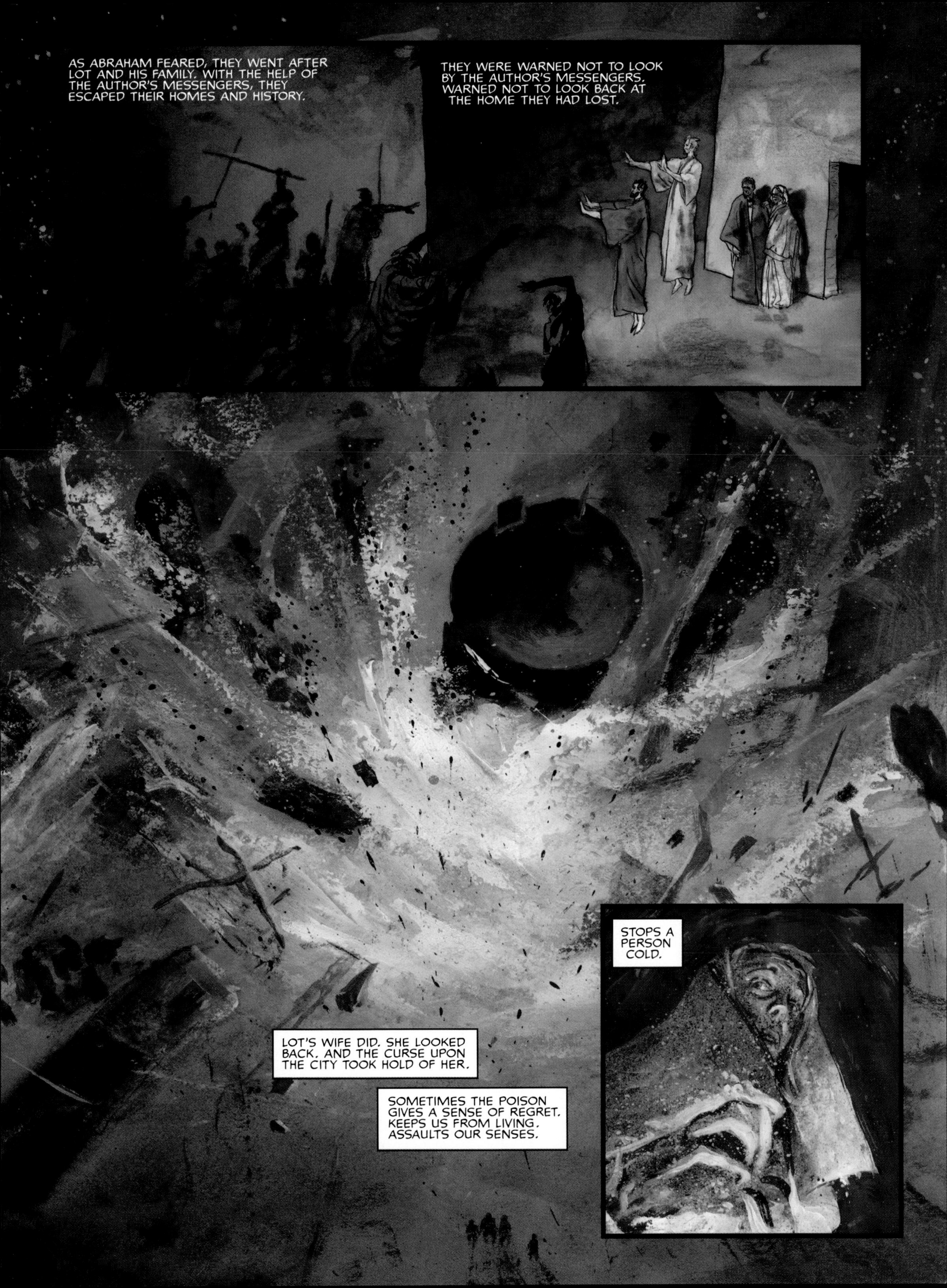
AS ABRAHAM FEARED, THEY WENT AFTER LOT AND HIS FAMILY. WITH THE HELP OF THE AUTHOR'S MESSENGERS, THEY ESCAPED THEIR HOMES AND HISTORY.
THEY WERE WARNED NOT TO LOOK BY THE AUTHOR'S MESSENGERS. WARNED NOT TO LOOK BACK AT THE HOME THEY HAD LOST.
LOT'S WIFE DID. SHE LOOKED BACK. AND THE CURSE UPON THE CITY TOOK HOLD OF HER.
SOMETIMES THE POISON GIVES A SENSE OF REGRET. KEEPS US FROM LIVING. ASSAULTS OUR SENSES.
STOPS A PERSON COLD.

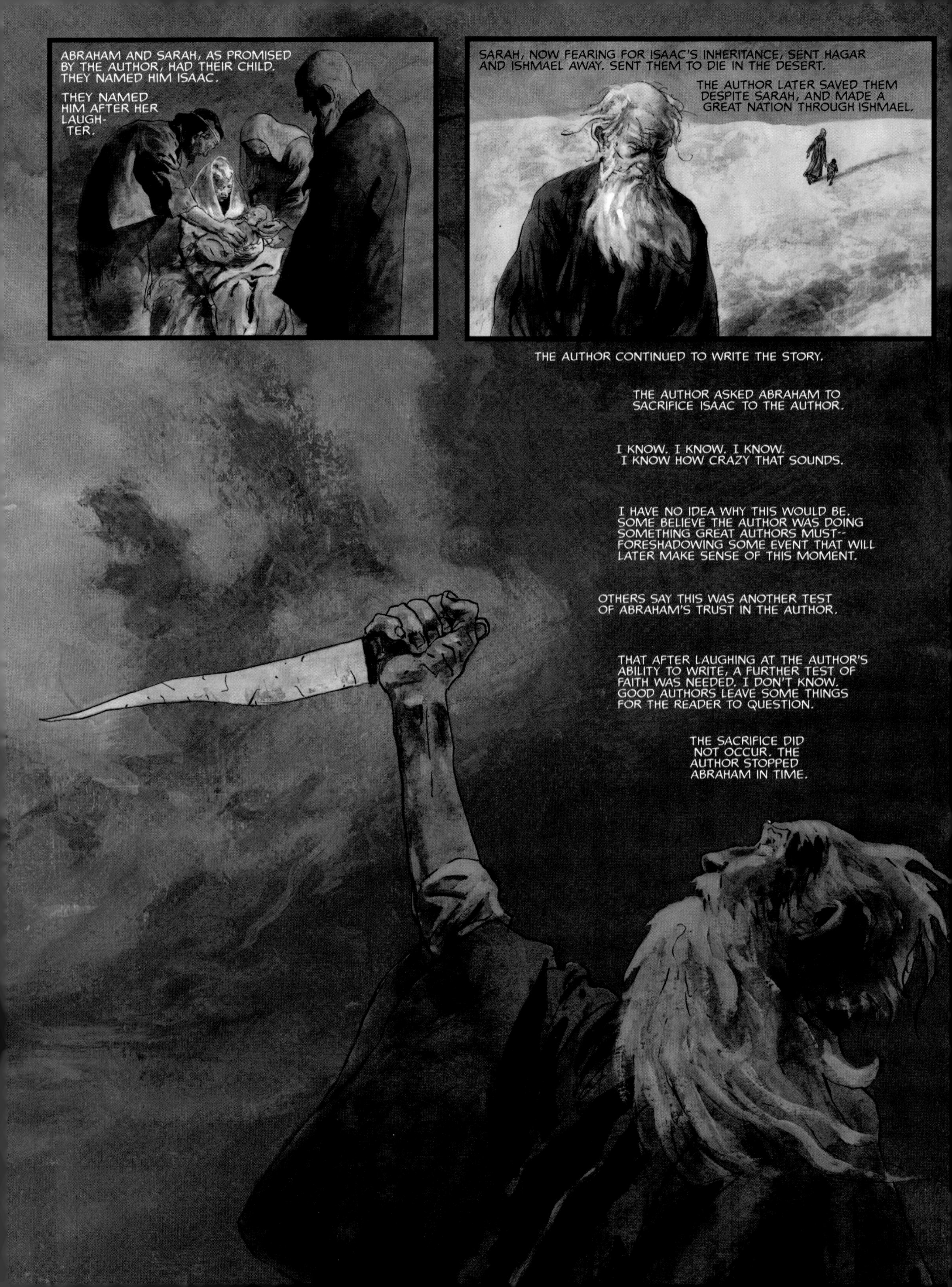
ABRAHAM AND SARAH, AS PROMISED BY THE AUTHOR, HAD THEIR CHILD. THEY NAMED HIM ISAAC.
THEY NAMED HIM AFTER HER LAUGH-TER.
SARAH, NOW FEARING FOR ISAAC'S INHERITANCE, SENT HAGAR AND ISHMAEL AWAY. SENT THEM TO DIE IN THE DESERT.
THE AUTHOR LATER SAVED THEM DESPITE SARAH, AND MADE A GREAT NATION THROUGH ISHMAEL.
THE AUTHOR CONTINUED TO WRITE THE STORY.
THE AUTHOR ASKED ABRAHAM TO SACRIFICE ISAAC TO THE AUTHOR.
I KNOW. I KNOW. I KNOW. I KNOW HOW CRAZY THAT SOUNDS.
I HAVE NO IDEA WHY THIS WOULD BE. SOME BELIEVE THE AUTHOR WAS DOING SOMETHING GREAT AUTHORS MUST-- FORESHADOWING SOME EVENT THAT WILL LATER MAKE SENSE OF THIS MOMENT.
OTHERS SAY THIS WAS ANOTHER TEST OF ABRAHAM'S TRUST IN THE AUTHOR.
THAT AFTER LAUGHING AT THE AUTHOR'S ABILITY TO WRITE, A FURTHER TEST OF FAITH WAS NEEDED. I DON'T KNOW. GOOD AUTHORS LEAVE SOME THINGS FOR THE READER TO QUESTION.
THE SACRIFICE DID NOT OCCUR. THE AUTHOR STOPPED ABRAHAM IN TIME.

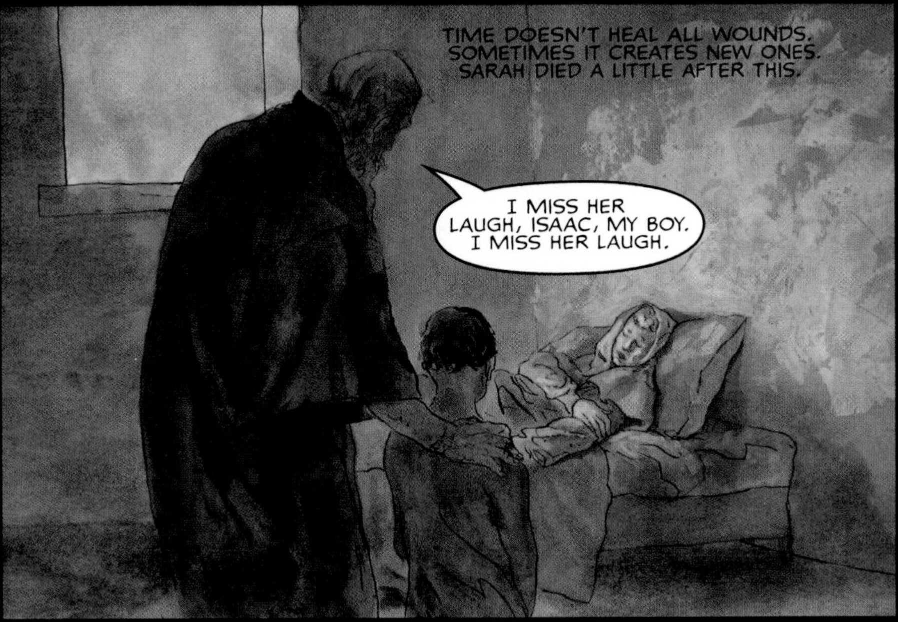
TIME DOESN'T HEAL ALL WOUNDS. SOMETIMES IT CREATES NEW ONES. SARAH DIED A LITTLE AFTER THIS.
I MISS HER LAUGH, ISAAC, MY BOY. I MISS HER LAUGH.

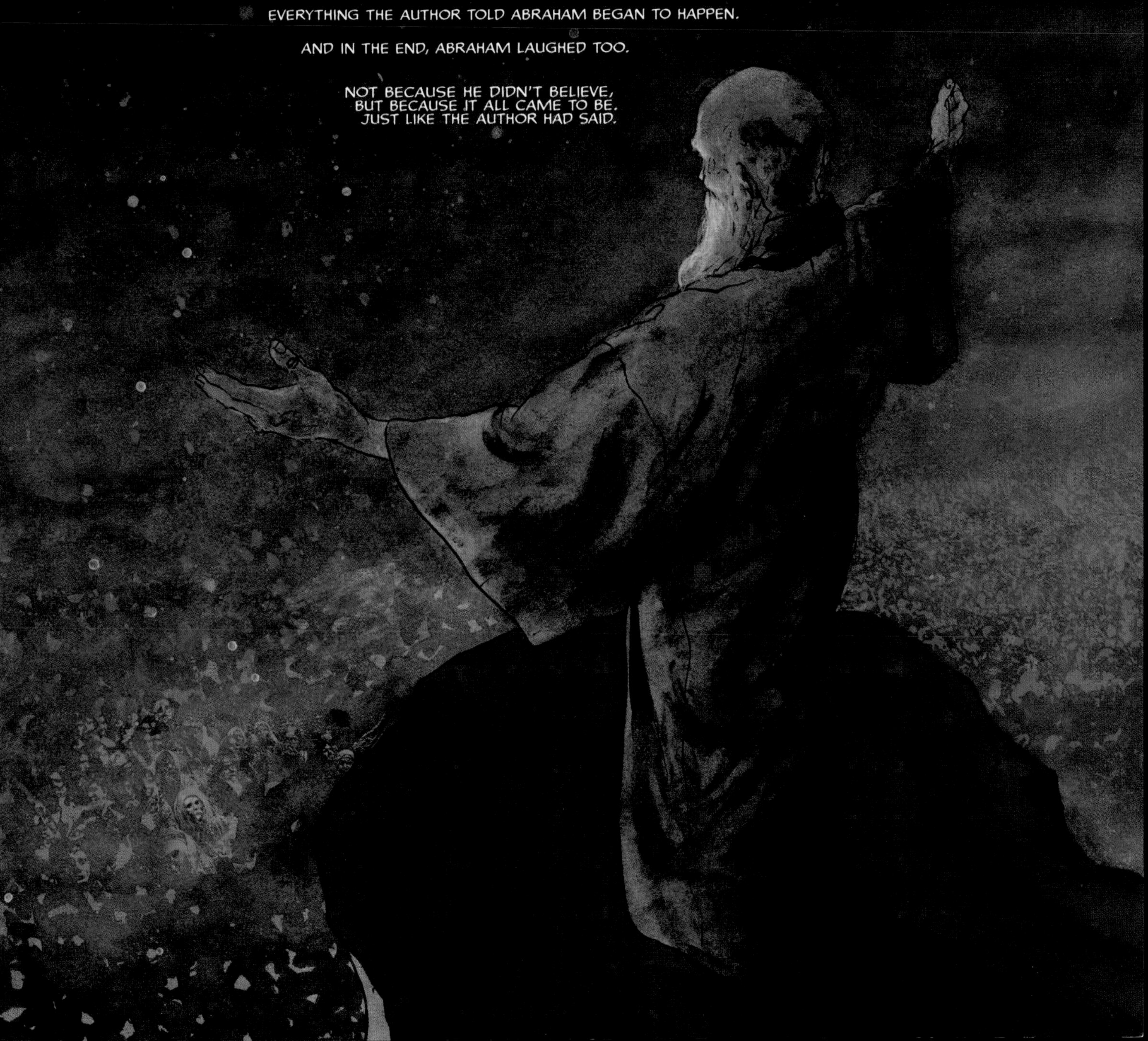
EVERYTHING THE AUTHOR TOLD ABRAHAM BEGAN TO HAPPEN.
AND IN THE END, ABRAHAM LAUGHED TOO.
NOT BECAUSE HE DIDN'T BELIEVE, BUT BECAUSE IT ALL CAME TO BE. JUST LIKE THE AUTHOR HAD SAID.

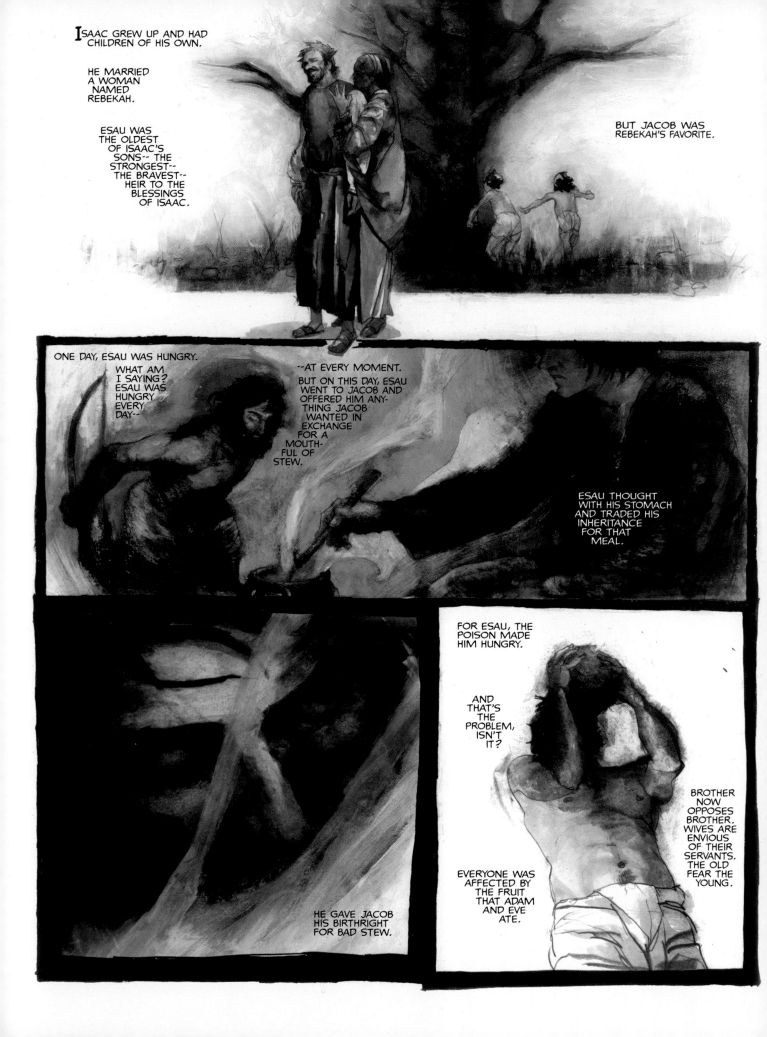

ISAAC GREW UP AND HAD CHILDREN OF HIS OWN.

HE MARRIED A WOMAN NAMED REBEKAH.

ESAU WAS THE OLDEST OF ISAAC'S SONS-- THE STRONGEST-- THE BRAVEST-- HEIR TO THE BLESSINGS OF ISAAC.

BUT JACOB WAS REBEKAH'S FAVORITE.

ONE DAY, ESAU WAS HUNGRY.

WHAT AM I SAYING? ESAU WAS HUNGRY EVERY DAY--

--AT EVERY MOMENT. BUT ON THIS DAY, ESAU WENT TO JACOB AND OFFERED HIM ANYTHING JACOB WANTED IN EXCHANGE FOR A MOUTHFUL OF STEW.

ESAU THOUGHT WITH HIS STOMACH AND TRADED HIS INHERITANCE FOR THAT MEAL.

HE GAVE JACOB HIS BIRTHRIGHT FOR BAD STEW.

FOR ESAU, THE POISON MADE HIM HUNGRY.

AND THAT'S THE PROBLEM, ISN'T IT?

EVERYONE WAS AFFECTED BY THE FRUIT THAT ADAM AND EVE ATE.

BROTHER NOW OPPOSES BROTHER. WIVES ARE ENVIOUS OF THEIR SERVANTS. THE OLD FEAR THE YOUNG.

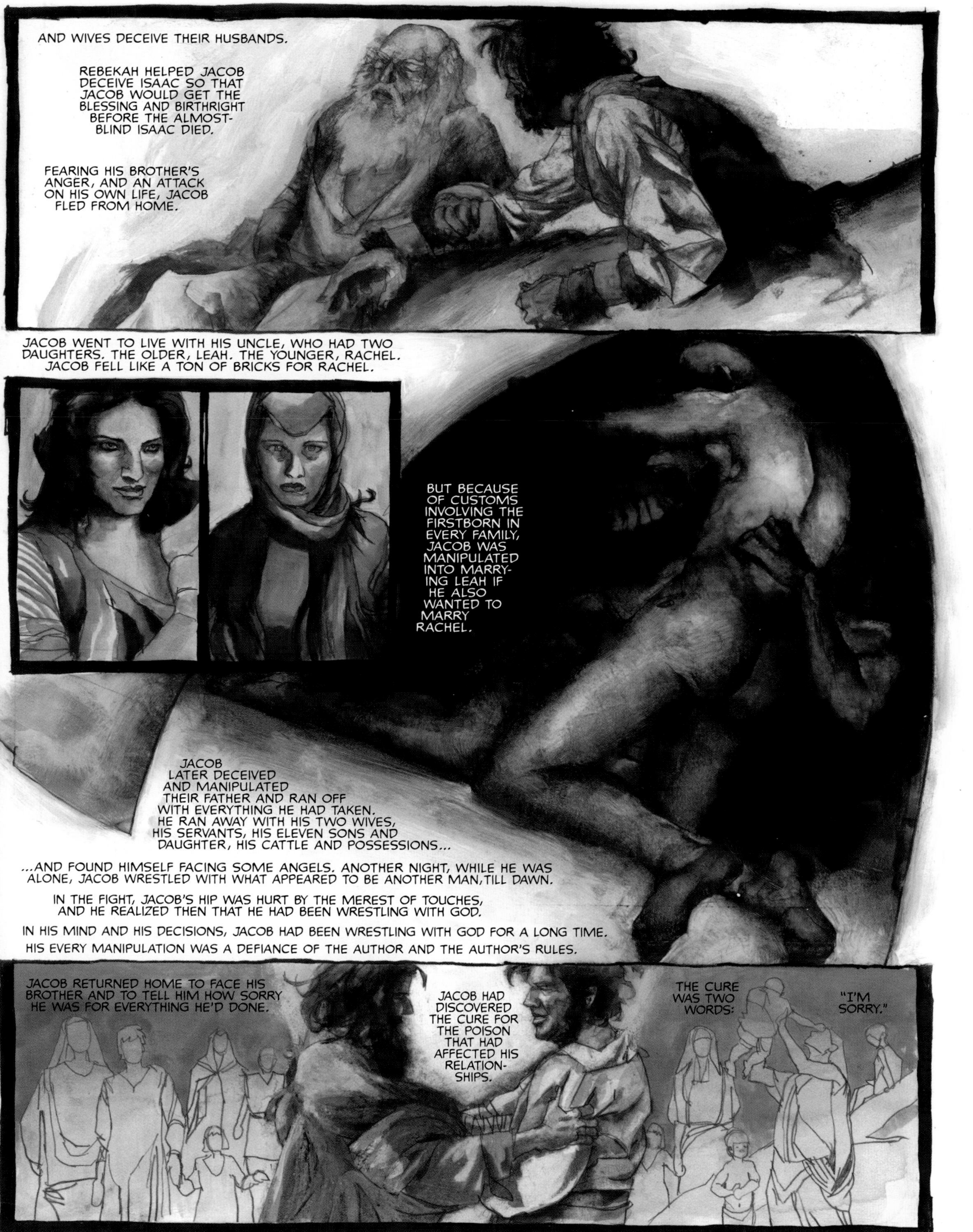
AND WIVES DECEIVE THEIR HUSBANDS.
REBEKAH HELPED JACOB DECEIVE ISAAC SO THAT JACOB WOULD GET THE BLESSING AND BIRTHRIGHT BEFORE THE ALMOST-BLIND ISAAC DIED.
FEARING HIS BROTHER'S ANGER, AND AN ATTACK ON HIS OWN LIFE, JACOB FLED FROM HOME.
JACOB WENT TO LIVE WITH HIS UNCLE, WHO HAD TWO DAUGHTERS. THE OLDER, LEAH. THE YOUNGER, RACHEL. JACOB FELL LIKE A TON OF BRICKS FOR RACHEL.
BUT BECAUSE OF CUSTOMS INVOLVING THE FIRSTBORN IN EVERY FAMILY, JACOB WAS MANIPULATED INTO MARRYING LEAH IF HE ALSO WANTED TO MARRY RACHEL.
JACOB LATER DECEIVED AND MANIPULATED THEIR FATHER AND RAN OFF WITH EVERYTHING HE HAD TAKEN. HE RAN AWAY WITH HIS TWO WIVES, HIS SERVANTS, HIS ELEVEN SONS AND DAUGHTER, HIS CATTLE AND POSSESSIONS...
...AND FOUND HIMSELF FACING SOME ANGELS. ANOTHER NIGHT, WHILE HE WAS ALONE, JACOB WRESTLED WITH WHAT APPEARED TO BE ANOTHER MAN, TILL DAWN.
IN THE FIGHT, JACOB'S HIP WAS HURT BY THE MEREST OF TOUCHES, AND HE REALIZED THEN THAT HE HAD BEEN WRESTLING WITH GOD.
IN HIS MIND AND HIS DECISIONS, JACOB HAD BEEN WRESTLING WITH GOD FOR A LONG TIME.
HIS EVERY MANIPULATION WAS A DEFIANCE OF THE AUTHOR AND THE AUTHOR'S RULES.
JACOB RETURNED HOME TO FACE HIS BROTHER AND TO TELL HIM HOW SORRY HE WAS FOR EVERYTHING HE'D DONE.
JACOB HAD DISCOVERED THE CURE FOR THE POISON THAT HAD AFFECTED HIS RELATIONSHIPS.
THE CURE WAS TWO WORDS:
"I'M SORRY."

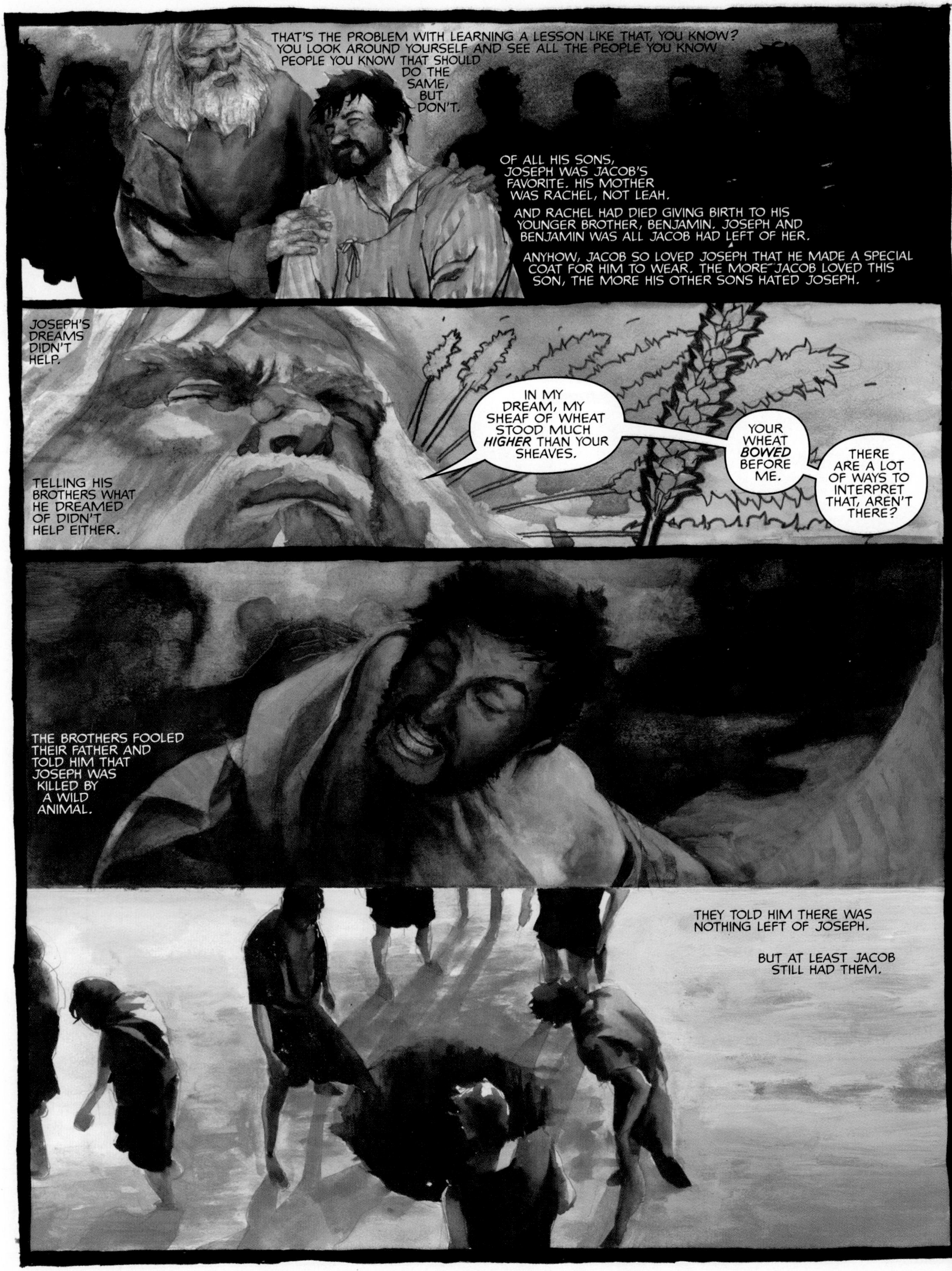
THAT'S THE PROBLEM WITH LEARNING A LESSON LIKE THAT, YOU KNOW? YOU LOOK AROUND YOURSELF AND SEE ALL THE PEOPLE YOU KNOW PEOPLE YOU KNOW THAT SHOULD DO THE SAME, BUT DON'T.
OF ALL HIS SONS, JOSEPH WAS JACOB'S FAVORITE. HIS MOTHER WAS RACHEL, NOT LEAH.
AND RACHEL HAD DIED GIVING BIRTH TO HIS YOUNGER BROTHER, BENJAMIN. JOSEPH AND BENJAMIN WAS ALL JACOB HAD LEFT OF HER.
ANYHOW, JACOB SO LOVED JOSEPH THAT HE MADE A SPECIAL COAT FOR HIM TO WEAR. THE MORE JACOB LOVED THIS SON, THE MORE HIS OTHER SONS HATED JOSEPH.
JOSEPH'S DREAMS DIDN'T HELP.
TELLING HIS BROTHERS WHAT HE DREAMED OF DIDN'T HELP EITHER.
IN MY DREAM, MY SHEAF OF WHEAT STOOD MUCH HIGHER THAN YOUR SHEAVES.
YOUR WHEAT BOWED BEFORE ME.
THERE ARE A LOT OF WAYS TO INTERPRET THAT, AREN'T THERE?
THE BROTHERS FOOLED THEIR FATHER AND TOLD HIM THAT JOSEPH WAS KILLED BY A WILD ANIMAL.
THEY TOLD HIM THERE WAS NOTHING LEFT OF JOSEPH.
BUT AT LEAST JACOB STILL HAD THEM.

THE TRUTH WAS THAT JOSEPH'S BROTHERS HAD SOLD HIM INTO SLAVERY.

HE BECAME ONE OF THE FAVORITE SERVANTS IN THE HOUSE OF POTIPHAR IN EGYPT.

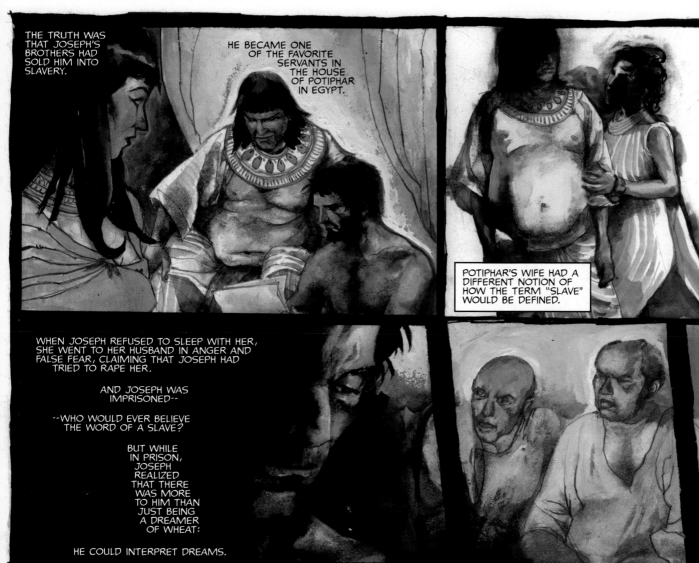

POTIPHAR'S WIFE HAD A DIFFERENT NOTION OF HOW THE TERM "SLAVE" WOULD BE DEFINED.

WHEN JOSEPH REFUSED TO SLEEP WITH HER, SHE WENT TO HER HUSBAND IN ANGER AND FALSE FEAR, CLAIMING THAT JOSEPH HAD TRIED TO RAPE HER.

AND JOSEPH WAS IMPRISONED--

--WHO WOULD EVER BELIEVE THE WORD OF A SLAVE?

BUT WHILE IN PRISON, JOSEPH REALIZED THAT THERE WAS MORE TO HIM THAN JUST BEING A DREAMER OF WHEAT:

HE COULD INTERPRET DREAMS.

FOR ANOTHER INMATE, A CUP-BEARER--

--JOSEPH TOLD HIM THAT HIS DREAM MEANT THAT HE WOULD BE RESTORED TO THE PHAROAH'S SERVICE.

BUT FOR THE BAKER--

--WHO'D DREAMED OF THREE BASKETS OF BREAD ON HIS HEAD BEING EATEN BY BIRDS--

--JOSEPH COULD ONLY SPEAK OF DEATH.

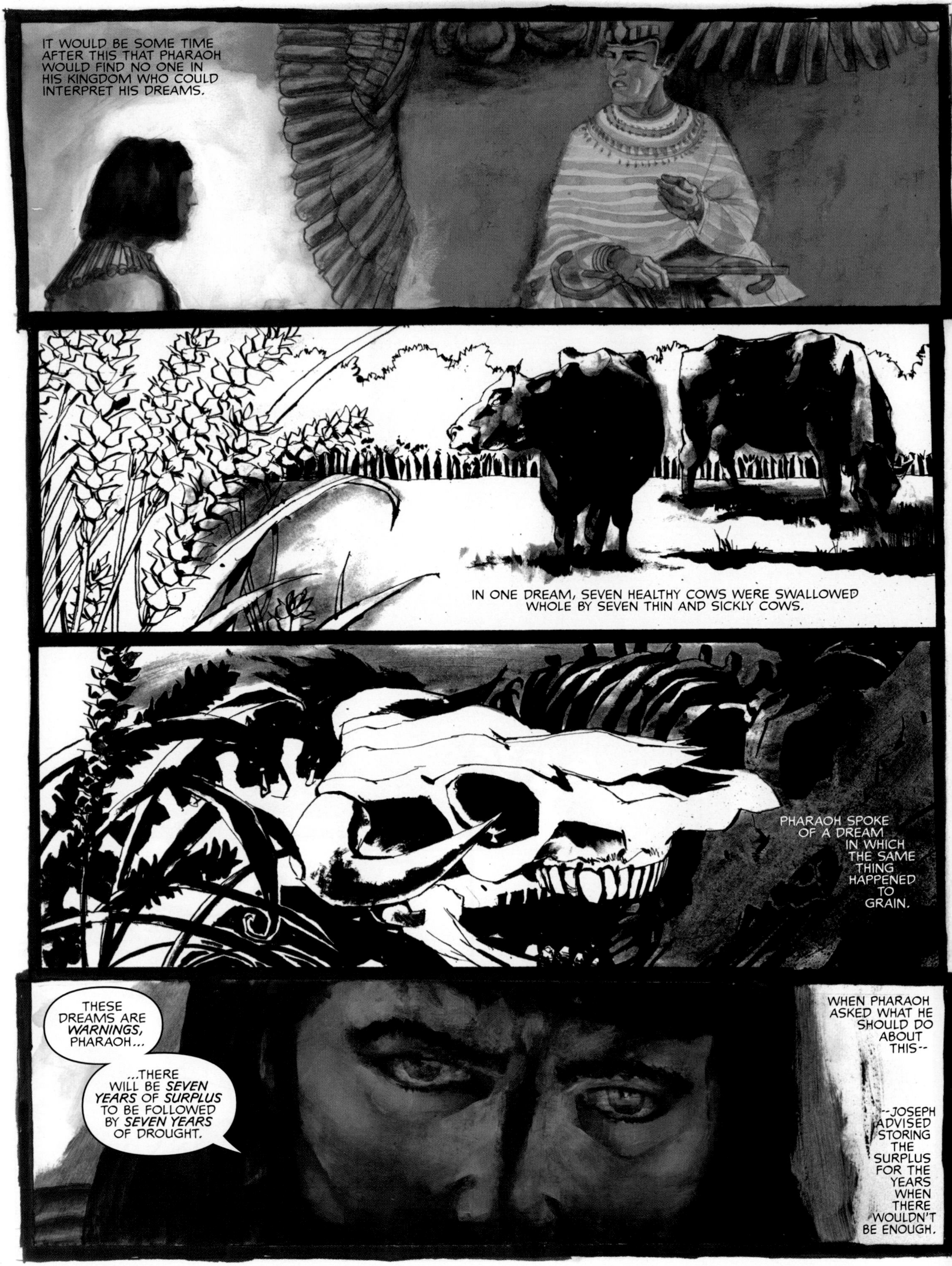
IT WOULD BE SOME TIME AFTER THIS THAT PHARAOH WOULD FIND NO ONE IN HIS KINGDOM WHO COULD INTERPRET HIS DREAMS.
IN ONE DREAM, SEVEN HEALTHY COWS WERE SWALLOWED WHOLE BY SEVEN THIN AND SICKLY COWS.
PHARAOH SPOKE OF A DREAM IN WHICH THE SAME THING HAPPENED TO GRAIN.
THESE DREAMS ARE *WARNINGS*, PHARAOH...
...THERE WILL BE *SEVEN YEARS* OF *SURPLUS* TO BE FOLLOWED BY *SEVEN YEARS* OF DROUGHT.
WHEN PHARAOH ASKED WHAT HE SHOULD DO ABOUT THIS--
--JOSEPH ADVISED STORING THE SURPLUS FOR THE YEARS WHEN THERE WOULDN'T BE ENOUGH.

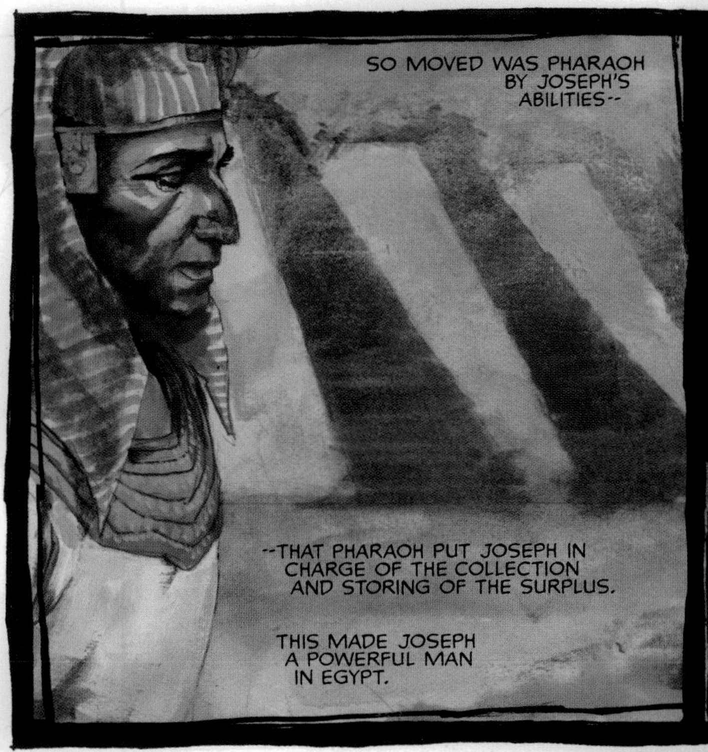
SO MOVED WAS PHARAOH BY JOSEPH'S ABILITIES--
--THAT PHARAOH PUT JOSEPH IN CHARGE OF THE COLLECTION AND STORING OF THE SURPLUS.
THIS MADE JOSEPH A POWERFUL MAN IN EGYPT.
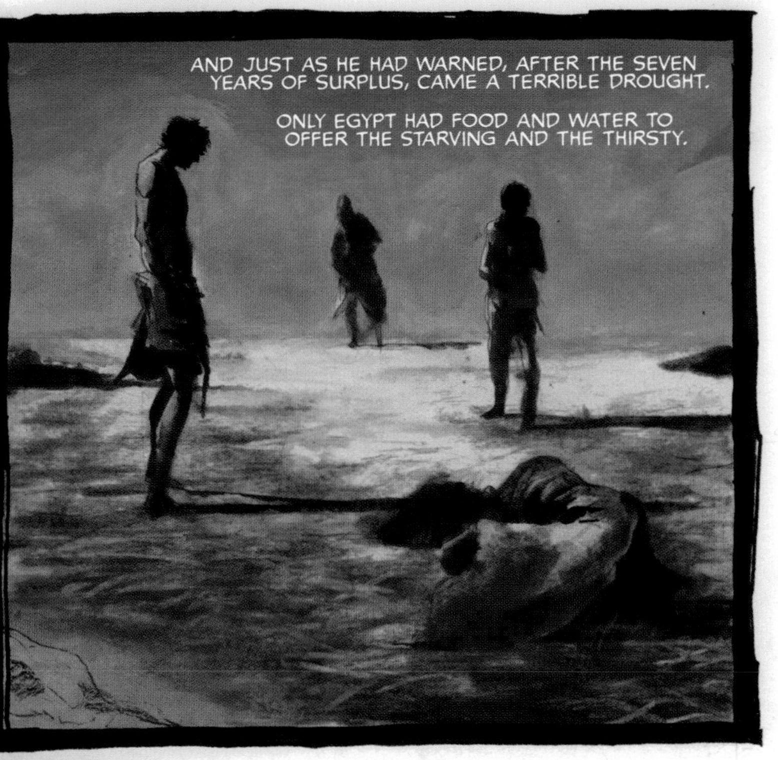
AND JUST AS HE HAD WARNED, AFTER THE SEVEN YEARS OF SURPLUS, CAME A TERRIBLE DROUGHT.
ONLY EGYPT HAD FOOD AND WATER TO OFFER THE STARVING AND THE THIRSTY.
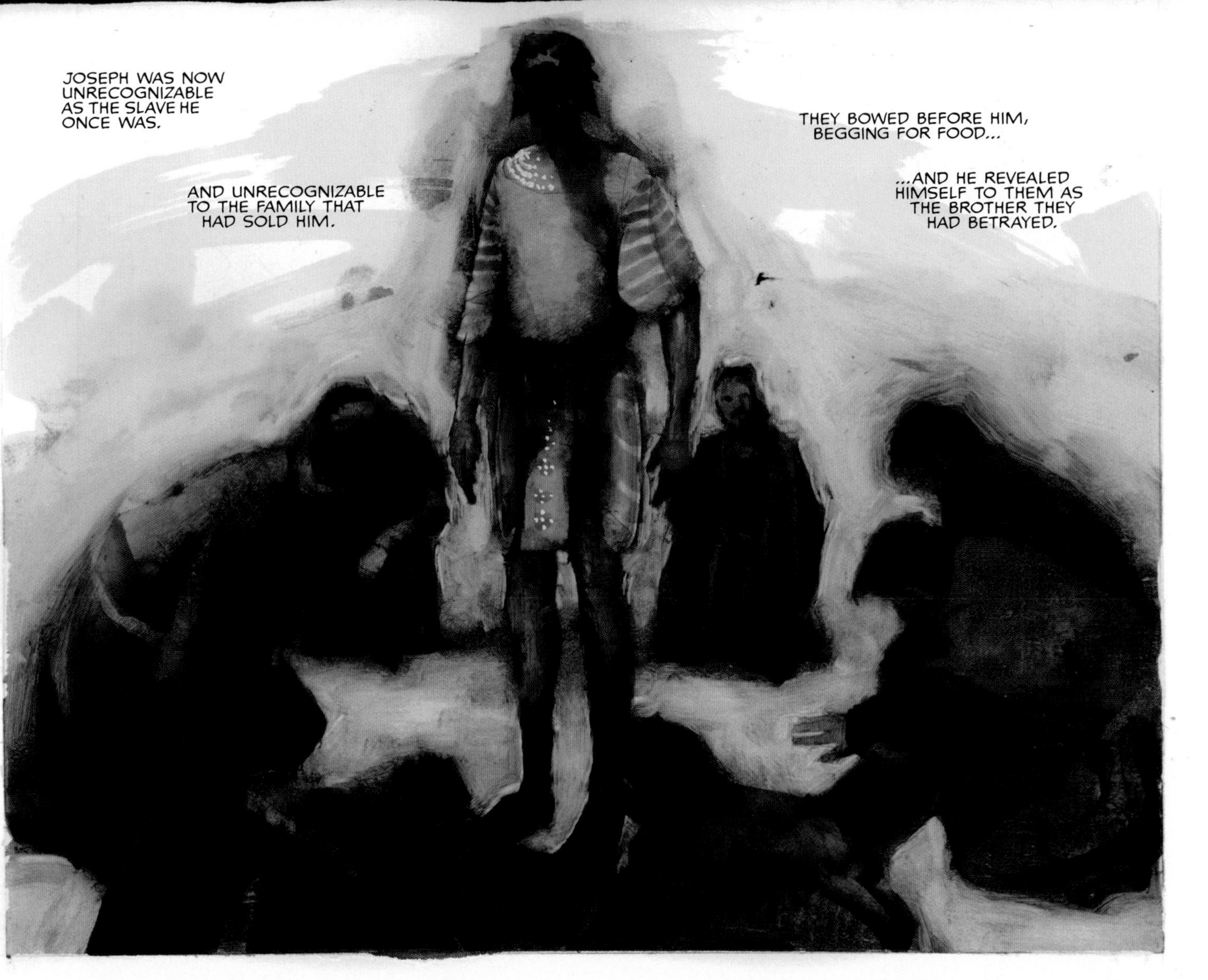
JOSEPH WAS NOW UNRECOGNIZABLE AS THE SLAVE HE ONCE WAS.
AND UNRECOGNIZABLE TO THE FAMILY THAT HAD SOLD HIM.
THEY BOWED BEFORE HIM, BEGGING FOR FOOD...
...AND HE REVEALED HIMSELF TO THEM AS THE BROTHER THEY HAD BETRAYED.

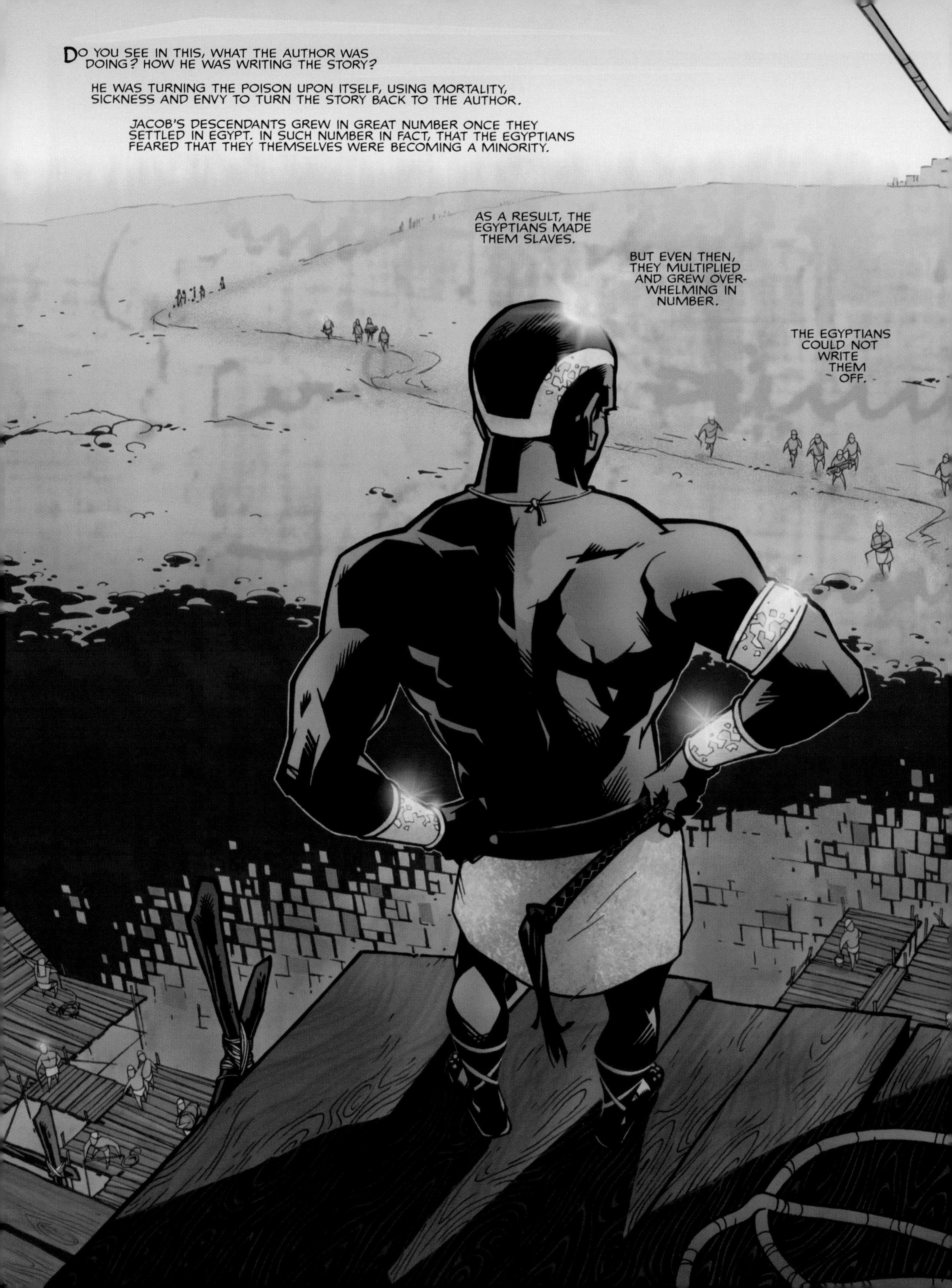

DO YOU SEE IN THIS, WHAT THE AUTHOR WAS DOING? HOW HE WAS WRITING THE STORY?
HE WAS TURNING THE POISON UPON ITSELF, USING MORTALITY, SICKNESS AND ENVY TO TURN THE STORY BACK TO THE AUTHOR.
JACOB'S DESCENDANTS GREW IN GREAT NUMBER ONCE THEY SETTLED IN EGYPT. IN SUCH NUMBER IN FACT, THAT THE EGYPTIANS FEARED THAT THEY THEMSELVES WERE BECOMING A MINORITY.
AS A RESULT, THE EGYPTIANS MADE THEM SLAVES.
BUT EVEN THEN, THEY MULTIPLIED AND GREW OVER-WHELMING IN NUMBER.
THE EGYPTIANS COULD NOT WRITE THEM OFF.

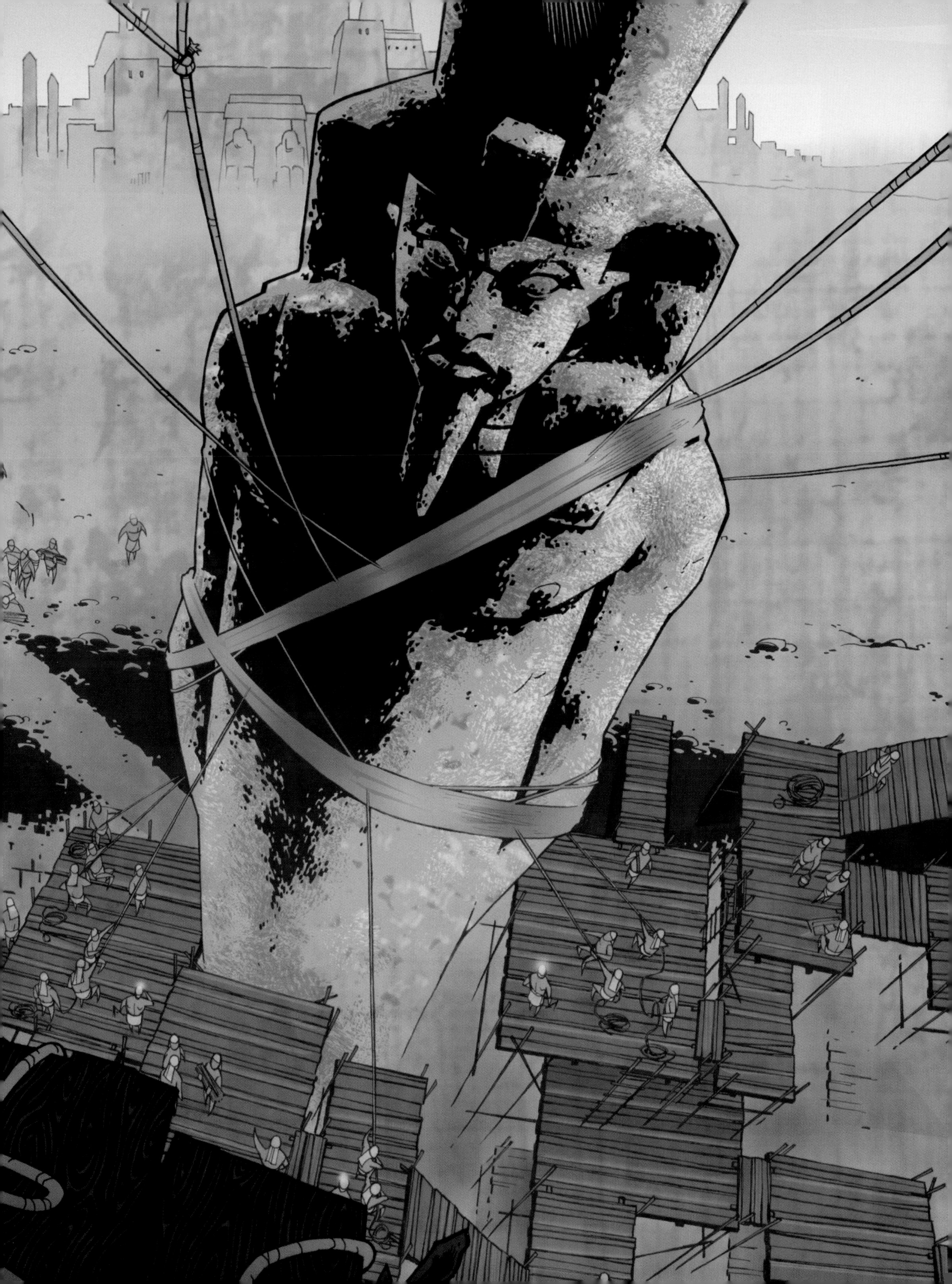

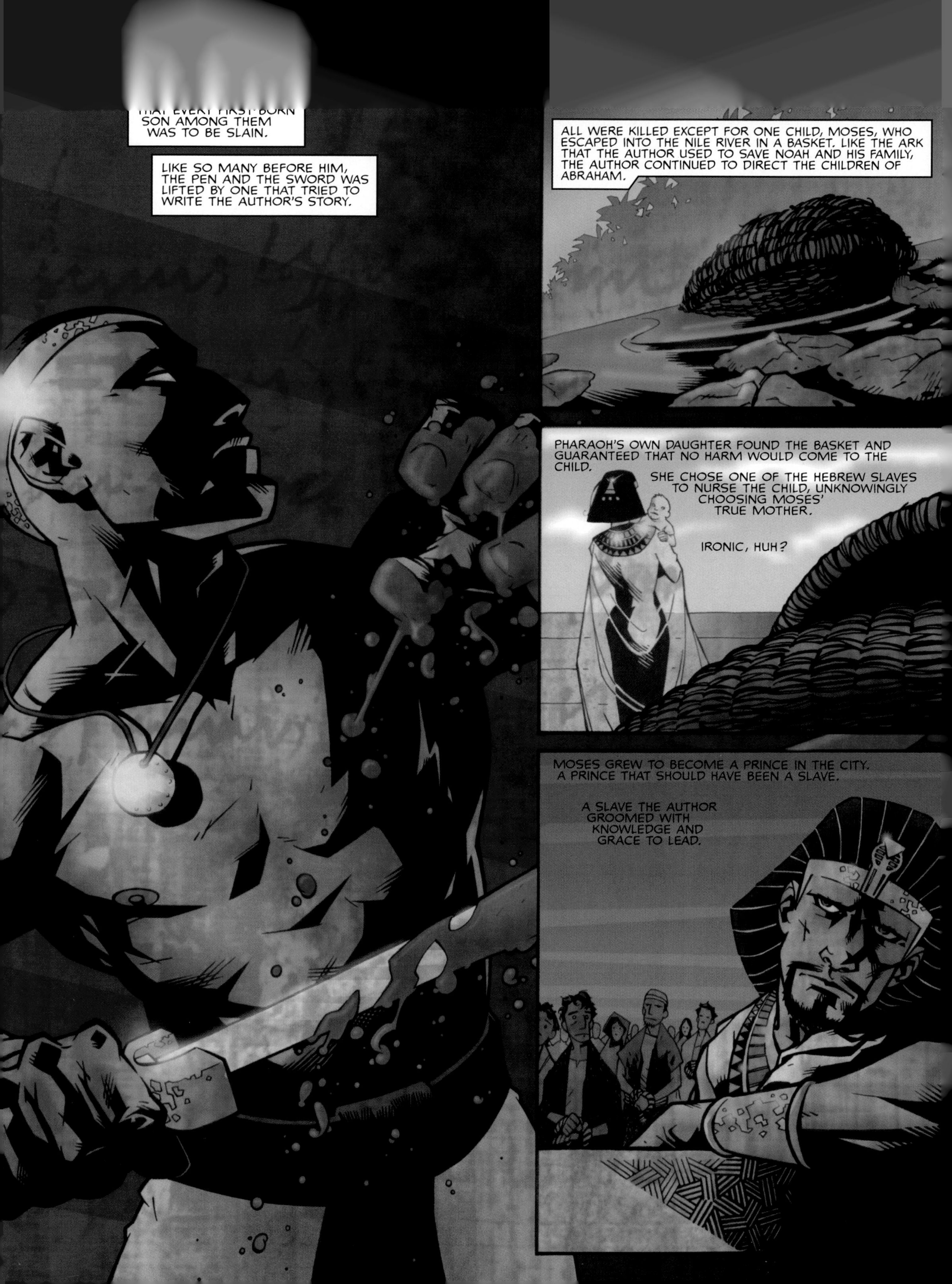
THAT EVERY FIRST-BORN SON AMONG THEM WAS TO BE SLAIN.
LIKE SO MANY BEFORE HIM, THE PEN AND THE SWORD WAS LIFTED BY ONE THAT TRIED TO WRITE THE AUTHOR'S STORY.
ALL WERE KILLED EXCEPT FOR ONE CHILD, MOSES, WHO ESCAPED INTO THE NILE RIVER IN A BASKET. LIKE THE ARK THAT THE AUTHOR USED TO SAVE NOAH AND HIS FAMILY, THE AUTHOR CONTINUED TO DIRECT THE CHILDREN OF ABRAHAM.
PHARAOH'S OWN DAUGHTER FOUND THE BASKET AND GUARANTEED THAT NO HARM WOULD COME TO THE CHILD.
SHE CHOSE ONE OF THE HEBREW SLAVES TO NURSE THE CHILD, UNKNOWINGLY CHOOSING MOSES' TRUE MOTHER.
IRONIC, HUH?
MOSES GREW TO BECOME A PRINCE IN THE CITY. A PRINCE THAT SHOULD HAVE BEEN A SLAVE.
A SLAVE THE AUTHOR GROOMED WITH KNOWLEDGE AND GRACE TO LEAD.

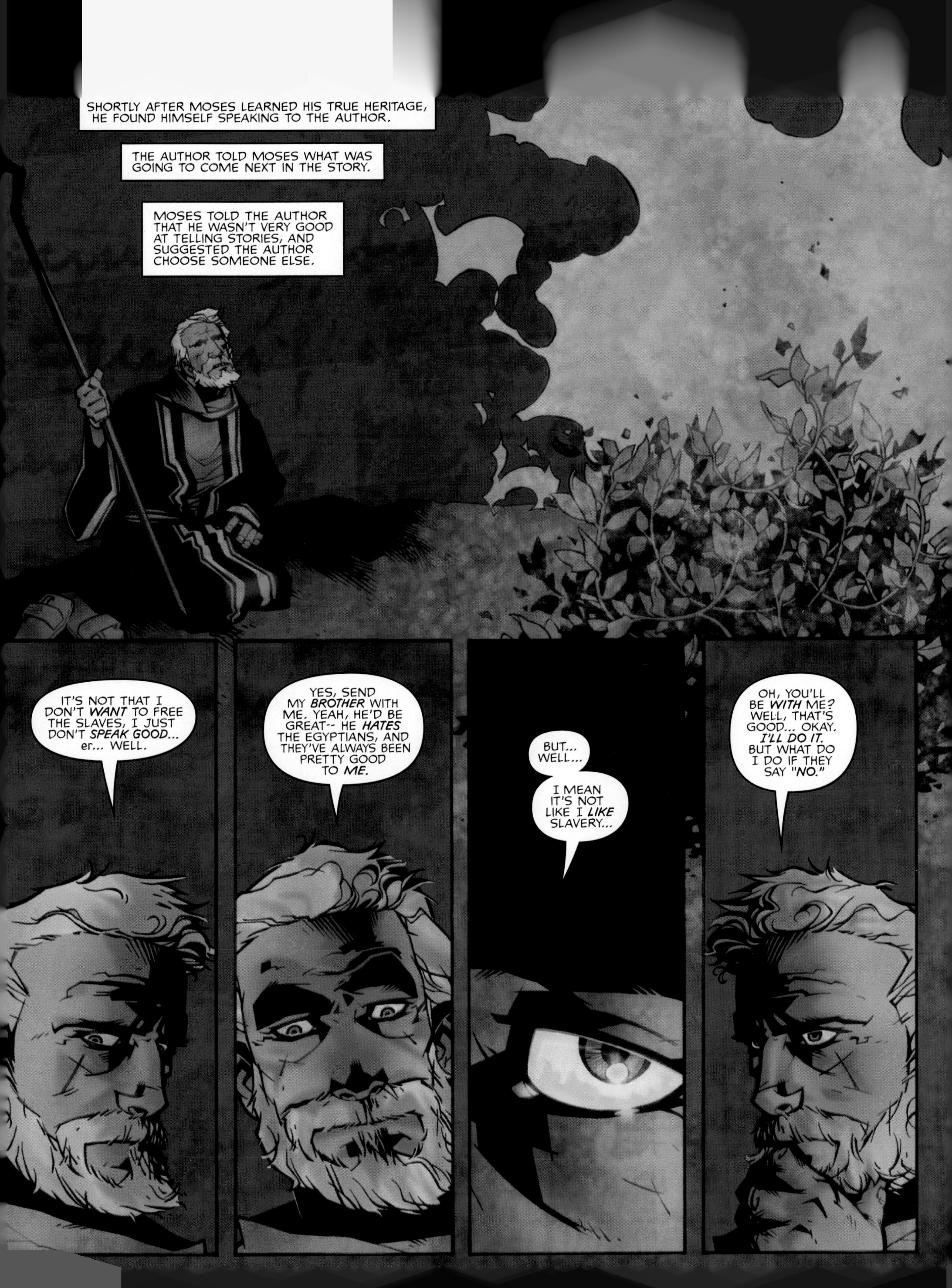
SHORTLY AFTER MOSES LEARNED HIS TRUE HERITAGE, HE FOUND HIMSELF SPEAKING TO THE AUTHOR.
THE AUTHOR TOLD MOSES WHAT WAS GOING TO COME NEXT IN THE STORY.
MOSES TOLD THE AUTHOR THAT HE WASN'T VERY GOOD AT TELLING STORIES, AND SUGGESTED THE AUTHOR CHOOSE SOMEONE ELSE.
IT'S NOT THAT I DON'T *WANT* TO FREE THE SLAVES, I JUST DON'T *SPEAK GOOD*... er... WELL.
YES, SEND MY *BROTHER* WITH ME. YEAH, HE'D BE GREAT-- HE *HATES* THE EGYPTIANS, AND THEY'VE ALWAYS BEEN PRETTY GOOD TO *ME*.
BUT... WELL...
I MEAN IT'S NOT LIKE I *LIKE* SLAVERY...
OH, YOU'LL BE *WITH* ME? WELL, THAT'S GOOD... OKAY. *I'LL DO IT.* BUT WHAT DO I DO IF THEY SAY "*NO.*"

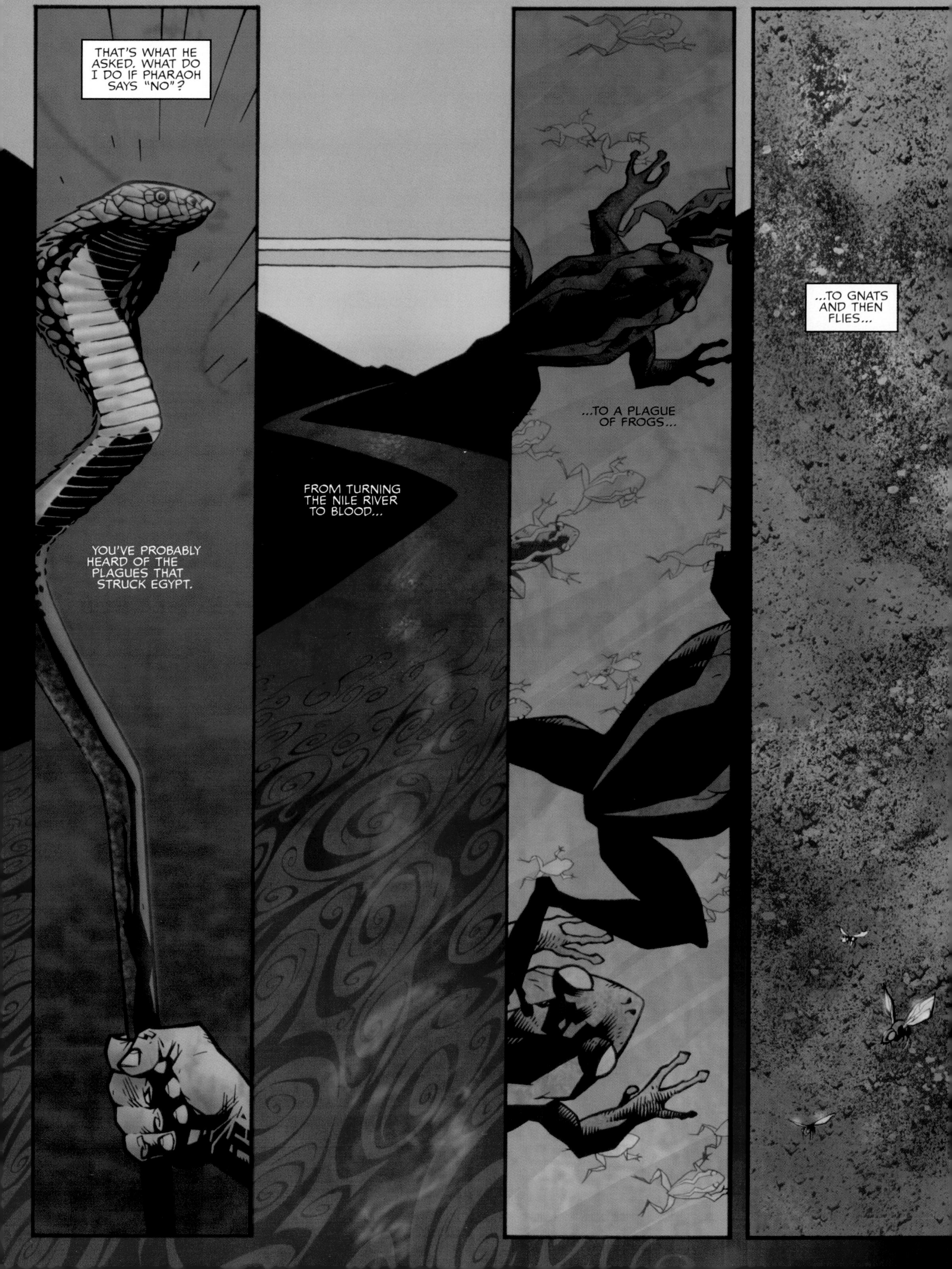
THAT'S WHAT HE ASKED. WHAT DO I DO IF PHARAOH SAYS "NO"?
YOU'VE PROBABLY HEARD OF THE PLAGUES THAT STRUCK EGYPT.
FROM TURNING THE NILE RIVER TO BLOOD...
...TO A PLAGUE OF FROGS...
...TO GNATS AND THEN FLIES...

...TO THE LIVESTOCK DYING...

...TO TERRIBLE BOILS.

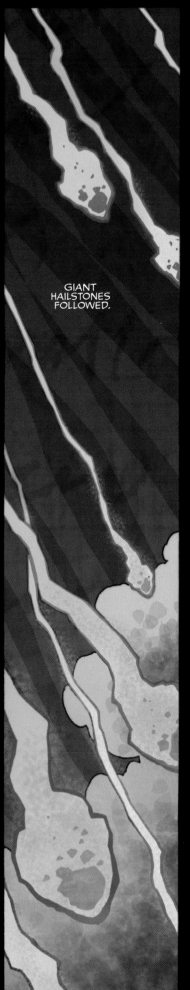

GIANT HAILSTONES FOLLOWED.

THEN LOCUSTS.

PHARAOH IGNORED THESE PLAGUES CITING THAT EACH WAS THE NATURAL LOGICAL EXTENSION OF THE OTHER.

THE NILE IS POLLUTED, AND SO THE FROGS CAN NO LONGER LIVE THERE. THE EGYPTIANS KILL THE FROGS THAT NOW OVERRUN THEIR HOMES, SO THERE'S NOTHING LEFT TO FEED UPON THE FLIES AND GNATS, WHICH SPREAD DISEASE TO THE LIVESTOCK AND ON AND ON.

MOSES REMINDED THE PHARAOH THAT THE GOD HE SERVED WAS THE AUTHOR OF THE NATURAL LAW AS WELL AS WHAT MIGHT BE CONSIDERED SUPERNATURAL.

BUT STILL, PHARAOH SAID "NO." THE SLAVES WOULD REMAIN SLAVES.

THIS FROM THE EGYPTIANS WHO HAD SO LONG WANTED TO LIMIT THE GROWTH OF THE HEBREW PEOPLE. HAD FOR SO LONG WANTED THEM GONE.

THE POISON THAT HAD NOW BEEN PASSED ON FOR SO LONG OFTEN TAKES THE FORM OF PRIDE.

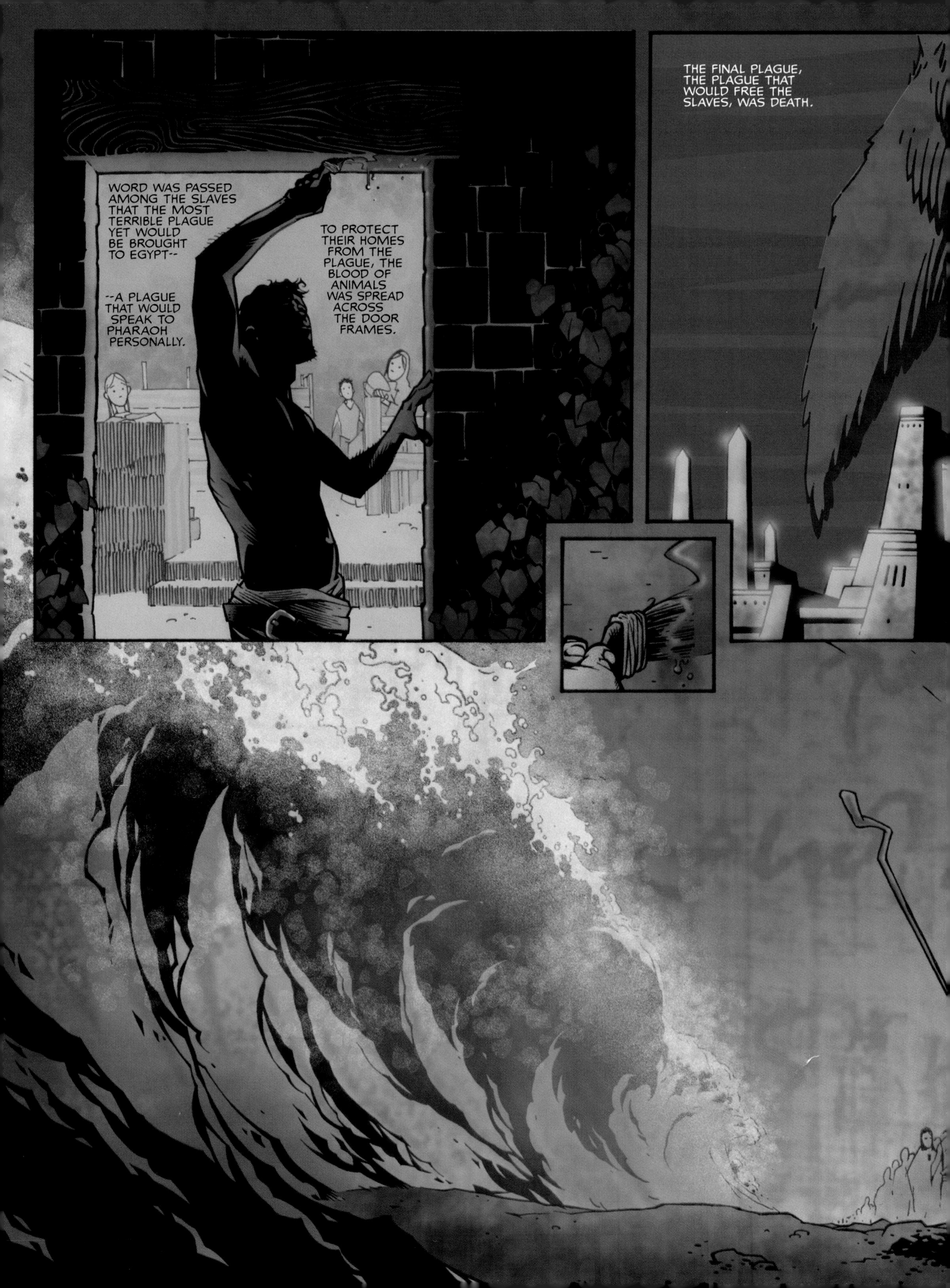
WORD WAS PASSED AMONG THE SLAVES THAT THE MOST TERRIBLE PLAGUE YET WOULD BE BROUGHT TO EGYPT--
--A PLAGUE THAT WOULD SPEAK TO PHARAOH PERSONALLY.
TO PROTECT THEIR HOMES FROM THE PLAGUE, THE BLOOD OF ANIMALS WAS SPREAD ACROSS THE DOOR FRAMES.
THE FINAL PLAGUE, THE PLAGUE THAT WOULD FREE THE SLAVES, WAS DEATH.

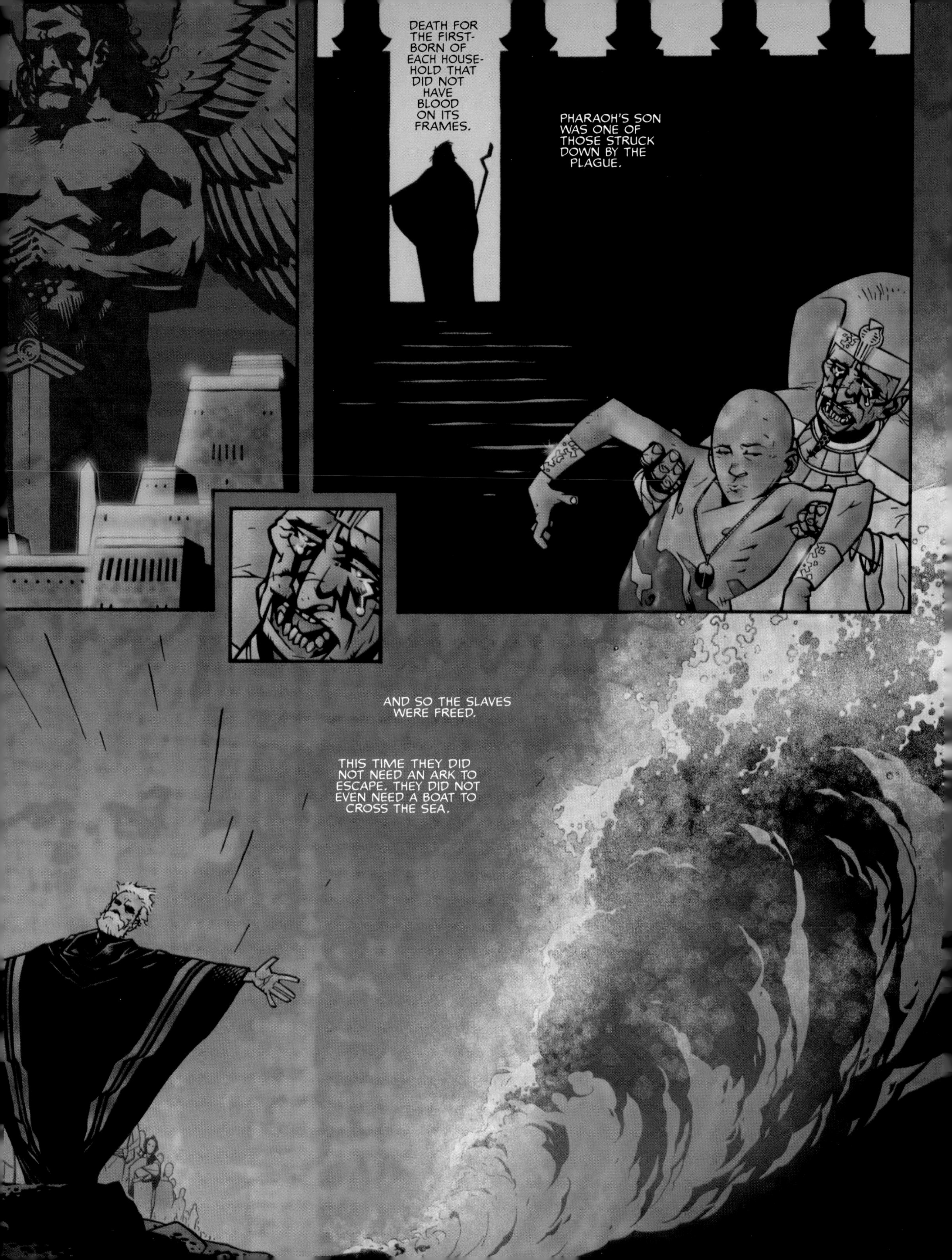

DEATH FOR THE FIRST-BORN OF EACH HOUSE-HOLD THAT DID NOT HAVE BLOOD ON ITS FRAMES.
PHARAOH'S SON WAS ONE OF THOSE STRUCK DOWN BY THE PLAGUE.
AND SO THE SLAVES WERE FREED.
THIS TIME THEY DID NOT NEED AN ARK TO ESCAPE. THEY DID NOT EVEN NEED A BOAT TO CROSS THE SEA.

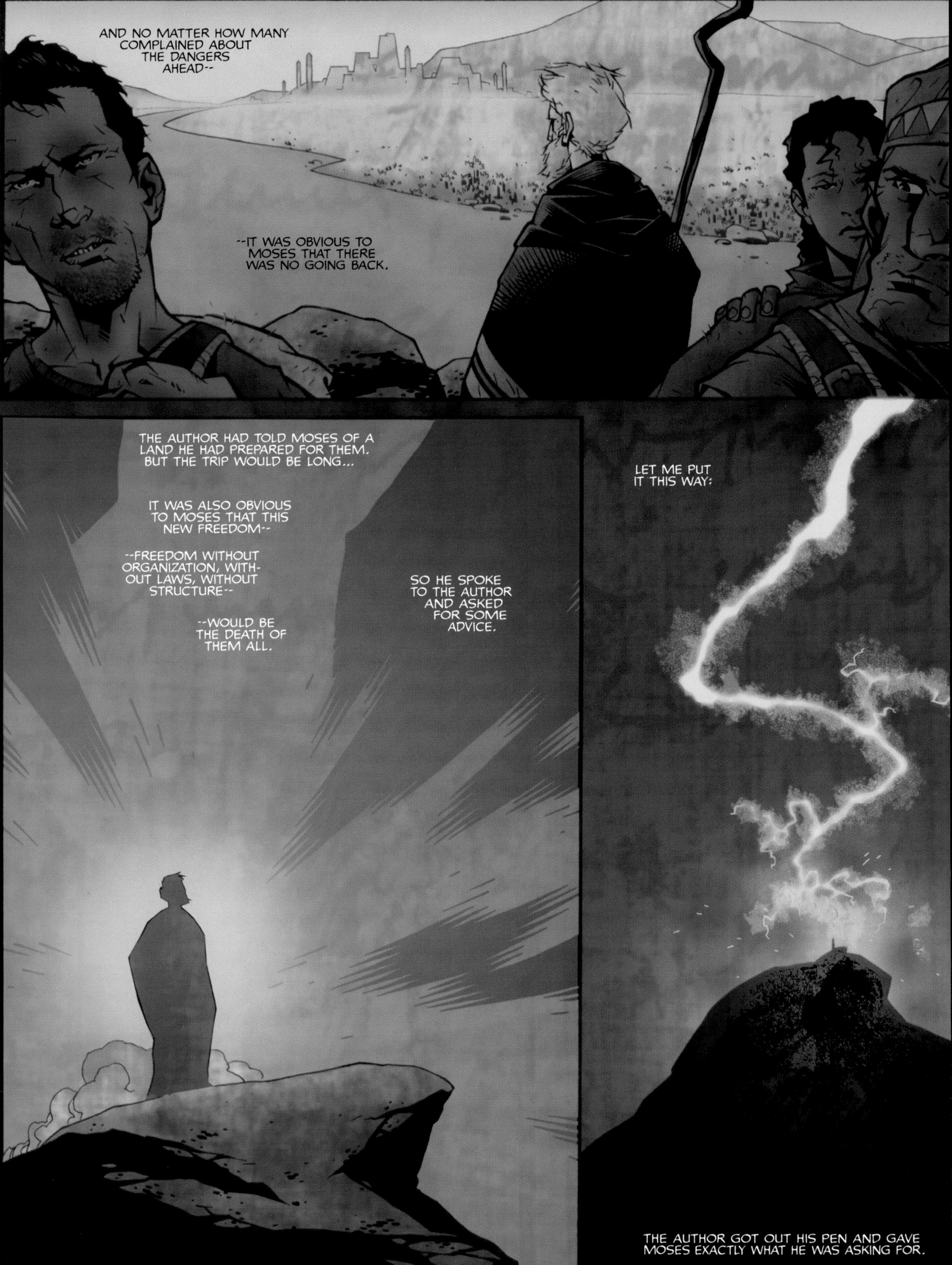
AND NO MATTER HOW MANY COMPLAINED ABOUT THE DANGERS AHEAD--
--IT WAS OBVIOUS TO MOSES THAT THERE WAS NO GOING BACK.
THE AUTHOR HAD TOLD MOSES OF A LAND HE HAD PREPARED FOR THEM. BUT THE TRIP WOULD BE LONG...
IT WAS ALSO OBVIOUS TO MOSES THAT THIS NEW FREEDOM--
--FREEDOM WITHOUT ORGANIZATION, WITH-OUT LAWS, WITHOUT STRUCTURE--
--WOULD BE THE DEATH OF THEM ALL.
SO HE SPOKE TO THE AUTHOR AND ASKED FOR SOME ADVICE.
LET ME PUT IT THIS WAY:
THE AUTHOR GOT OUT HIS PEN AND GAVE MOSES EXACTLY WHAT HE WAS ASKING FOR.

THE ONLY THING HARDER THAN THE PAPER THE AUTHOR USED, WAS ATTEMPTING TO OBEY EACH AND EVERY COMMANDMENT AND LAW.

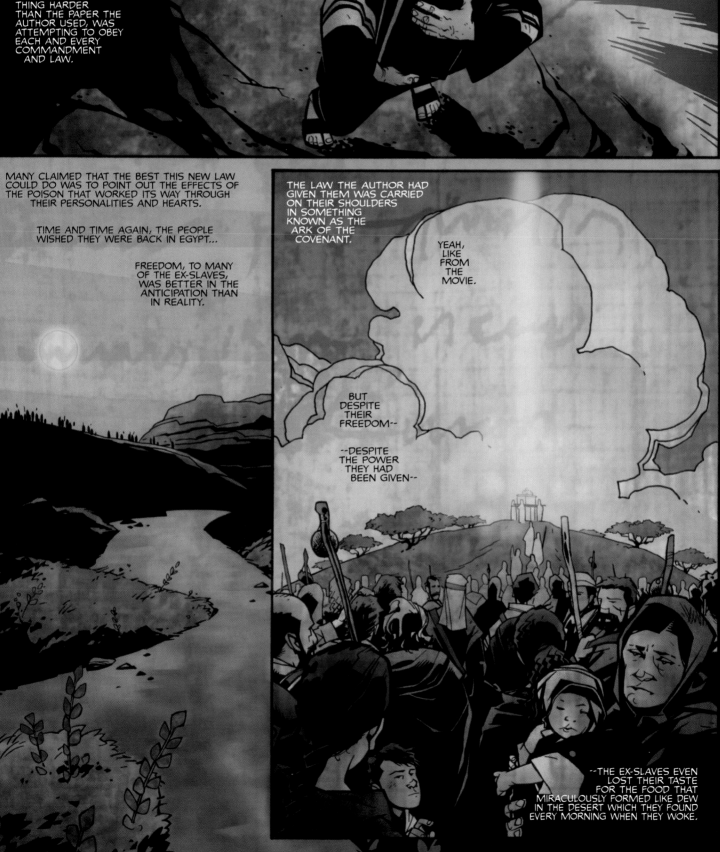

MANY CLAIMED THAT THE BEST THIS NEW LAW COULD DO WAS TO POINT OUT THE EFFECTS OF THE POISON THAT WORKED ITS WAY THROUGH THEIR PERSONALITIES AND HEARTS.

TIME AND TIME AGAIN, THE PEOPLE WISHED THEY WERE BACK IN EGYPT...

FREEDOM, TO MANY OF THE EX-SLAVES, WAS BETTER IN THE ANTICIPATION THAN IN REALITY.

THE LAW THE AUTHOR HAD GIVEN THEM WAS CARRIED ON THEIR SHOULDERS IN SOMETHING KNOWN AS THE ARK OF THE COVENANT.

YEAH, LIKE FROM THE MOVIE.

BUT DESPITE THEIR FREEDOM--

--DESPITE THE POWER THEY HAD BEEN GIVEN--

--THE EX-SLAVES EVEN LOST THEIR TASTE FOR THE FOOD THAT MIRACULOUSLY FORMED LIKE DEW IN THE DESERT WHICH THEY FOUND EVERY MORNING WHEN THEY WOKE.

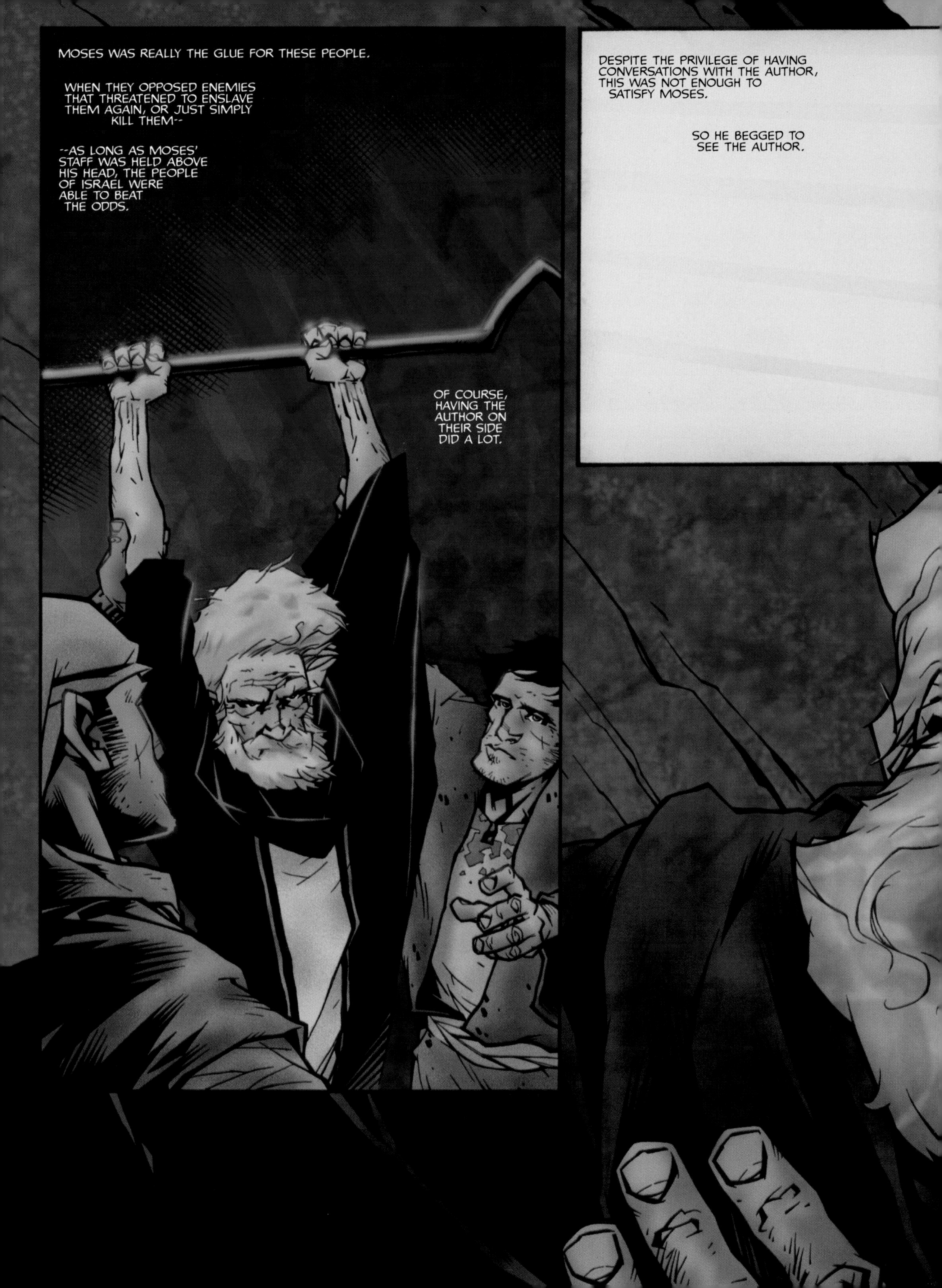
MOSES WAS REALLY THE GLUE FOR THESE PEOPLE.
WHEN THEY OPPOSED ENEMIES THAT THREATENED TO ENSLAVE THEM AGAIN, OR JUST SIMPLY KILL THEM--
--AS LONG AS MOSES' STAFF WAS HELD ABOVE HIS HEAD, THE PEOPLE OF ISRAEL WERE ABLE TO BEAT THE ODDS.
OF COURSE, HAVING THE AUTHOR ON THEIR SIDE DID A LOT.
DESPITE THE PRIVILEGE OF HAVING CONVERSATIONS WITH THE AUTHOR, THIS WAS NOT ENOUGH TO SATISFY MOSES.
SO HE BEGGED TO SEE THE AUTHOR.

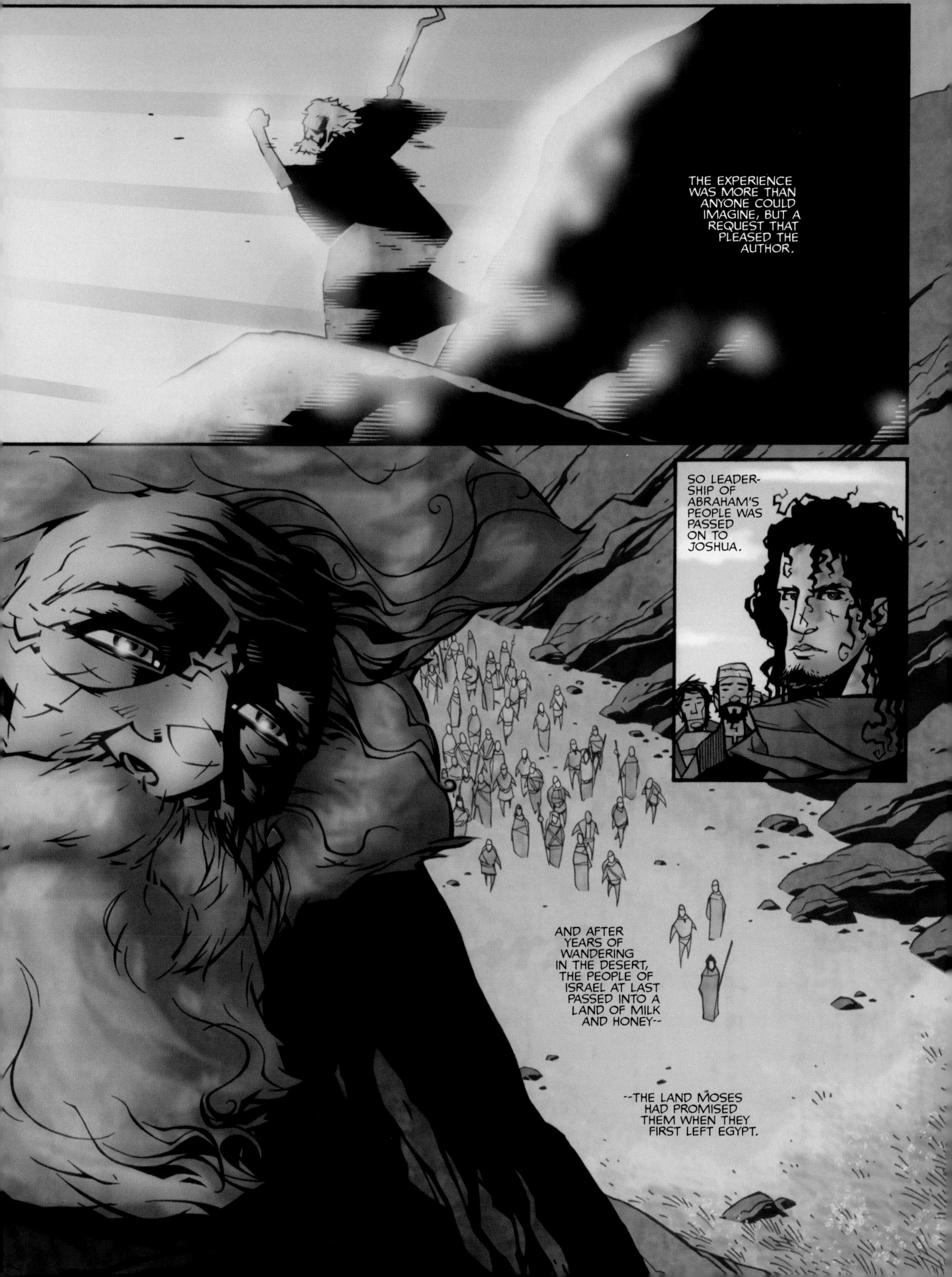
THE EXPERIENCE WAS MORE THAN ANYONE COULD IMAGINE, BUT A REQUEST THAT PLEASED THE AUTHOR.
SO LEADERSHIP OF ABRAHAM'S PEOPLE WAS PASSED ON TO JOSHUA.
AND AFTER YEARS OF WANDERING IN THE DESERT, THE PEOPLE OF ISRAEL AT LAST PASSED INTO A LAND OF MILK AND HONEY--
--THE LAND MOSES HAD PROMISED THEM WHEN THEY FIRST LEFT EGYPT.

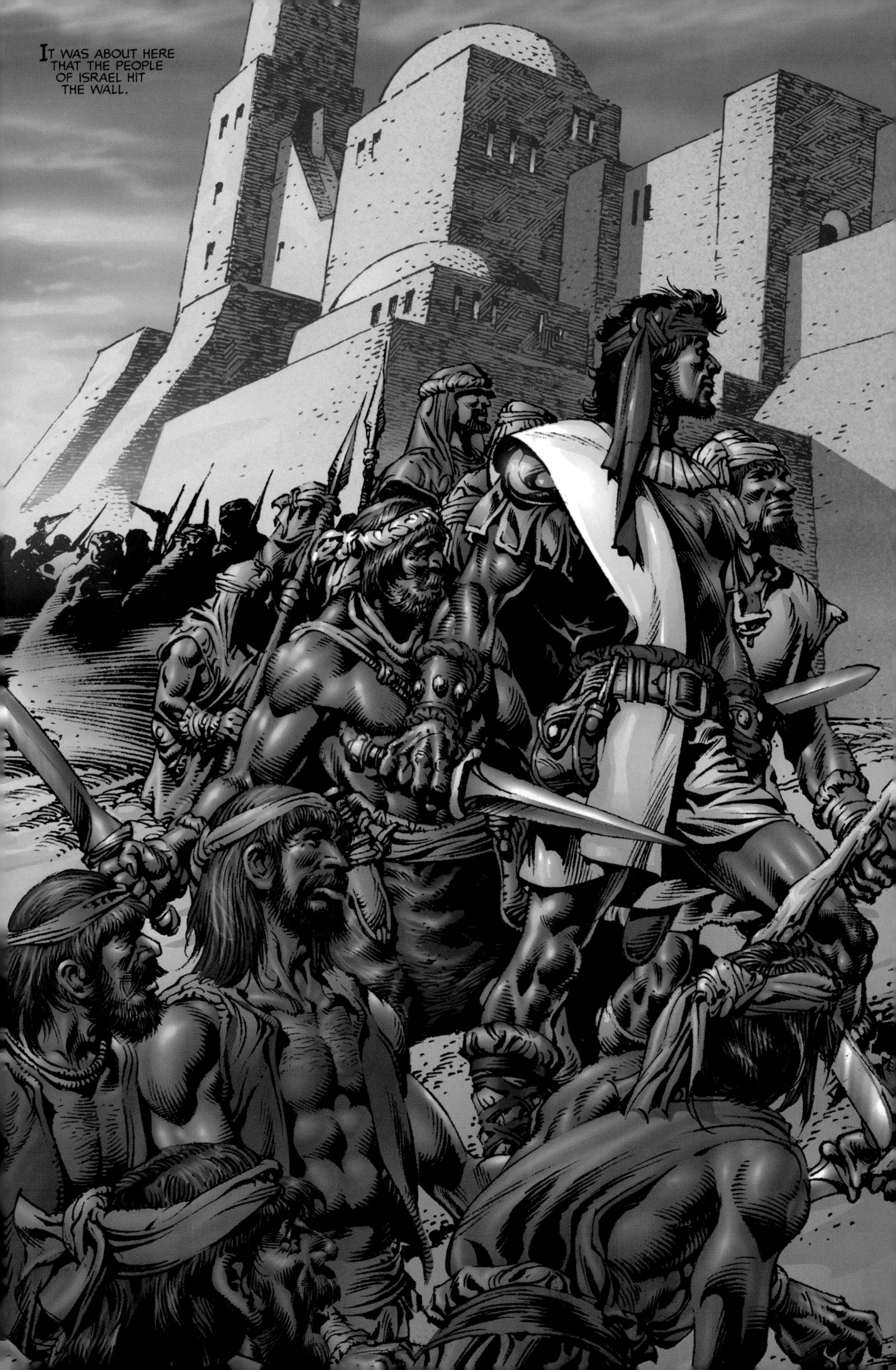
IT WAS ABOUT HERE THAT THE PEOPLE OF ISRAEL HIT THE WALL.

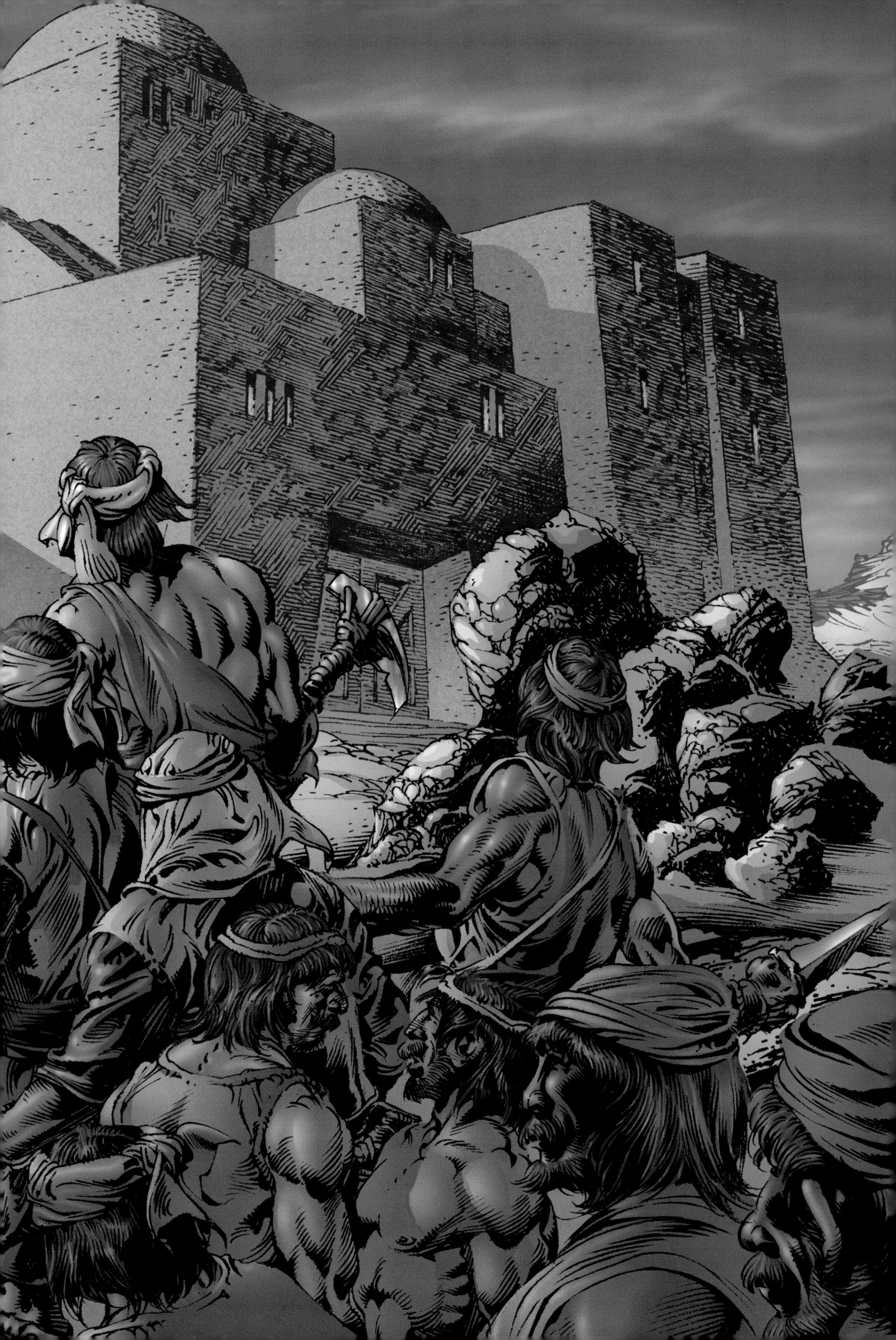

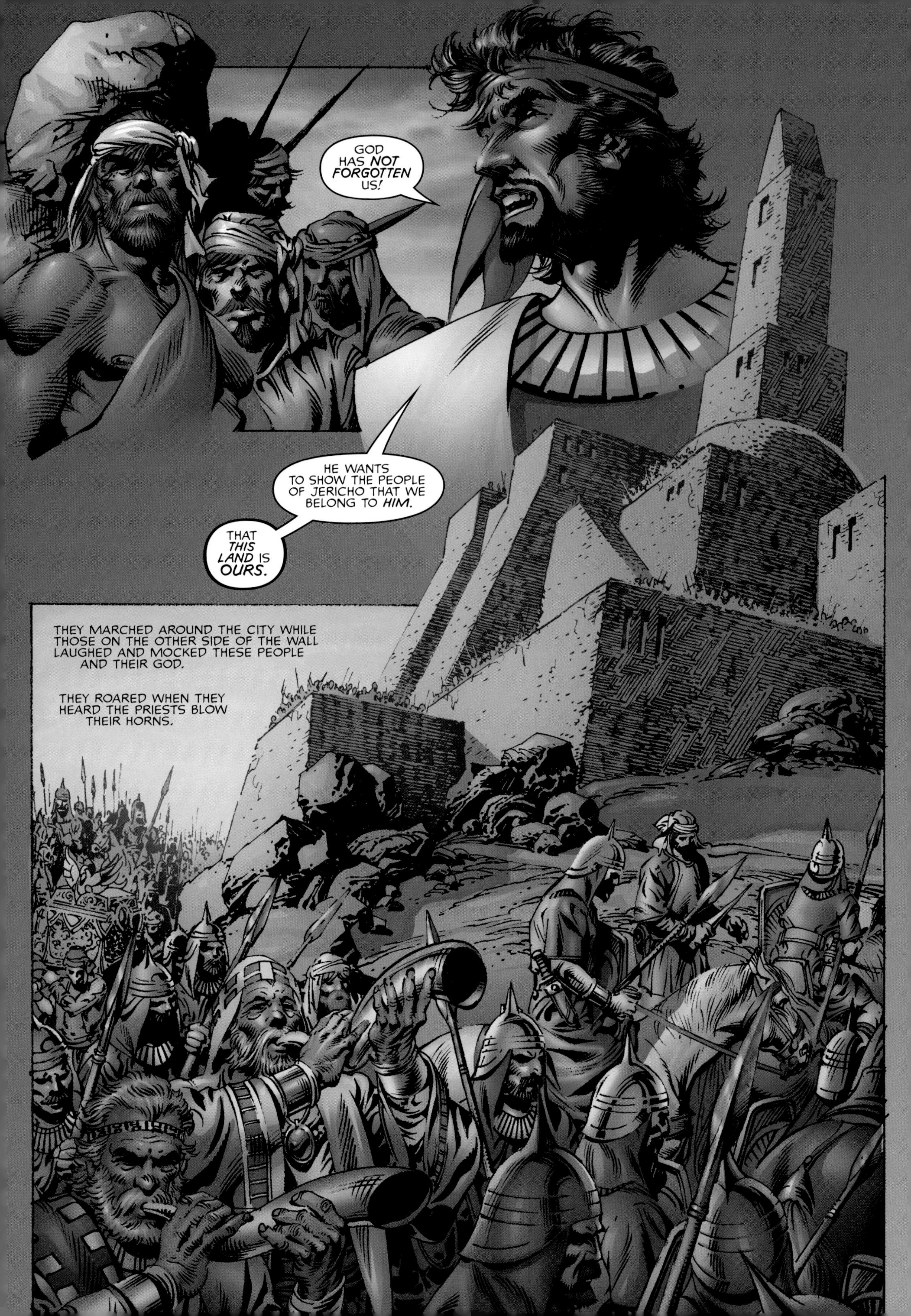
GOD HAS NOT FORGOTTEN US!
HE WANTS TO SHOW THE PEOPLE OF JERICHO THAT WE BELONG TO HIM.
THAT THIS LAND IS OURS.
THEY MARCHED AROUND THE CITY WHILE THOSE ON THE OTHER SIDE OF THE WALL LAUGHED AND MOCKED THESE PEOPLE AND THEIR GOD.
THEY ROARED WHEN THEY HEARD THE PRIESTS BLOW THEIR HORNS.

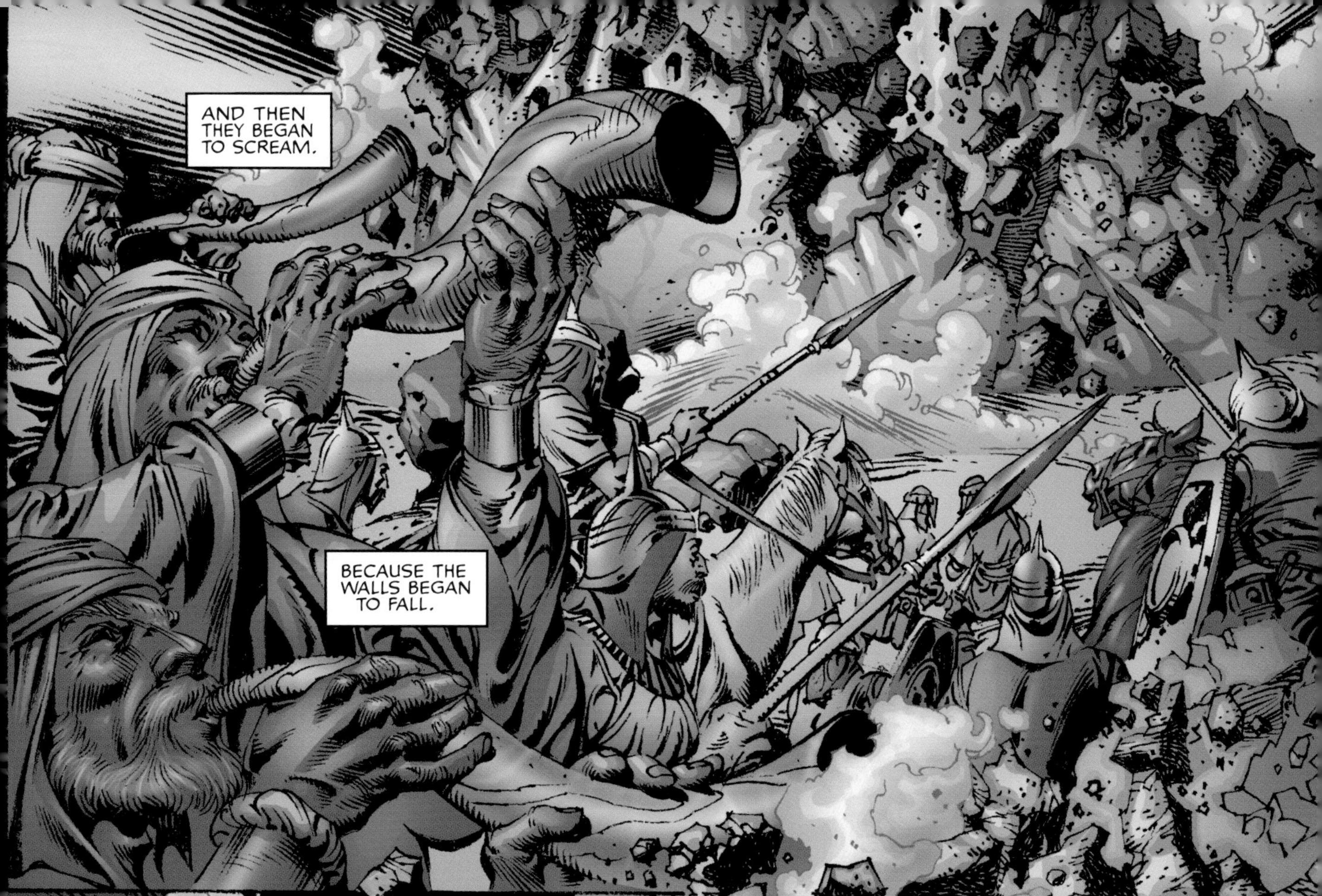
AND THEN THEY BEGAN TO SCREAM.
BECAUSE THE WALLS BEGAN TO FALL.

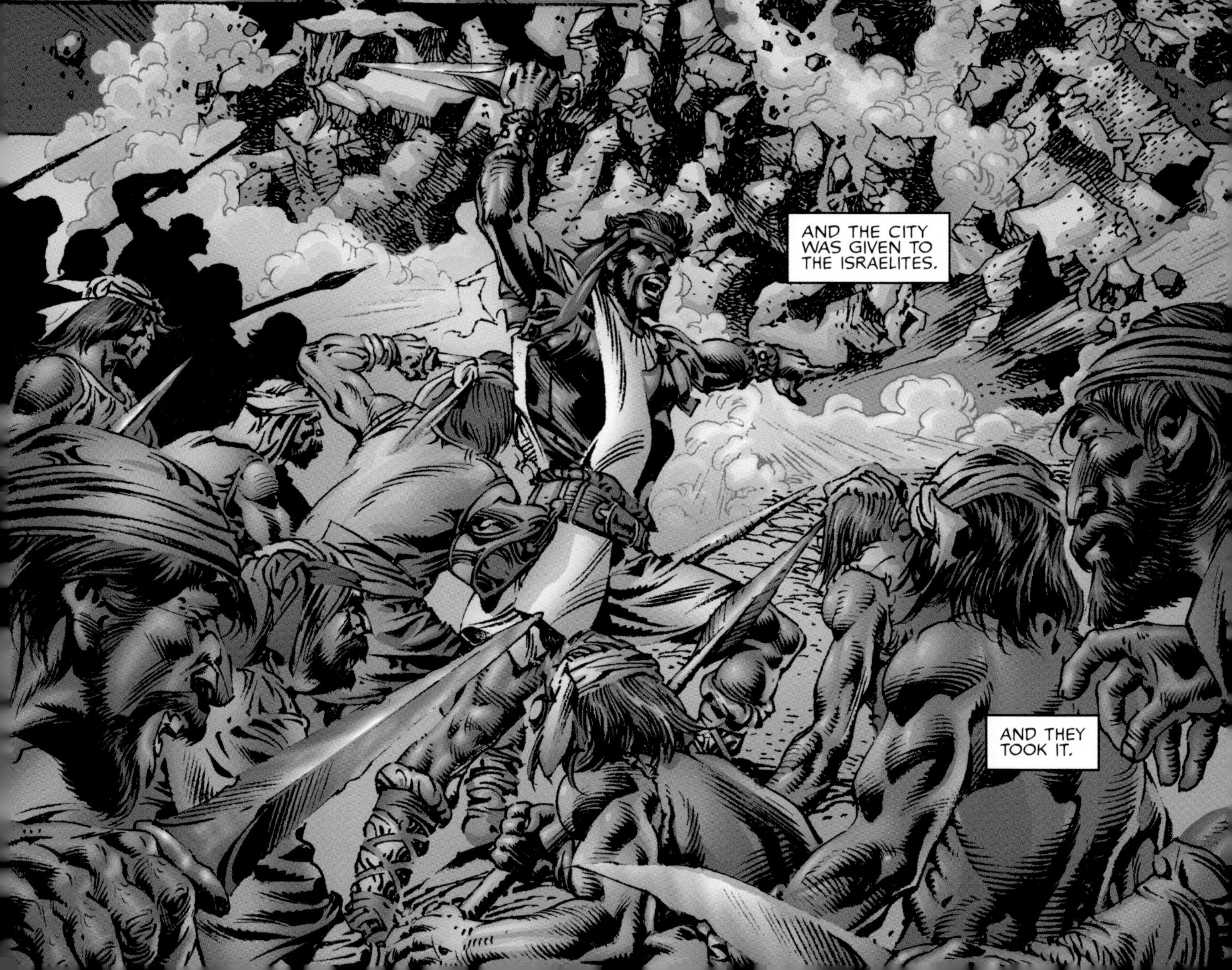
AND THE CITY WAS GIVEN TO THE ISRAELITES.
AND THEY TOOK IT.

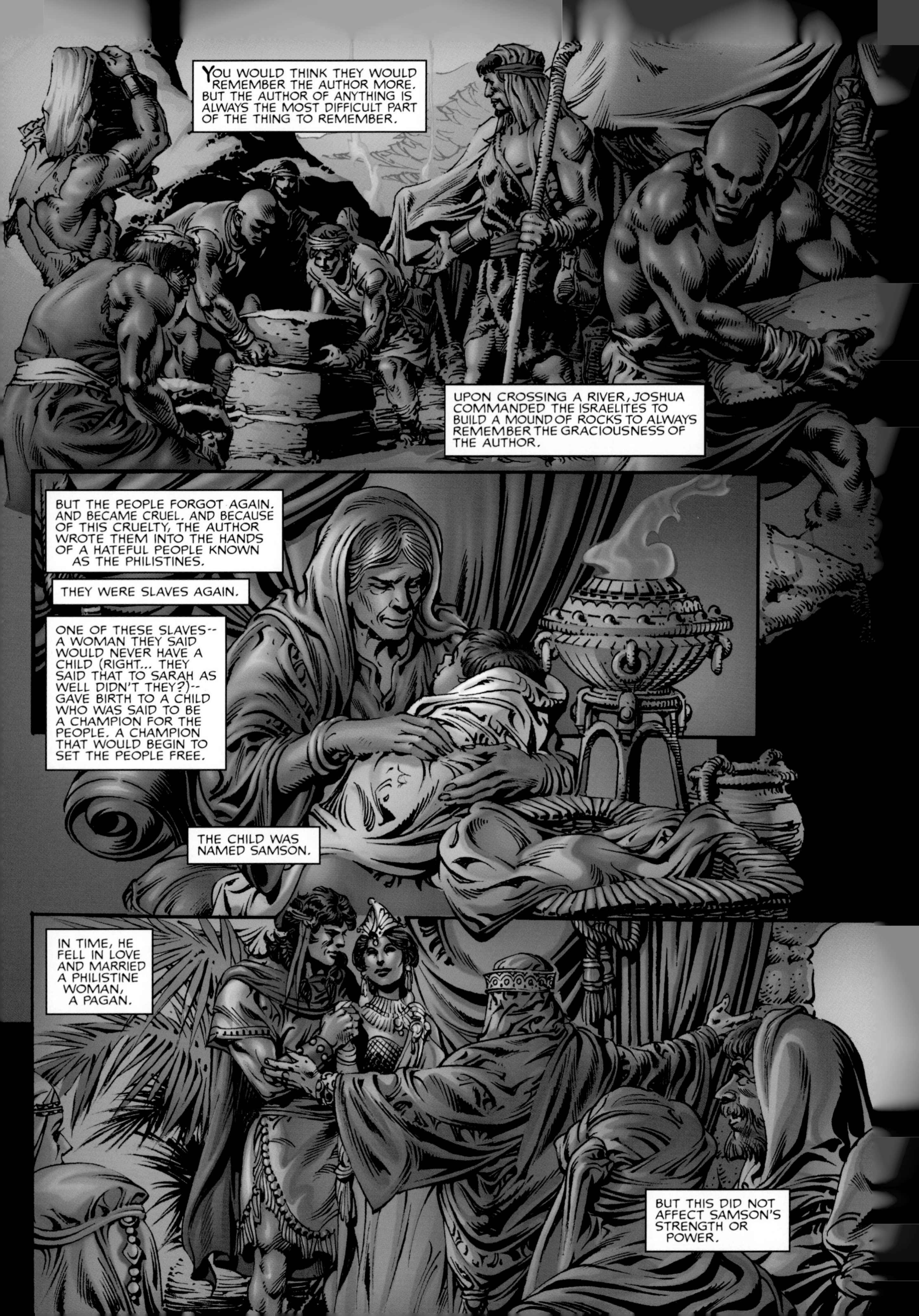
YOU WOULD THINK THEY WOULD REMEMBER THE AUTHOR MORE. BUT THE AUTHOR OF ANYTHING IS ALWAYS THE MOST DIFFICULT PART OF THE THING TO REMEMBER.
UPON CROSSING A RIVER, JOSHUA COMMANDED THE ISRAELITES TO BUILD A MOUND OF ROCKS TO ALWAYS REMEMBER THE GRACIOUSNESS OF THE AUTHOR.
BUT THE PEOPLE FORGOT AGAIN. AND BECAME CRUEL. AND BECAUSE OF THIS CRUELTY, THE AUTHOR WROTE THEM INTO THE HANDS OF A HATEFUL PEOPLE KNOWN AS THE PHILISTINES.
THEY WERE SLAVES AGAIN.
ONE OF THESE SLAVES-- A WOMAN THEY SAID WOULD NEVER HAVE A CHILD (RIGHT... THEY SAID THAT TO SARAH AS WELL DIDN'T THEY?)-- GAVE BIRTH TO A CHILD WHO WAS SAID TO BE A CHAMPION FOR THE PEOPLE. A CHAMPION THAT WOULD BEGIN TO SET THE PEOPLE FREE.
THE CHILD WAS NAMED SAMSON.
IN TIME, HE FELL IN LOVE AND MARRIED A PHILISTINE WOMAN, A PAGAN.
BUT THIS DID NOT AFFECT SAMSON'S STRENGTH OR POWER.

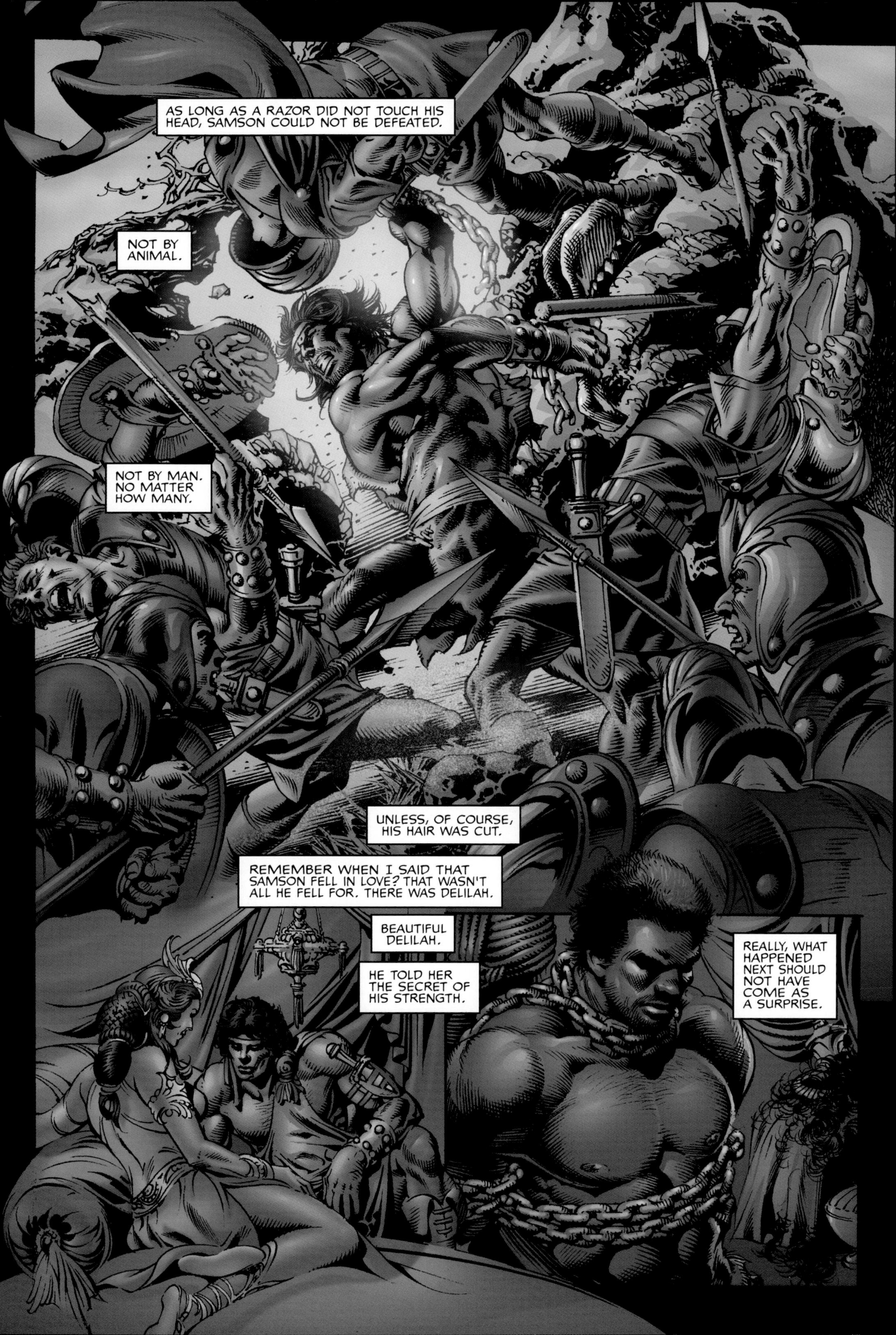
AS LONG AS A RAZOR DID NOT TOUCH HIS HEAD, SAMSON COULD NOT BE DEFEATED.
NOT BY ANIMAL.
NOT BY MAN. NO MATTER HOW MANY.
UNLESS, OF COURSE, HIS HAIR WAS CUT.
REMEMBER WHEN I SAID THAT SAMSON FELL IN LOVE? THAT WASN'T ALL HE FELL FOR. THERE WAS DELILAH.
BEAUTIFUL DELILAH.
HE TOLD HER THE SECRET OF HIS STRENGTH.
REALLY, WHAT HAPPENED NEXT SHOULD NOT HAVE COME AS A SURPRISE.

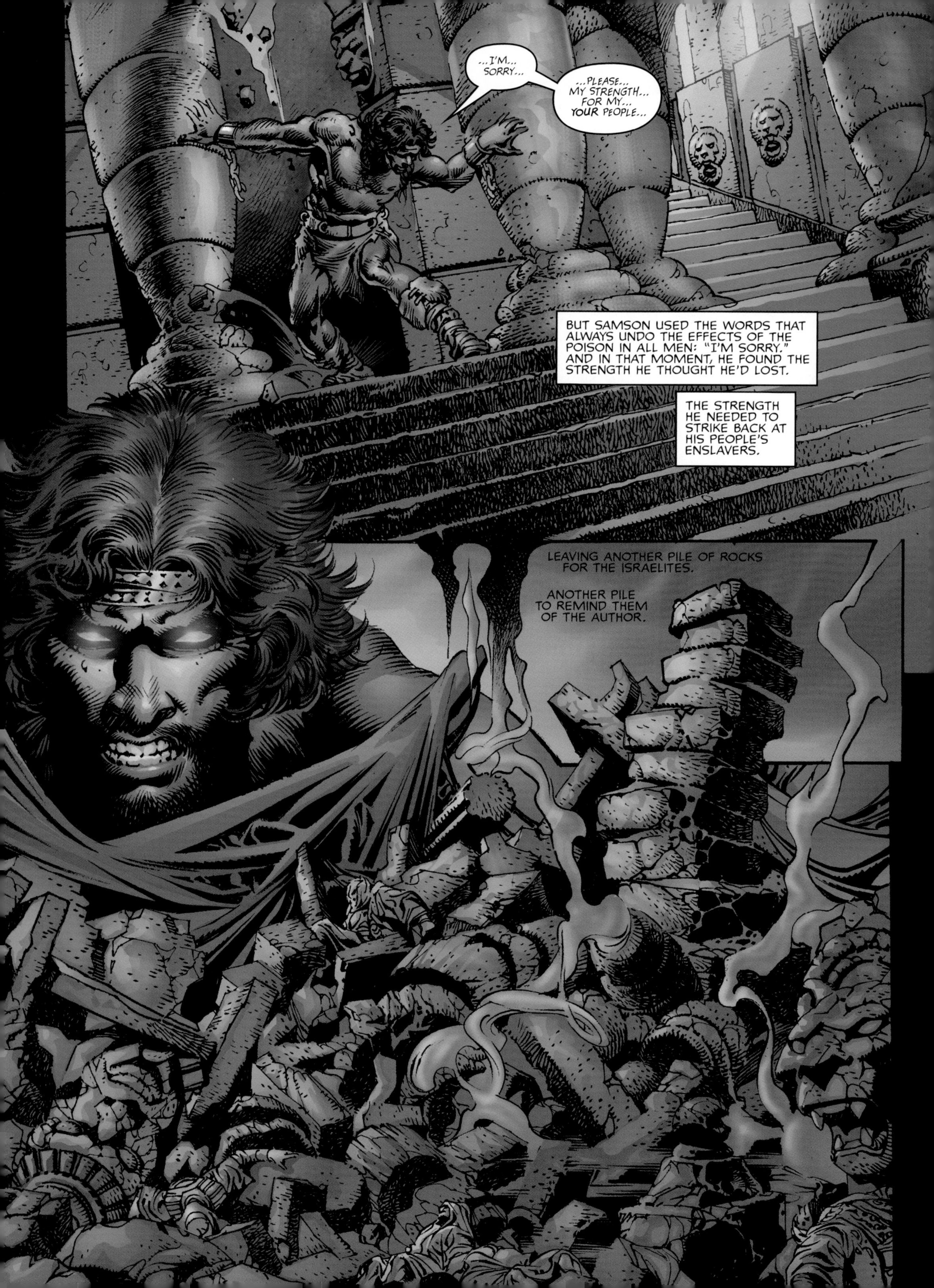
...I'M... SORRY...
...PLEASE... MY STRENGTH... FOR MY... YOUR PEOPLE...
BUT SAMSON USED THE WORDS THAT ALWAYS UNDO THE EFFECTS OF THE POISON IN ALL MEN: "I'M SORRY." AND IN THAT MOMENT, HE FOUND THE STRENGTH HE THOUGHT HE'D LOST.
THE STRENGTH HE NEEDED TO STRIKE BACK AT HIS PEOPLE'S ENSLAVERS.
LEAVING ANOTHER PILE OF ROCKS FOR THE ISRAELITES.
ANOTHER PILE TO REMIND THEM OF THE AUTHOR.

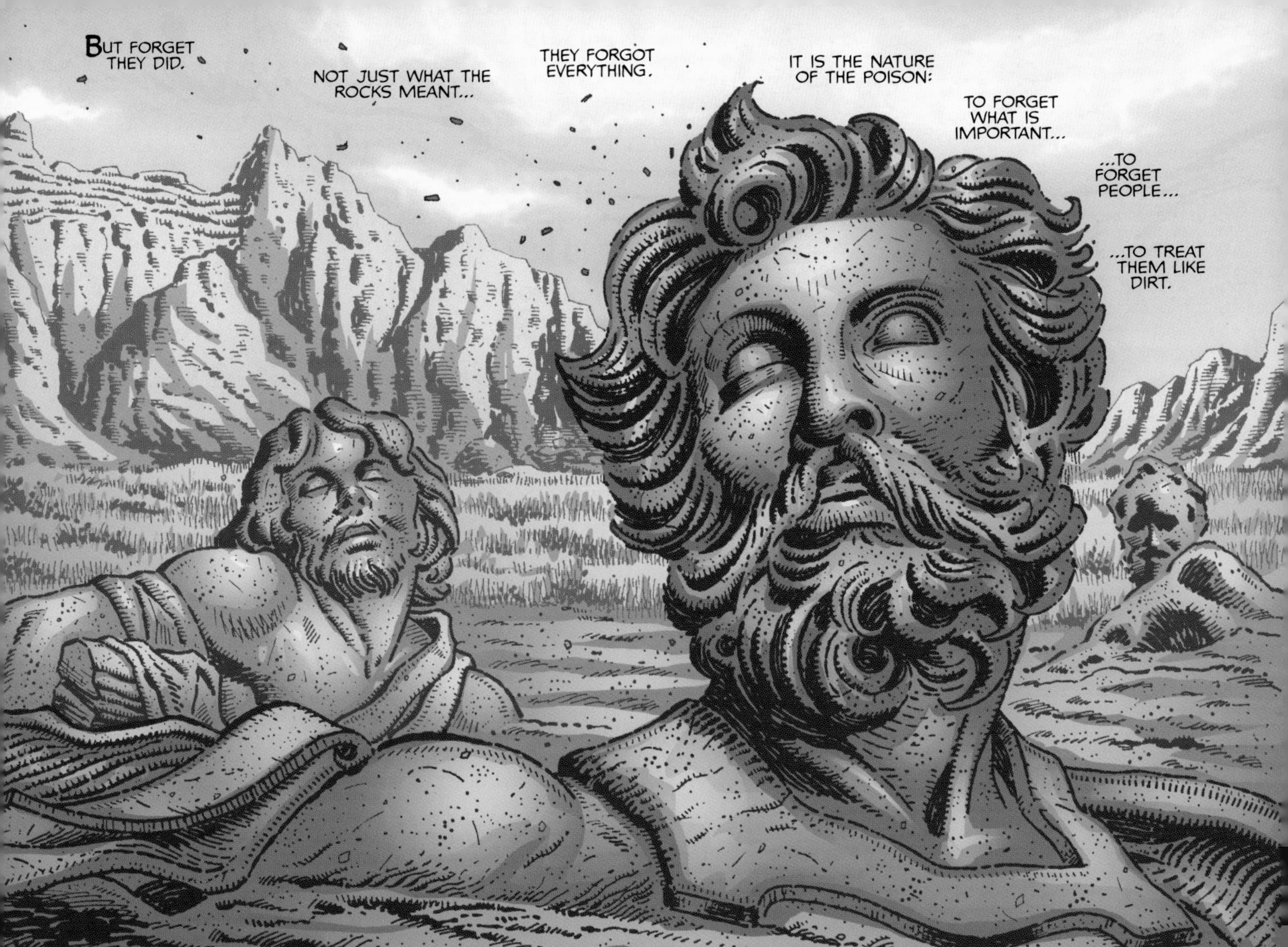
BUT FORGET THEY DID.
NOT JUST WHAT THE ROCKS MEANT...
THEY FORGOT EVERYTHING.
IT IS THE NATURE OF THE POISON:
TO FORGET WHAT IS IMPORTANT...
...TO FORGET PEOPLE...
...TO TREAT THEM LIKE DIRT.

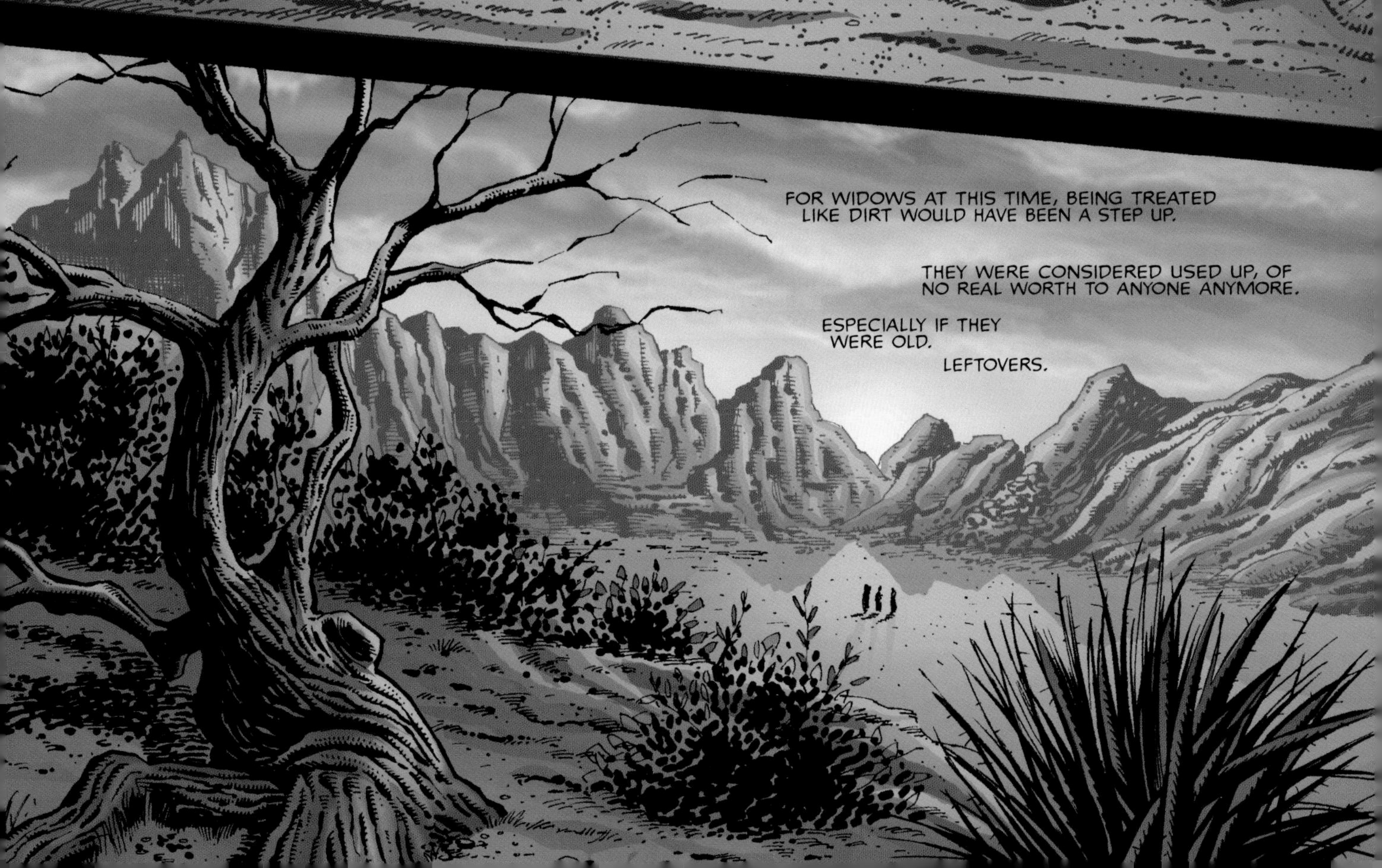
FOR WIDOWS AT THIS TIME, BEING TREATED LIKE DIRT WOULD HAVE BEEN A STEP UP.
THEY WERE CONSIDERED USED UP, OF NO REAL WORTH TO ANYONE ANYMORE.
ESPECIALLY IF THEY WERE OLD.
LEFTOVERS.

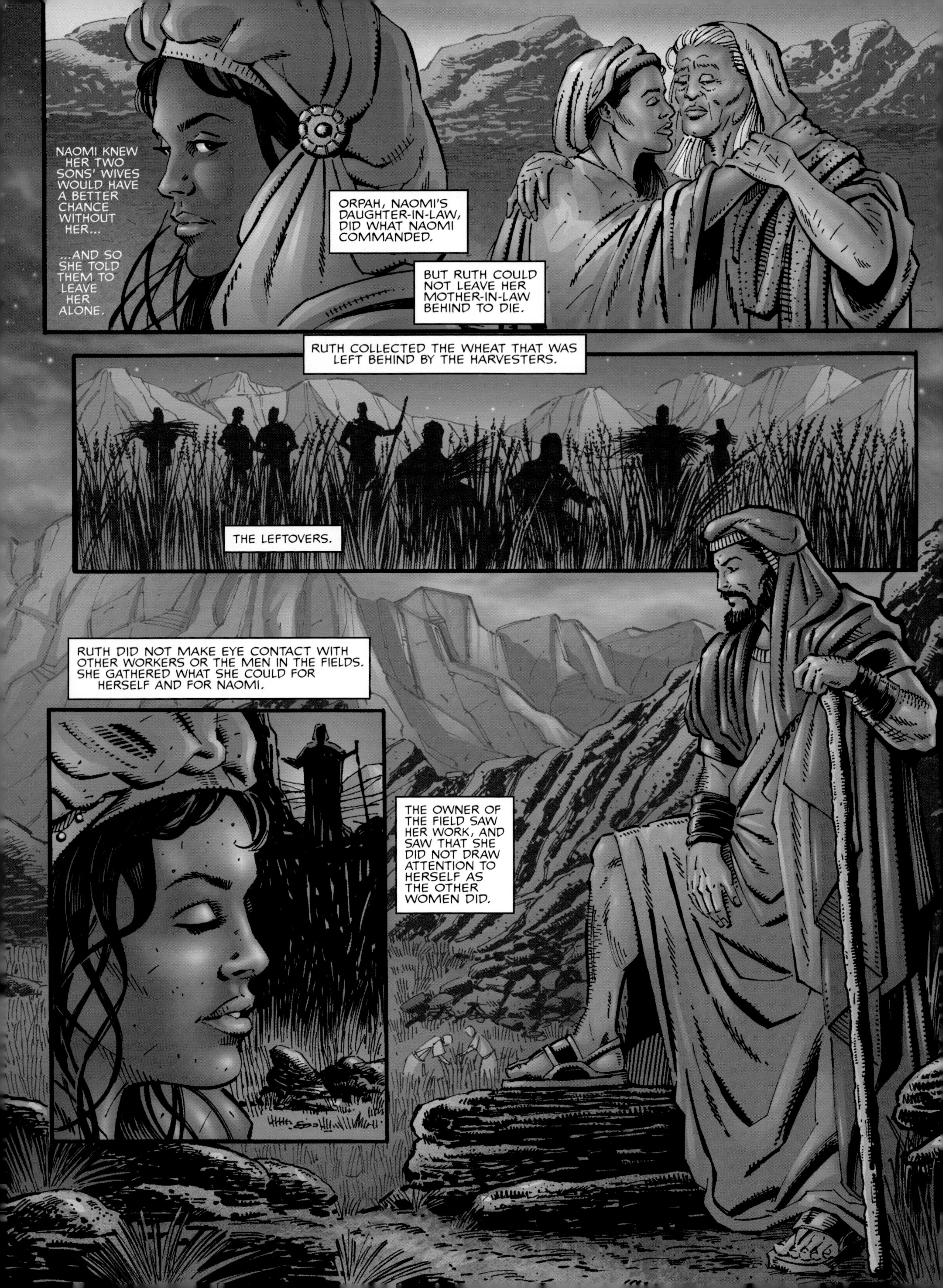
NAOMI KNEW HER TWO SONS' WIVES WOULD HAVE A BETTER CHANCE WITHOUT HER...
...AND SO SHE TOLD THEM TO LEAVE HER ALONE.
ORPAH, NAOMI'S DAUGHTER-IN-LAW, DID WHAT NAOMI COMMANDED.
BUT RUTH COULD NOT LEAVE HER MOTHER-IN-LAW BEHIND TO DIE.
RUTH COLLECTED THE WHEAT THAT WAS LEFT BEHIND BY THE HARVESTERS.
THE LEFTOVERS.
RUTH DID NOT MAKE EYE CONTACT WITH OTHER WORKERS OR THE MEN IN THE FIELDS. SHE GATHERED WHAT SHE COULD FOR HERSELF AND FOR NAOMI.
THE OWNER OF THE FIELD SAW HER WORK, AND SAW THAT SHE DID NOT DRAW ATTENTION TO HERSELF AS THE OTHER WOMEN DID.

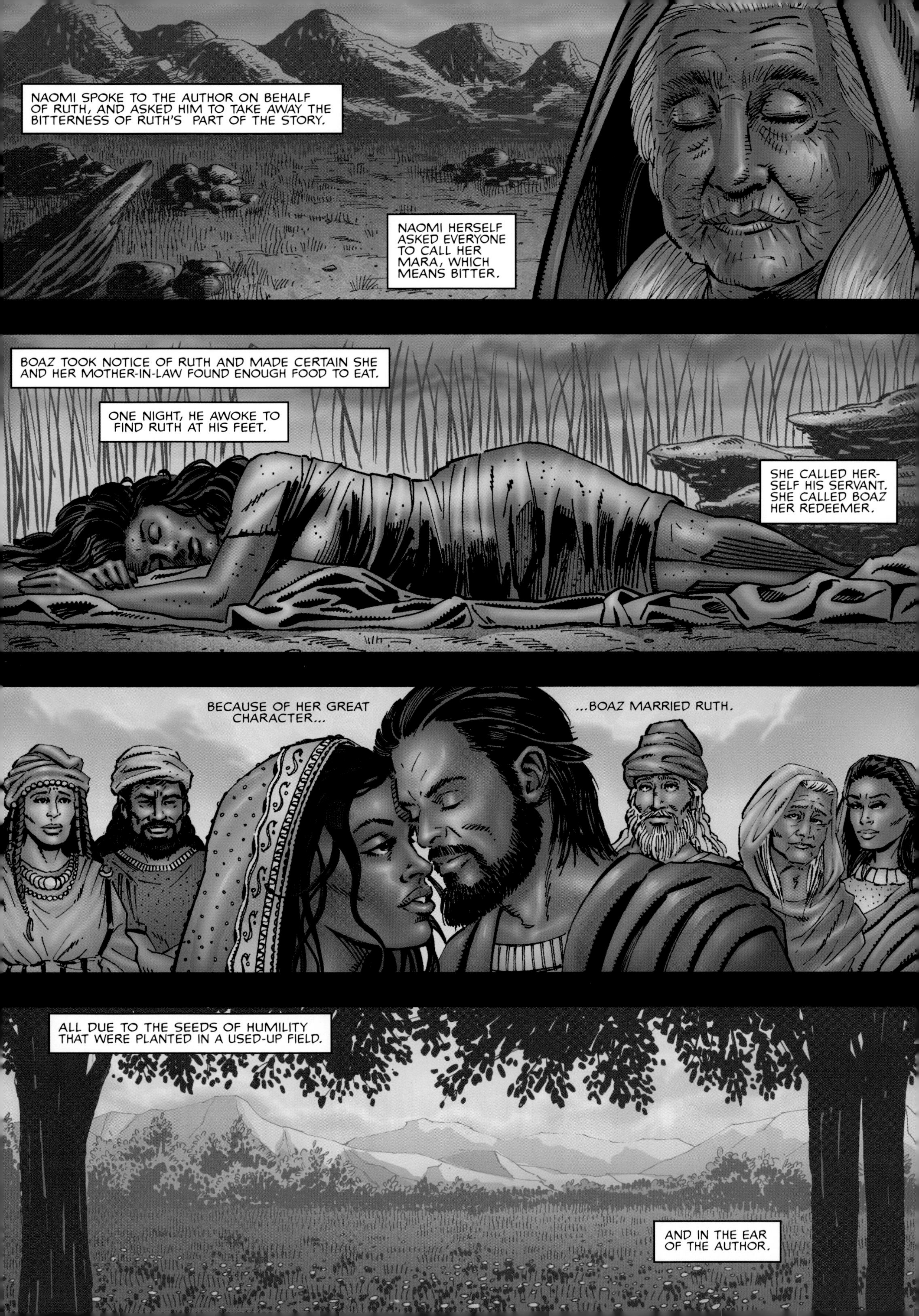
NAOMI SPOKE TO THE AUTHOR ON BEHALF OF RUTH, AND ASKED HIM TO TAKE AWAY THE BITTERNESS OF RUTH'S PART OF THE STORY.
NAOMI HERSELF ASKED EVERYONE TO CALL HER MARA, WHICH MEANS BITTER.
BOAZ TOOK NOTICE OF RUTH AND MADE CERTAIN SHE AND HER MOTHER-IN-LAW FOUND ENOUGH FOOD TO EAT.
ONE NIGHT, HE AWOKE TO FIND RUTH AT HIS FEET.
SHE CALLED HER-SELF HIS SERVANT. SHE CALLED BOAZ HER REDEEMER.
BECAUSE OF HER GREAT CHARACTER...
...BOAZ MARRIED RUTH.
ALL DUE TO THE SEEDS OF HUMILITY THAT WERE PLANTED IN A USED-UP FIELD.
AND IN THE EAR OF THE AUTHOR.

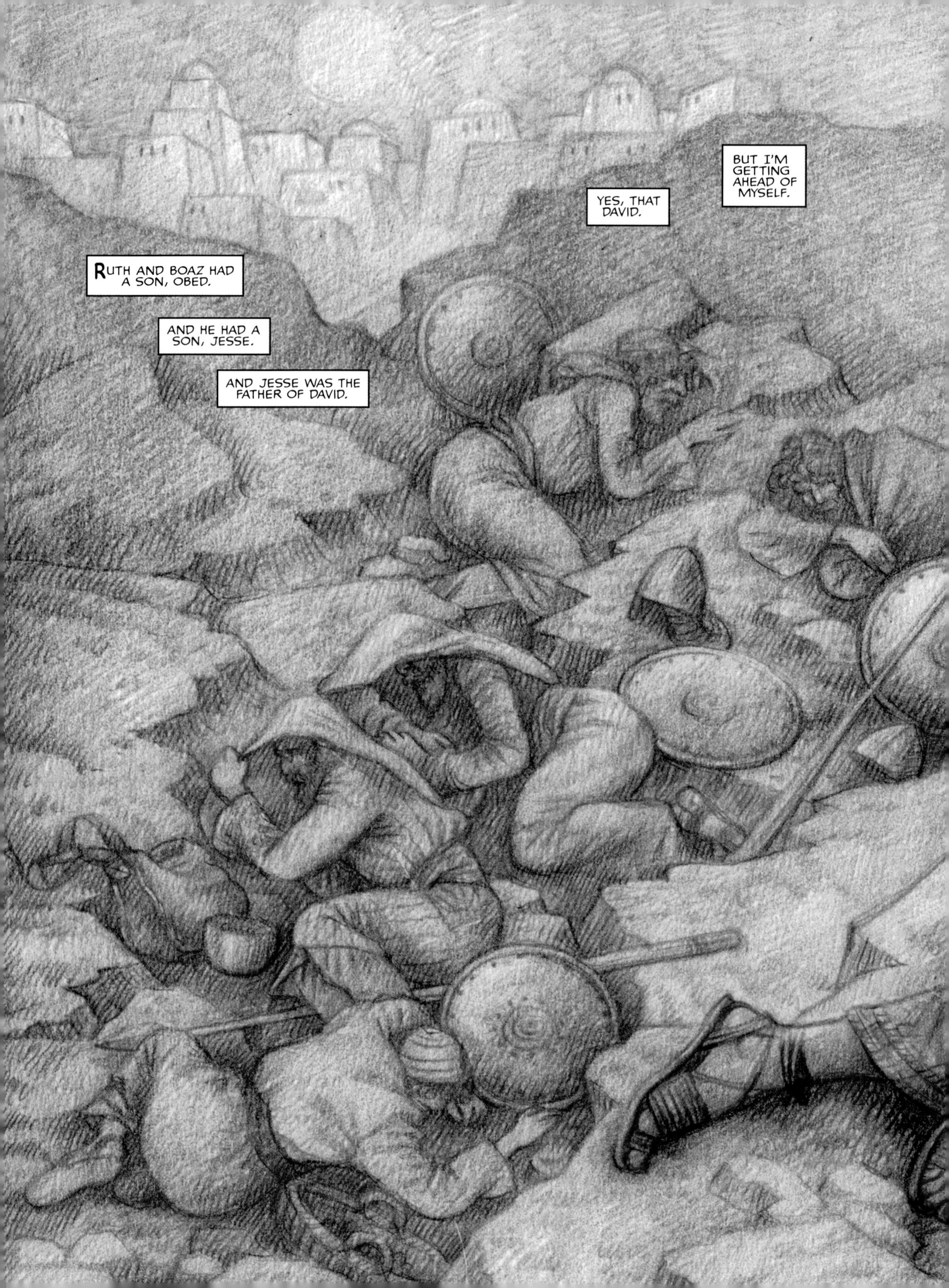
RUTH AND BOAZ HAD A SON, OBED.
AND HE HAD A SON, JESSE.
AND JESSE WAS THE FATHER OF DAVID.
YES, THAT DAVID.
BUT I'M GETTING AHEAD OF MYSELF.

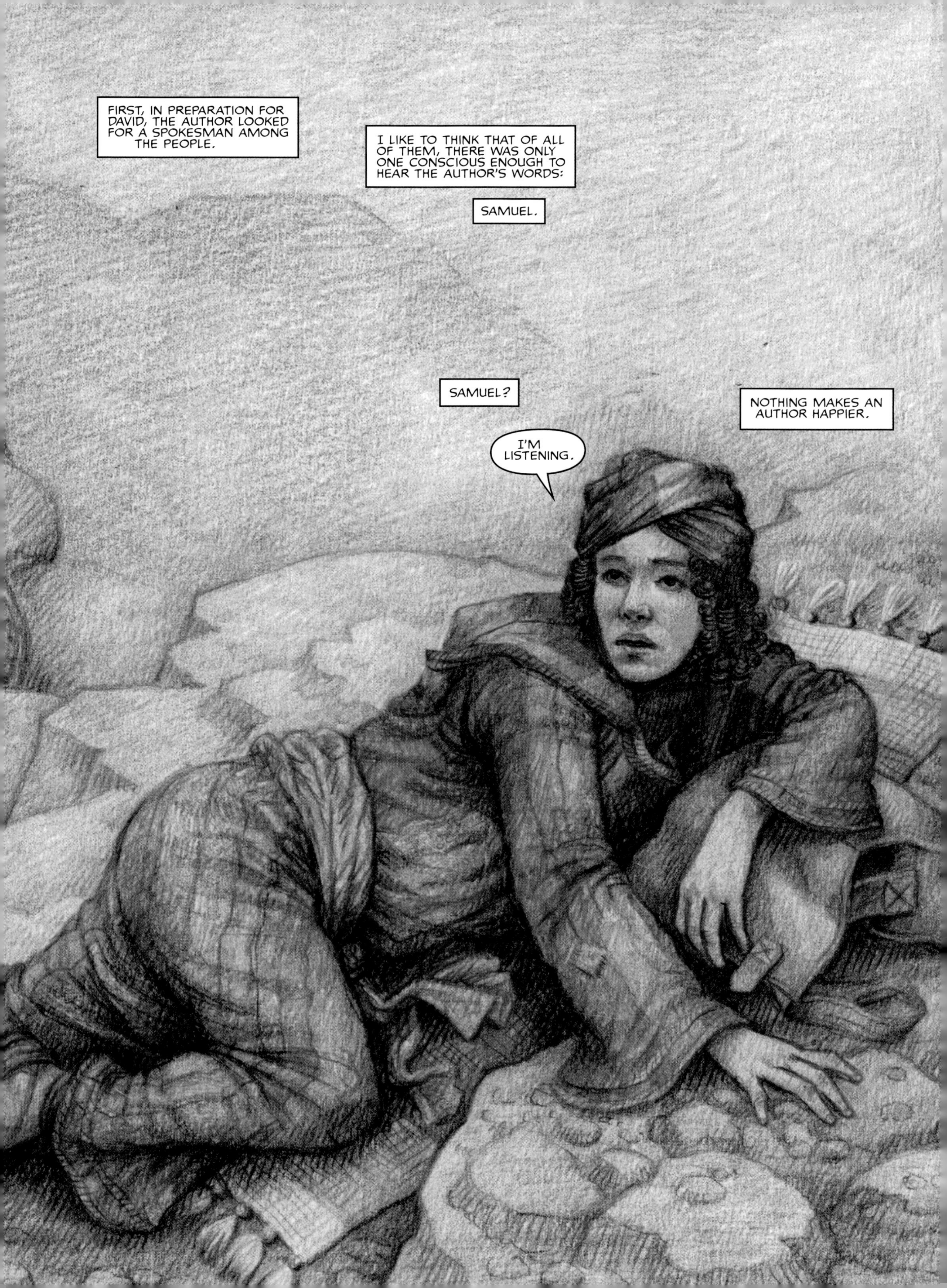
FIRST, IN PREPARATION FOR DAVID, THE AUTHOR LOOKED FOR A SPOKESMAN AMONG THE PEOPLE.
I LIKE TO THINK THAT OF ALL OF THEM, THERE WAS ONLY ONE CONSCIOUS ENOUGH TO HEAR THE AUTHOR'S WORDS:
SAMUEL.
SAMUEL?
I'M LISTENING.
NOTHING MAKES AN AUTHOR HAPPIER.

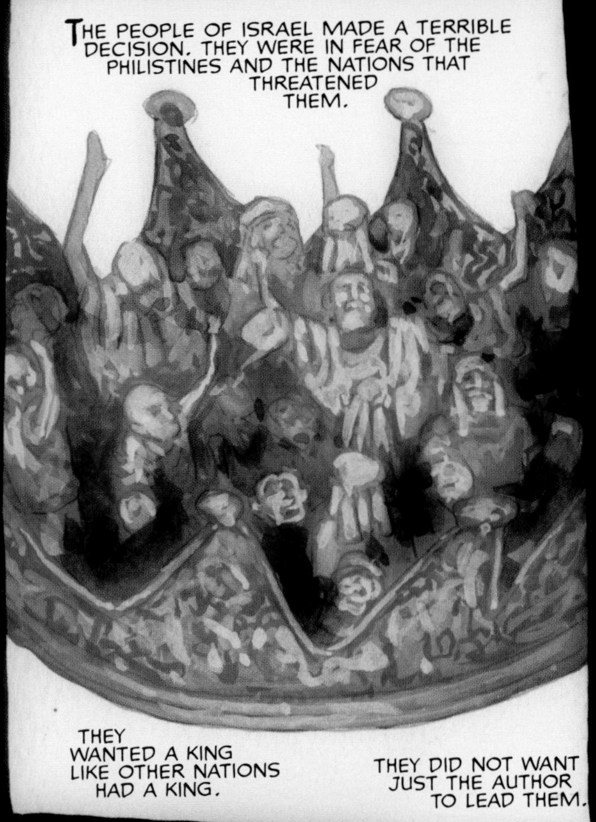
THE PEOPLE OF ISRAEL MADE A TERRIBLE DECISION. THEY WERE IN FEAR OF THE PHILISTINES AND THE NATIONS THAT THREATENED THEM.
THEY WANTED A KING LIKE OTHER NATIONS HAD A KING.
THEY DID NOT WANT JUST THE AUTHOR TO LEAD THEM.

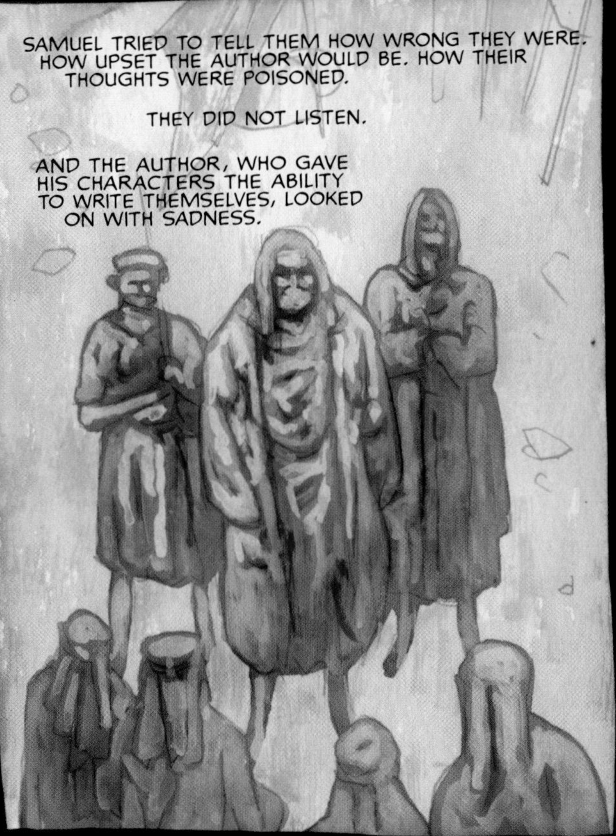
SAMUEL TRIED TO TELL THEM HOW WRONG THEY WERE. HOW UPSET THE AUTHOR WOULD BE. HOW THEIR THOUGHTS WERE POISONED.
THEY DID NOT LISTEN.
AND THE AUTHOR, WHO GAVE HIS CHARACTERS THE ABILITY TO WRITE THEMSELVES, LOOKED ON WITH SADNESS.

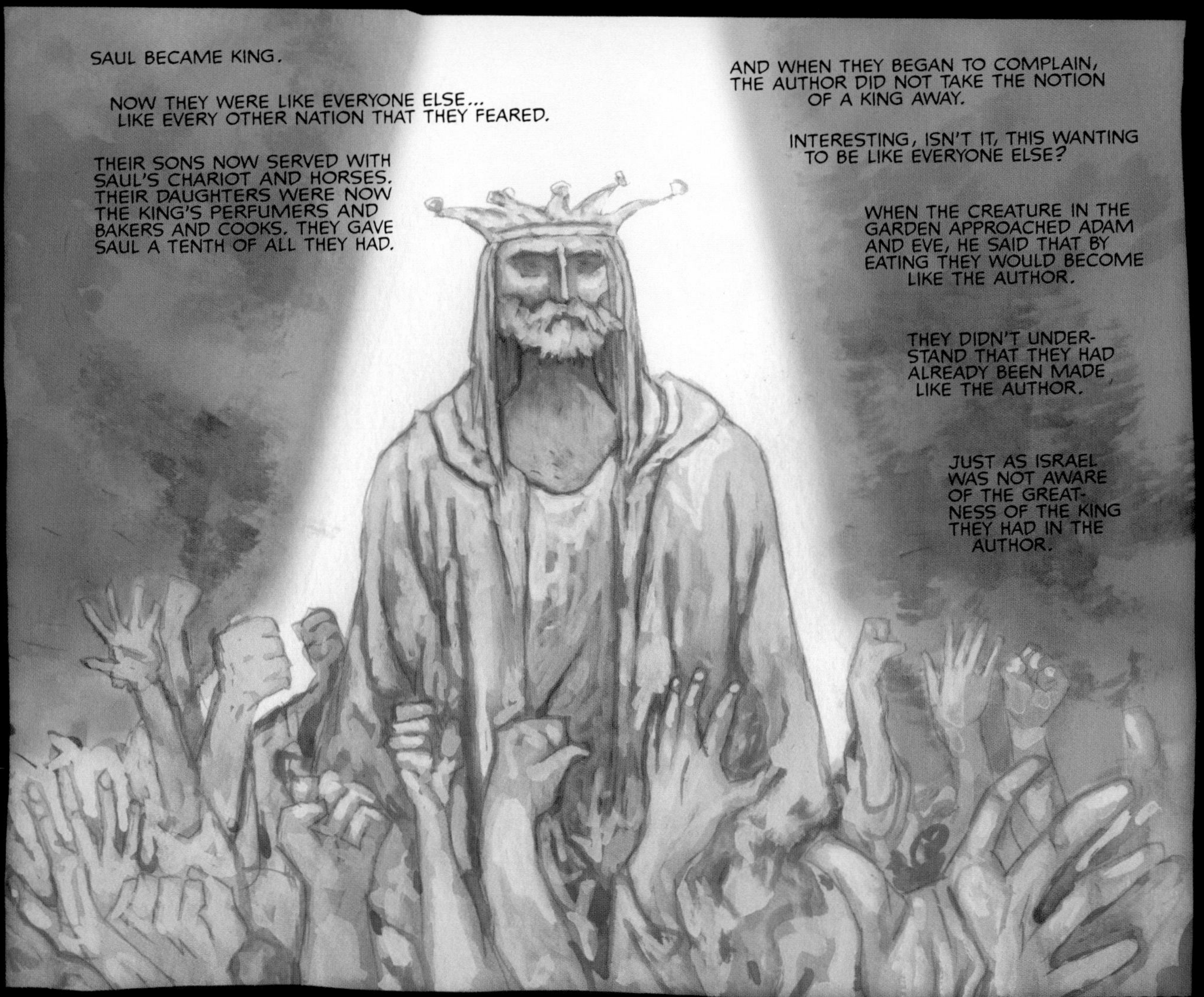
SAUL BECAME KING.
NOW THEY WERE LIKE EVERYONE ELSE... LIKE EVERY OTHER NATION THAT THEY FEARED.
THEIR SONS NOW SERVED WITH SAUL'S CHARIOT AND HORSES. THEIR DAUGHTERS WERE NOW THE KING'S PERFUMERS AND BAKERS AND COOKS. THEY GAVE SAUL A TENTH OF ALL THEY HAD.
AND WHEN THEY BEGAN TO COMPLAIN, THE AUTHOR DID NOT TAKE THE NOTION OF A KING AWAY.
INTERESTING, ISN'T IT, THIS WANTING TO BE LIKE EVERYONE ELSE?
WHEN THE CREATURE IN THE GARDEN APPROACHED ADAM AND EVE, HE SAID THAT BY EATING THEY WOULD BECOME LIKE THE AUTHOR.
THEY DIDN'T UNDER-STAND THAT THEY HAD ALREADY BEEN MADE LIKE THE AUTHOR.
JUST AS ISRAEL WAS NOT AWARE OF THE GREAT-NESS OF THE KING THEY HAD IN THE AUTHOR.

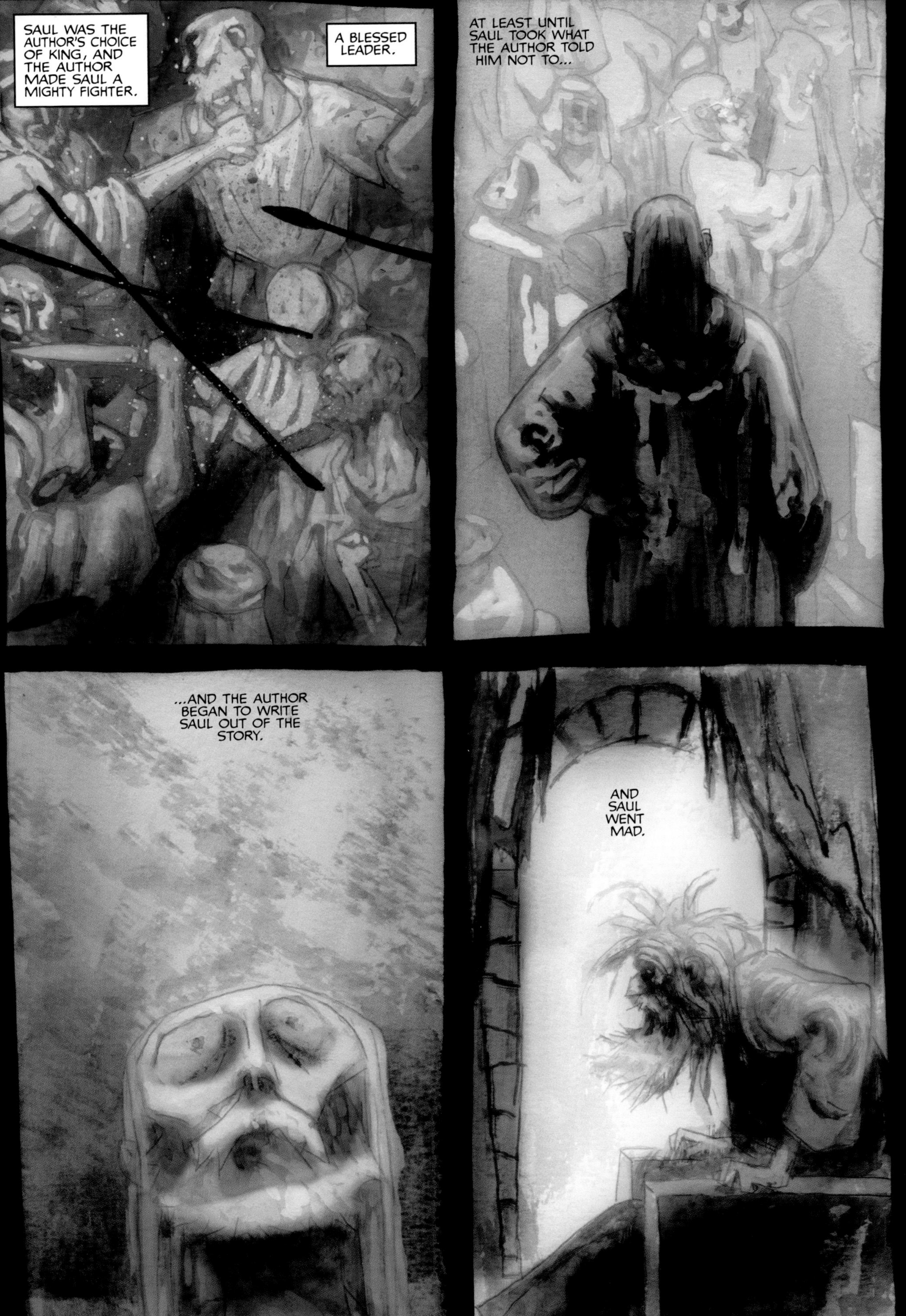
SAUL WAS THE AUTHOR'S CHOICE OF KING, AND THE AUTHOR MADE SAUL A MIGHTY FIGHTER.
A BLESSED LEADER.
AT LEAST UNTIL SAUL TOOK WHAT THE AUTHOR TOLD HIM NOT TO...
...AND THE AUTHOR BEGAN TO WRITE SAUL OUT OF THE STORY.
AND SAUL WENT MAD.

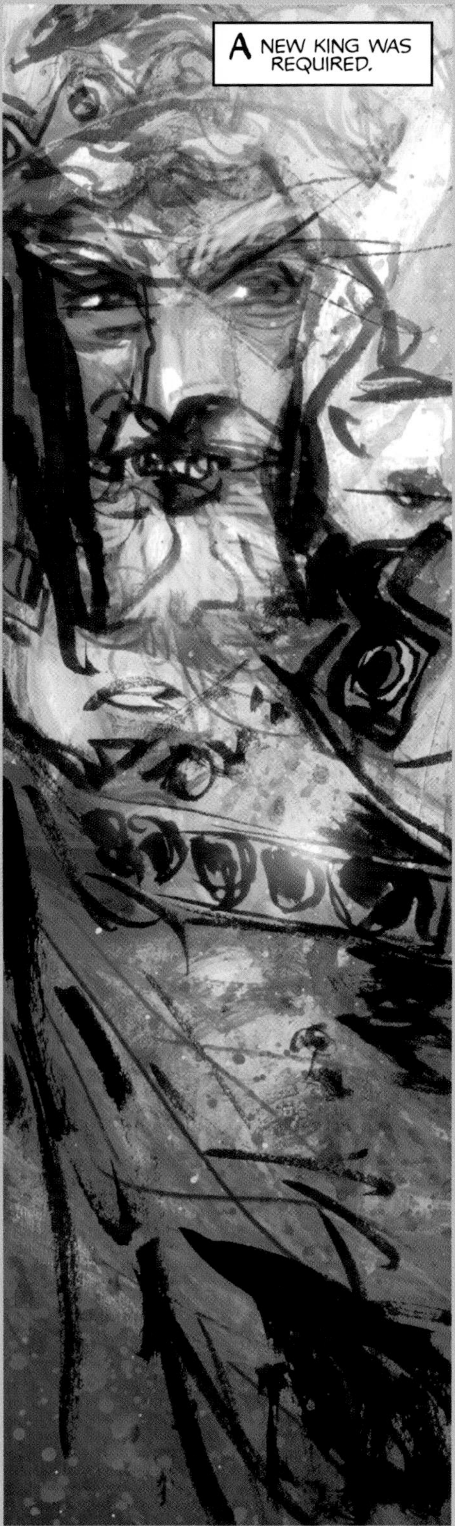
A NEW KING WAS REQUIRED.

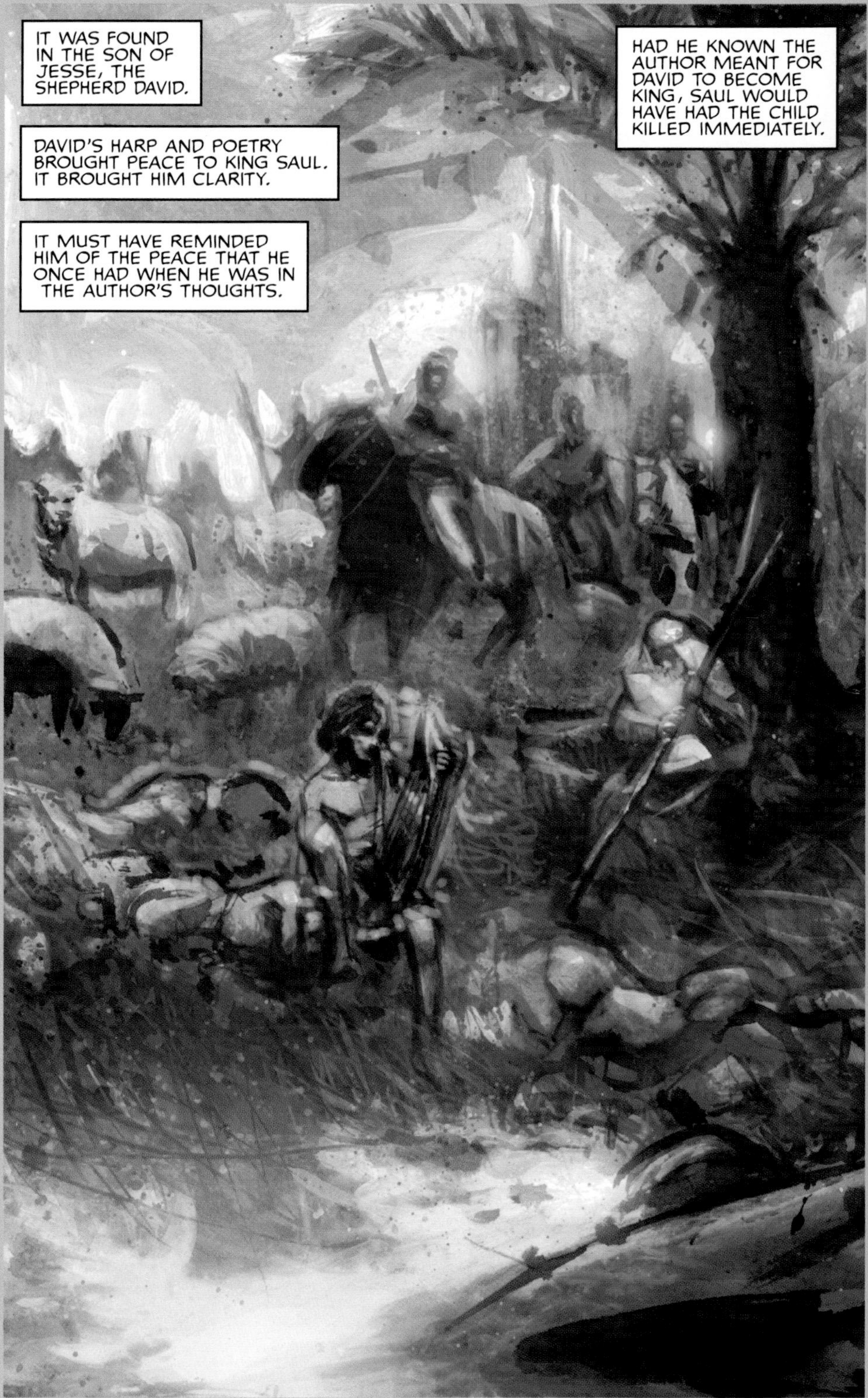
IT WAS FOUND IN THE SON OF JESSE, THE SHEPHERD DAVID.
DAVID'S HARP AND POETRY BROUGHT PEACE TO KING SAUL. IT BROUGHT HIM CLARITY.
IT MUST HAVE REMINDED HIM OF THE PEACE THAT HE ONCE HAD WHEN HE WAS IN THE AUTHOR'S THOUGHTS.
HAD HE KNOWN THE AUTHOR MEANT FOR DAVID TO BECOME KING, SAUL WOULD HAVE HAD THE CHILD KILLED IMMEDIATELY.

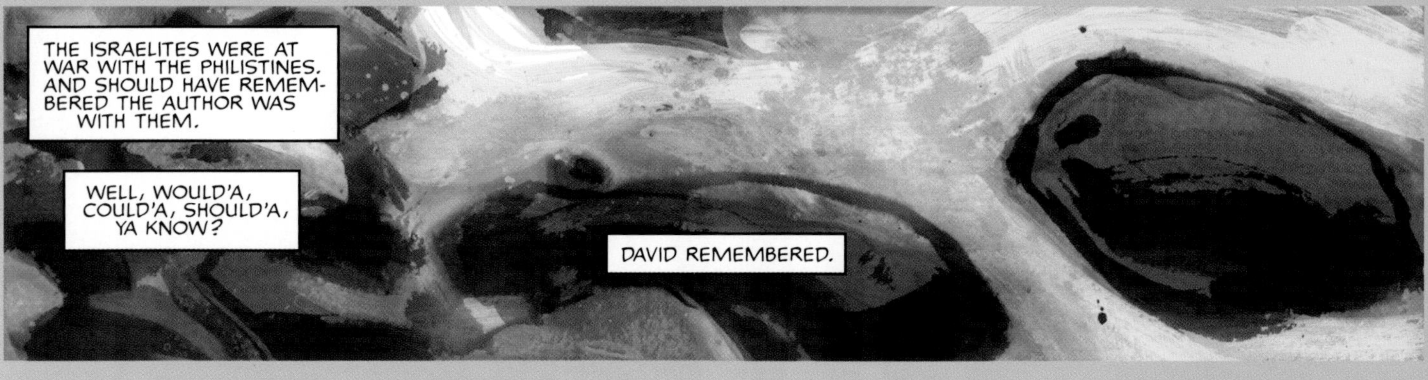
THE ISRAELITES WERE AT WAR WITH THE PHILISTINES. AND SHOULD HAVE REMEMBERED THE AUTHOR WAS WITH THEM.
WELL, WOULD'A, COULD'A, SHOULD'A, YA KNOW?
DAVID REMEMBERED.

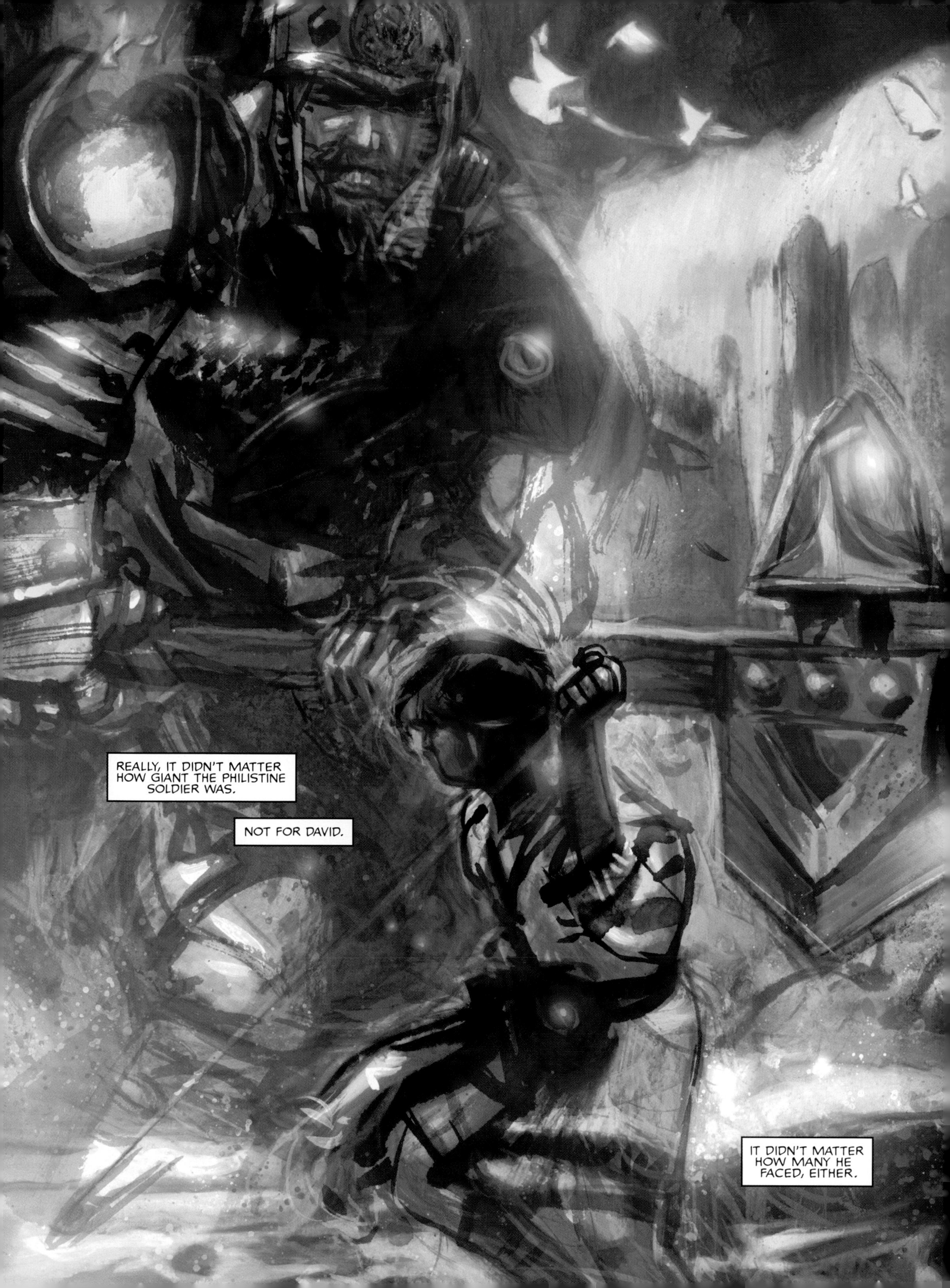
REALLY, IT DIDN'T MATTER HOW GIANT THE PHILISTINE SOLDIER WAS.
NOT FOR DAVID.
IT DIDN'T MATTER HOW MANY HE FACED, EITHER.

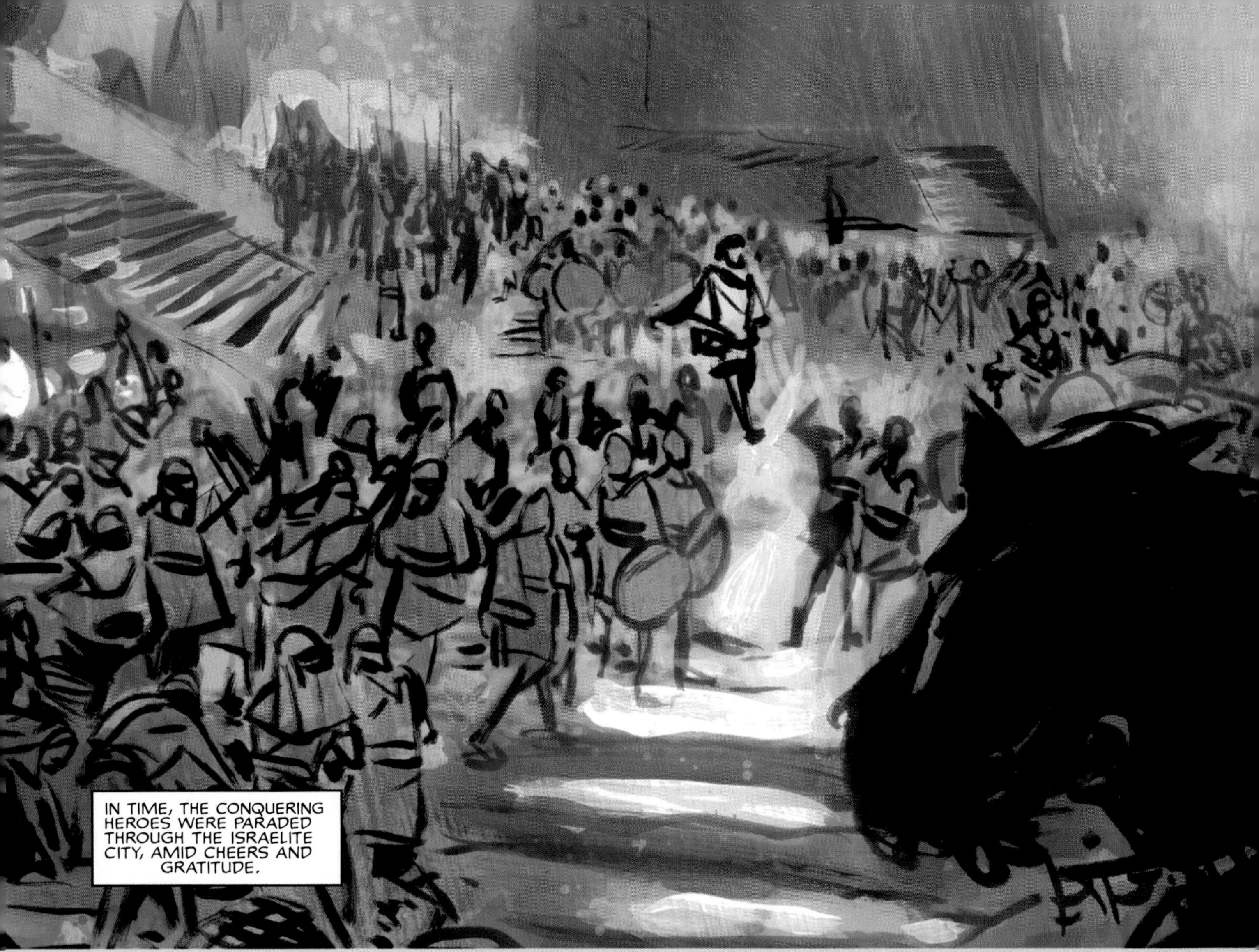
IN TIME, THE CONQUERING HEROES WERE PARADED THROUGH THE ISRAELITE CITY, AMID CHEERS AND GRATITUDE.

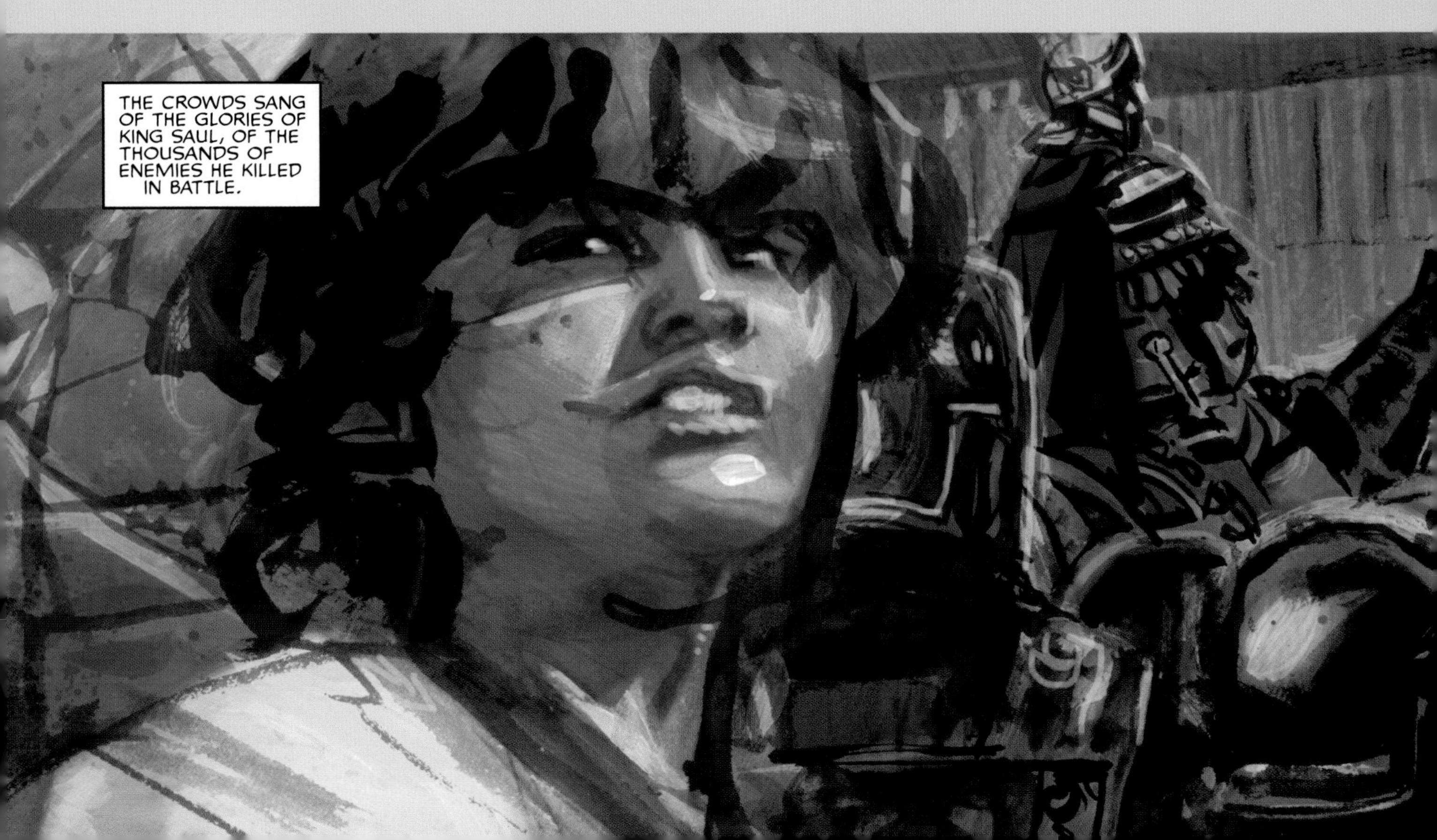
THE CROWDS SANG OF THE GLORIES OF KING SAUL, OF THE THOUSANDS OF ENEMIES HE KILLED IN BATTLE.

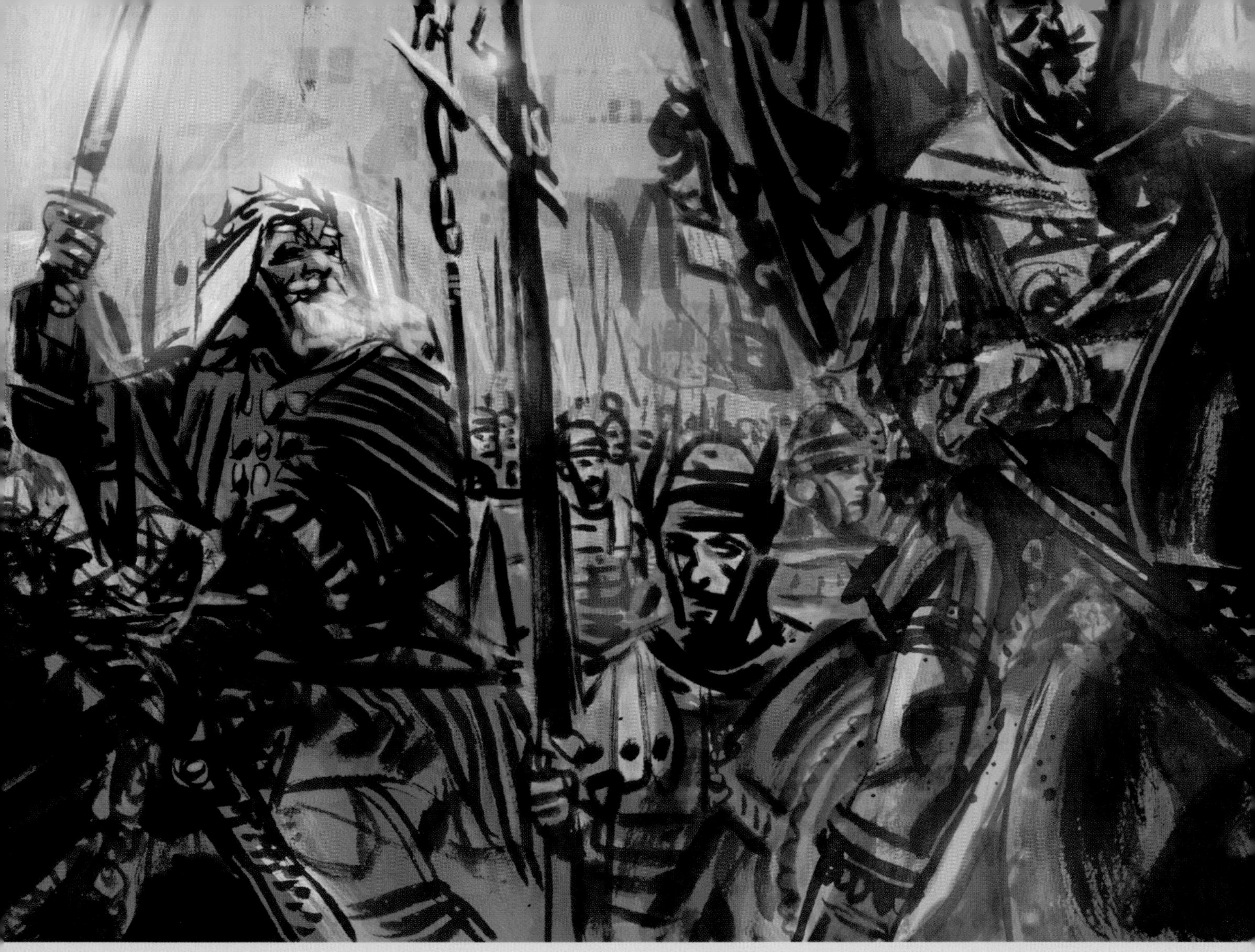
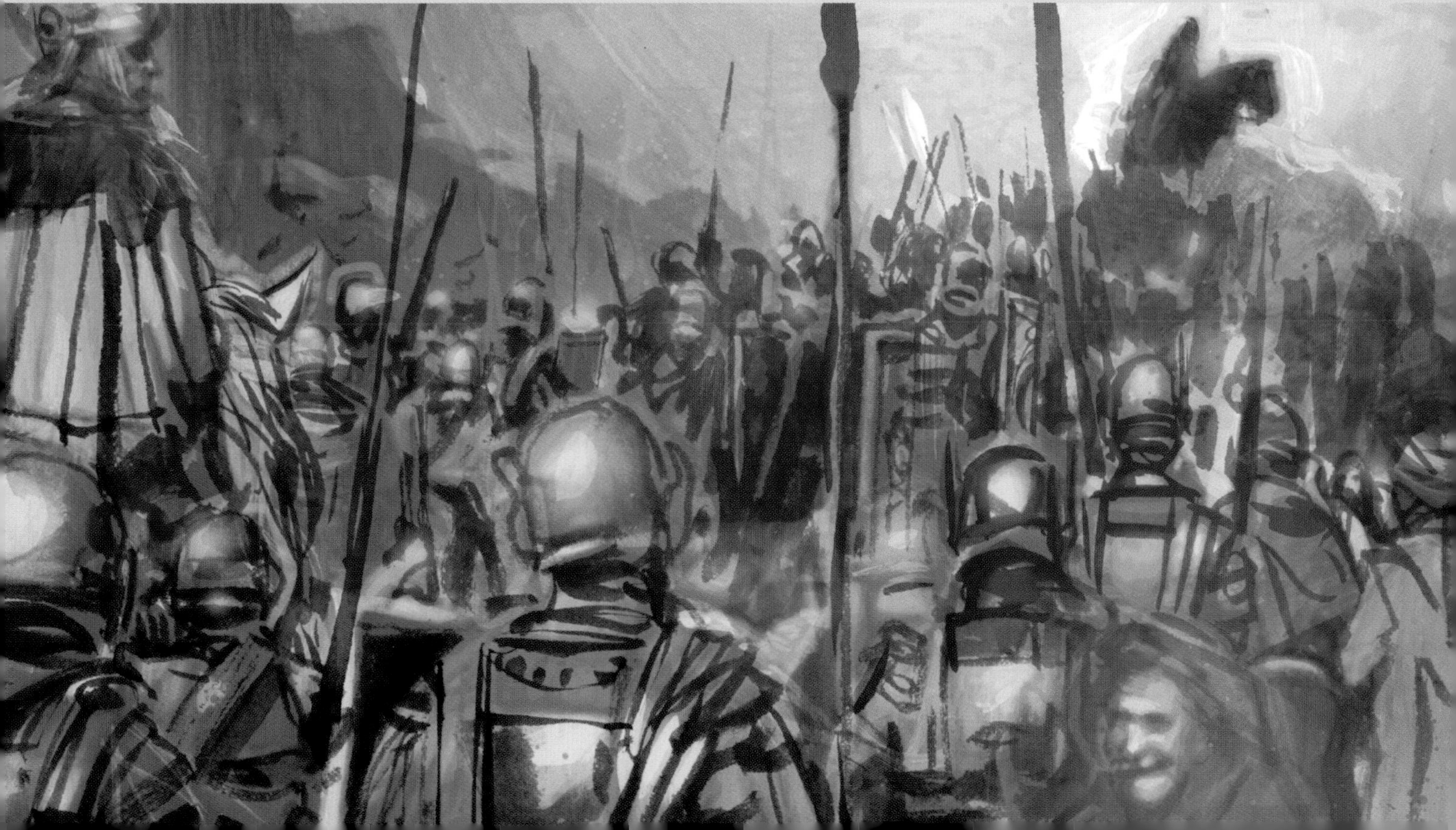

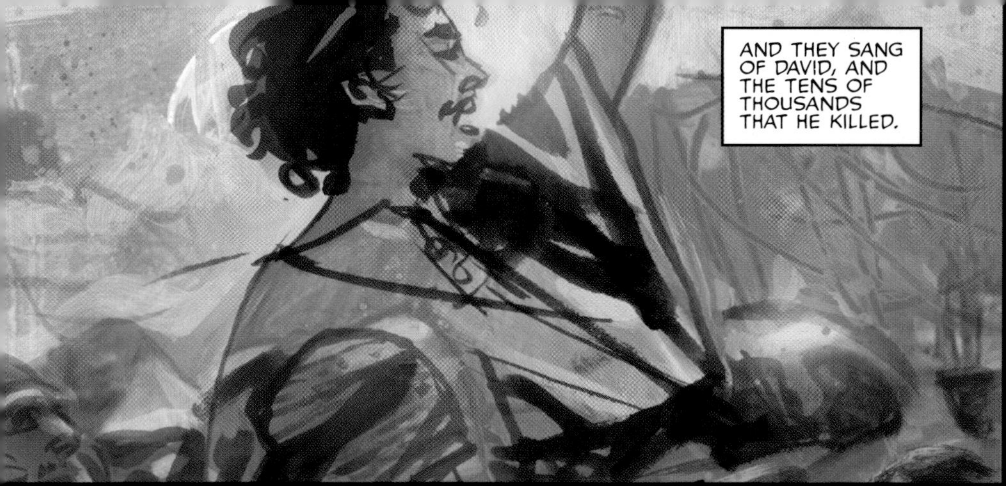
AND THEY SANG OF DAVID, AND THE TENS OF THOUSANDS THAT HE KILLED.

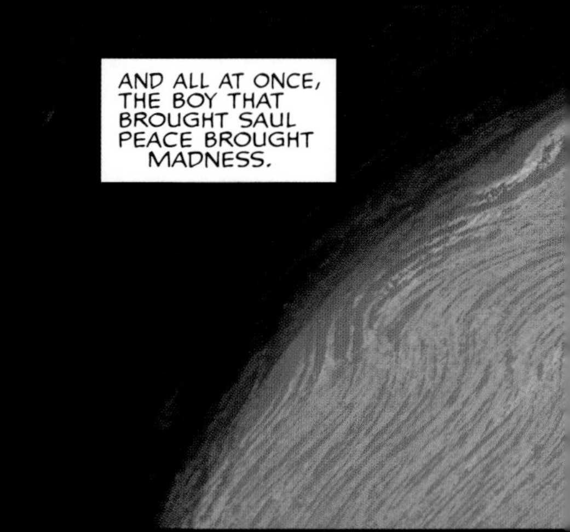
AND ALL AT ONCE, THE BOY THAT BROUGHT SAUL PEACE BROUGHT MADNESS.

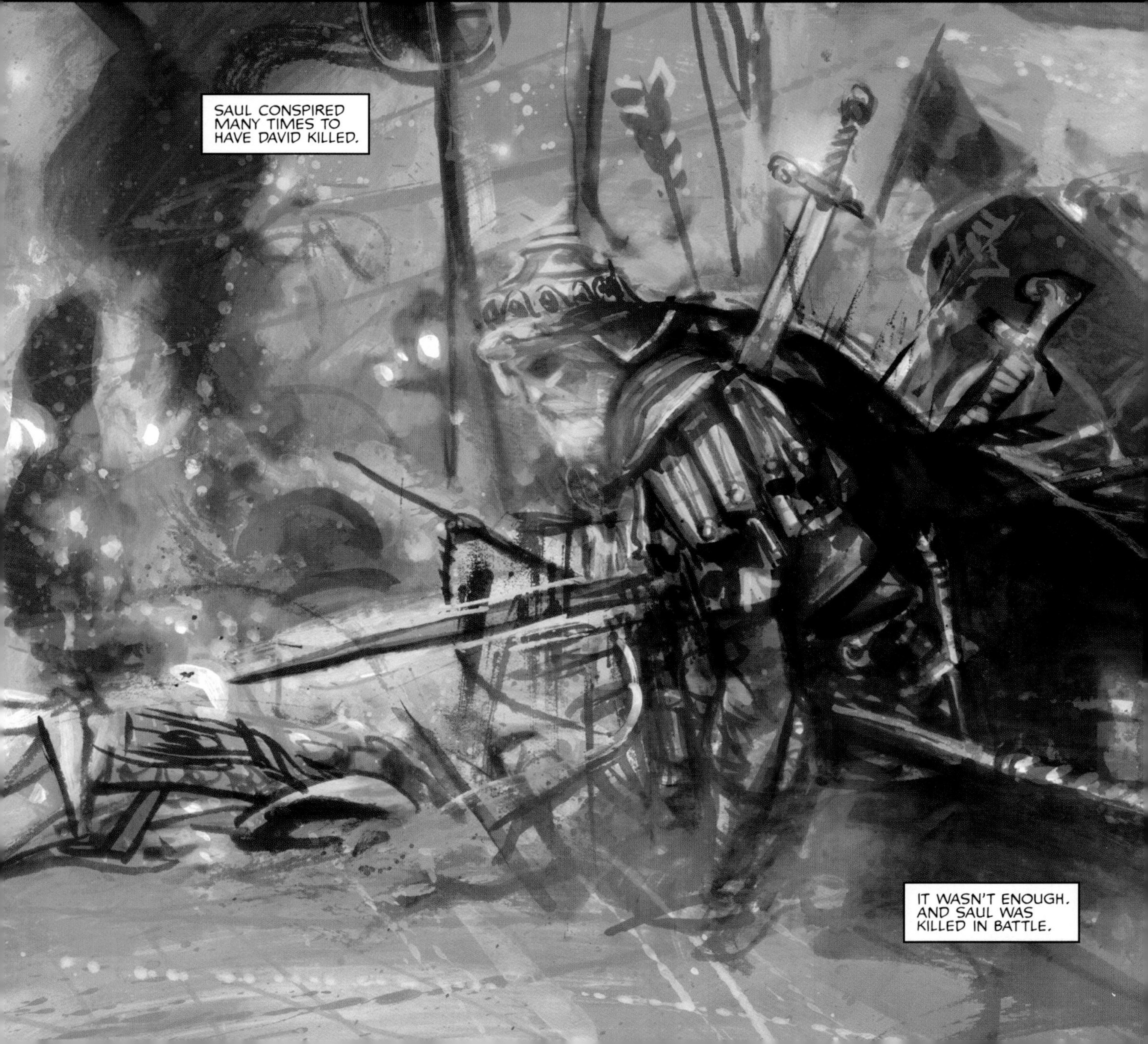
SAUL CONSPIRED MANY TIMES TO HAVE DAVID KILLED.
IT WASN'T ENOUGH. AND SAUL WAS KILLED IN BATTLE.

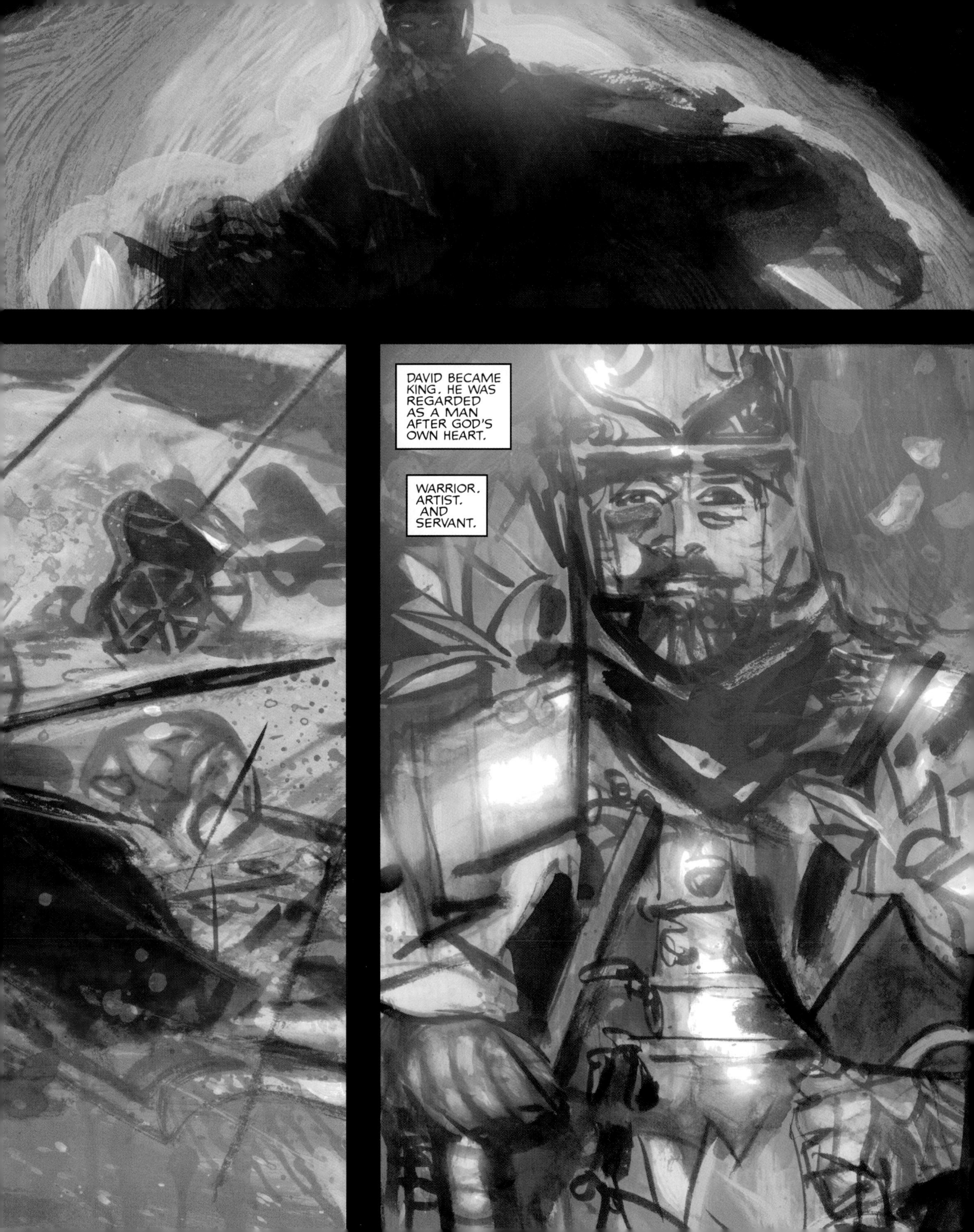
DAVID BECAME KING. HE WAS REGARDED AS A MAN AFTER GOD'S OWN HEART.
WARRIOR. ARTIST. AND SERVANT.

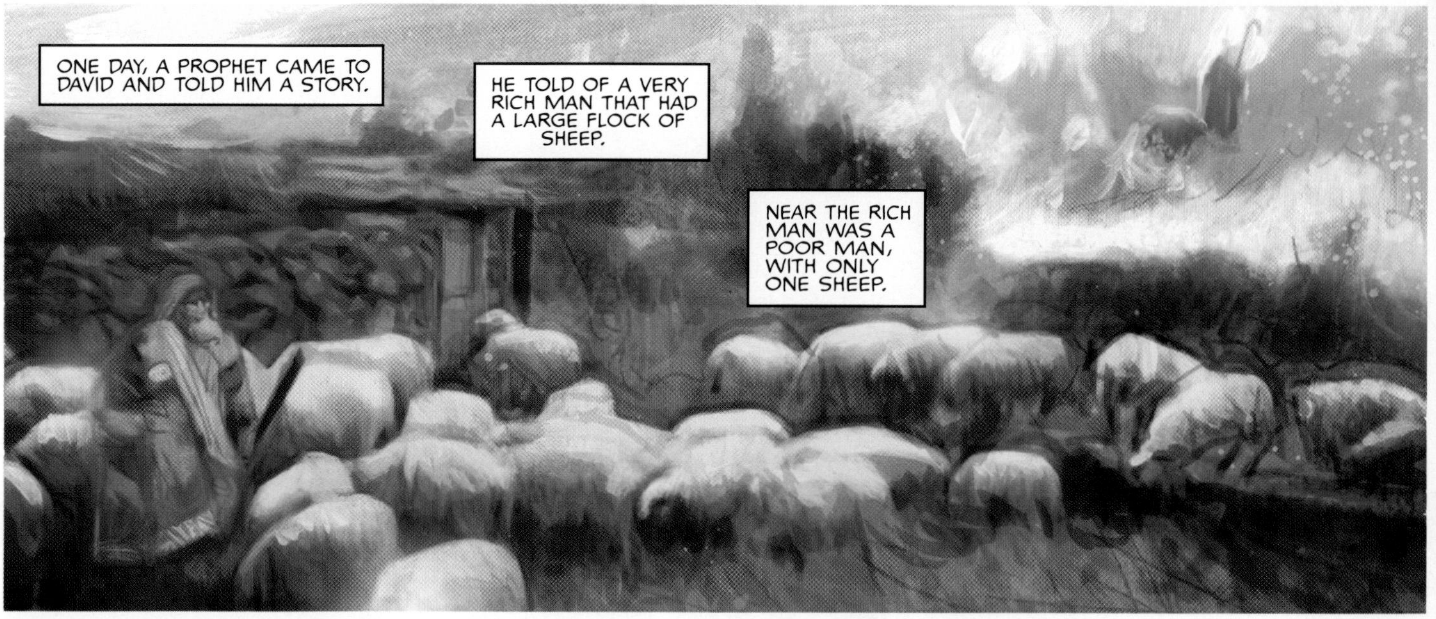
ONE DAY, A PROPHET CAME TO DAVID AND TOLD HIM A STORY.
HE TOLD OF A VERY RICH MAN THAT HAD A LARGE FLOCK OF SHEEP.
NEAR THE RICH MAN WAS A POOR MAN, WITH ONLY ONE SHEEP.

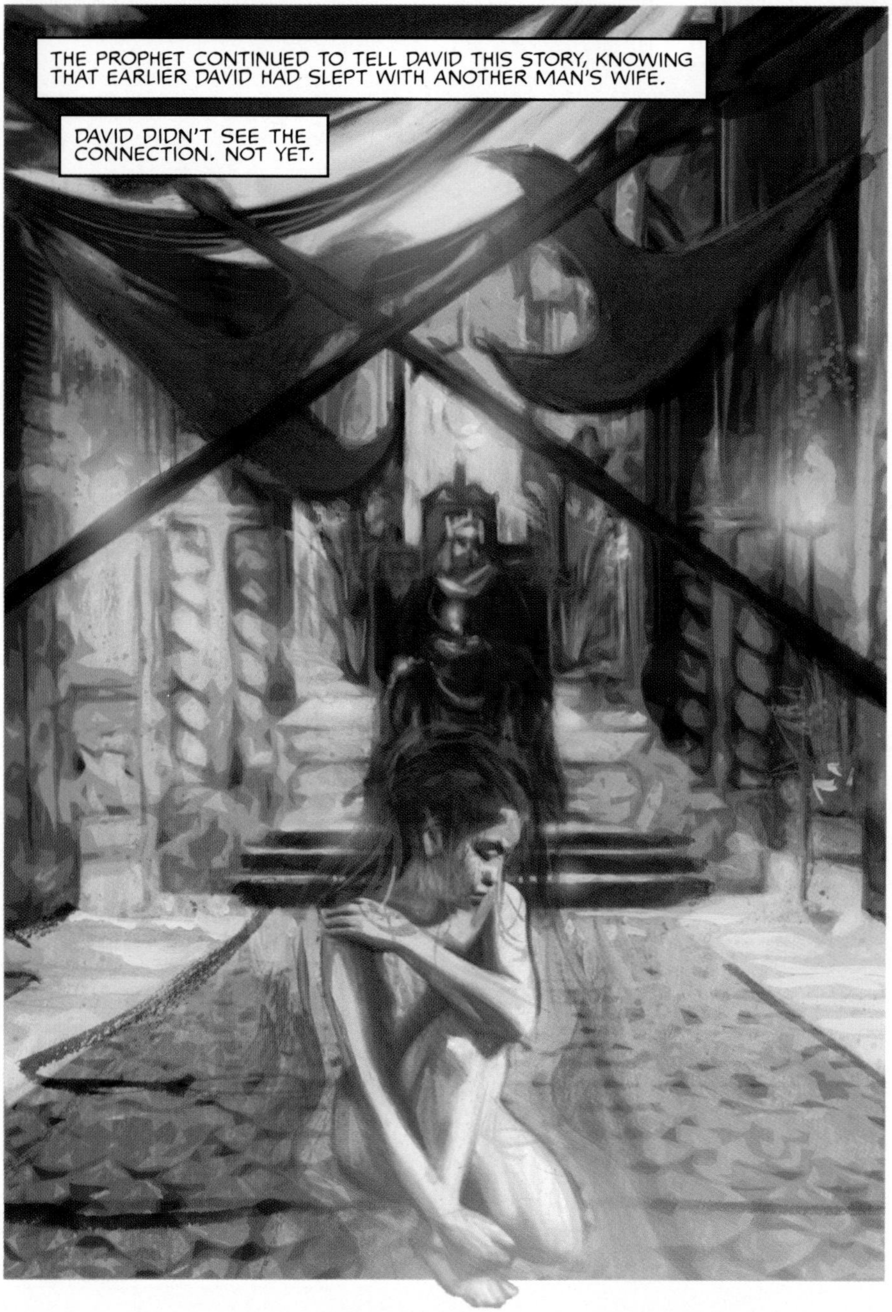
THE PROPHET CONTINUED TO TELL DAVID THIS STORY, KNOWING THAT EARLIER DAVID HAD SLEPT WITH ANOTHER MAN'S WIFE.
DAVID DIDN'T SEE THE CONNECTION. NOT YET.

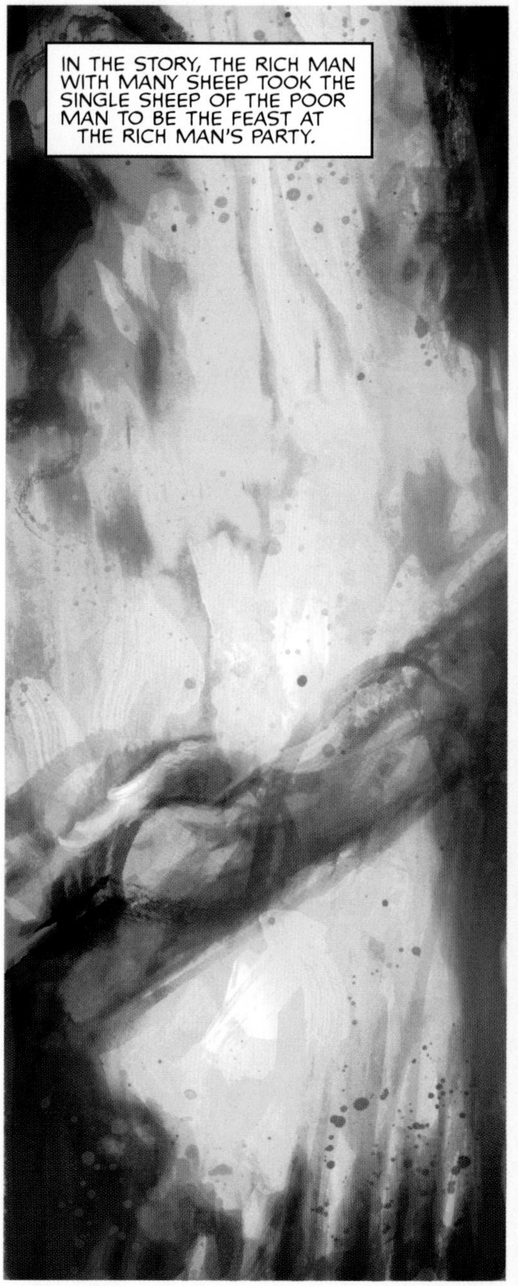
IN THE STORY, THE RICH MAN WITH MANY SHEEP TOOK THE SINGLE SHEEP OF THE POOR MAN TO BE THE FEAST AT THE RICH MAN'S PARTY.

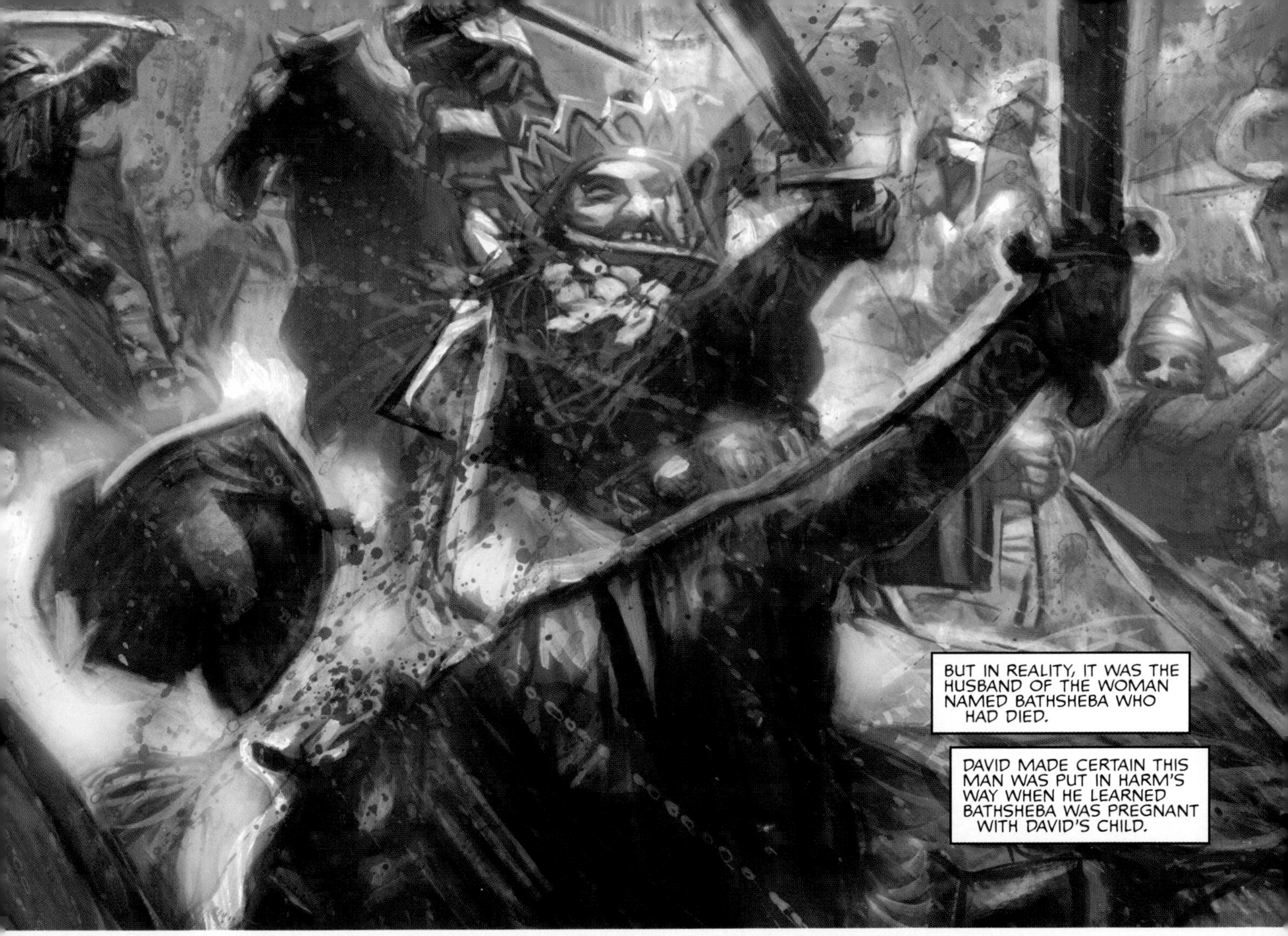
BUT IN REALITY, IT WAS THE HUSBAND OF THE WOMAN NAMED BATHSHEBA WHO HAD DIED.
DAVID MADE CERTAIN THIS MAN WAS PUT IN HARM'S WAY WHEN HE LEARNED BATHSHEBA WAS PREGNANT WITH DAVID'S CHILD.
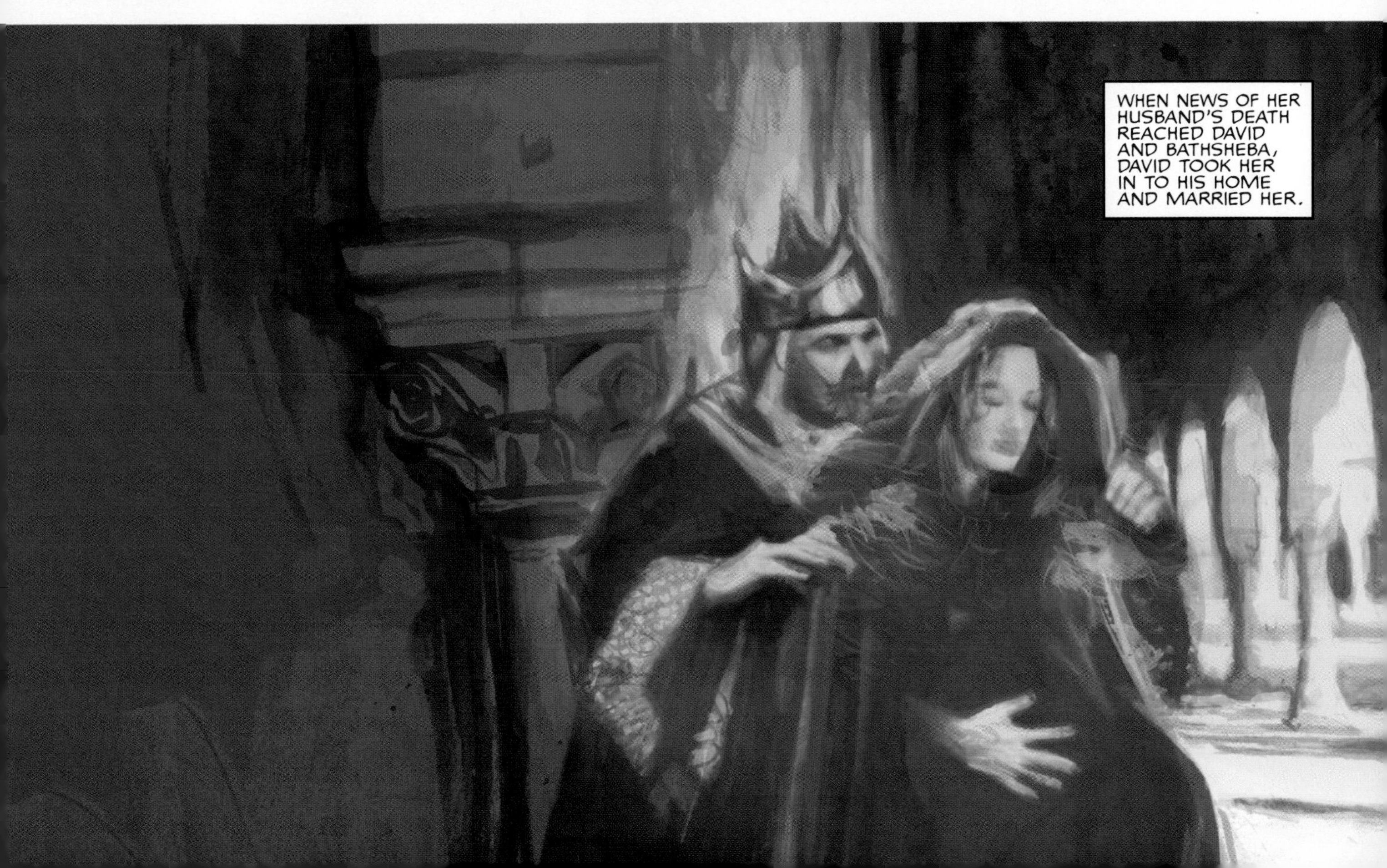
WHEN NEWS OF HER HUSBAND'S DEATH REACHED DAVID AND BATHSHEBA, DAVID TOOK HER IN TO HIS HOME AND MARRIED HER.

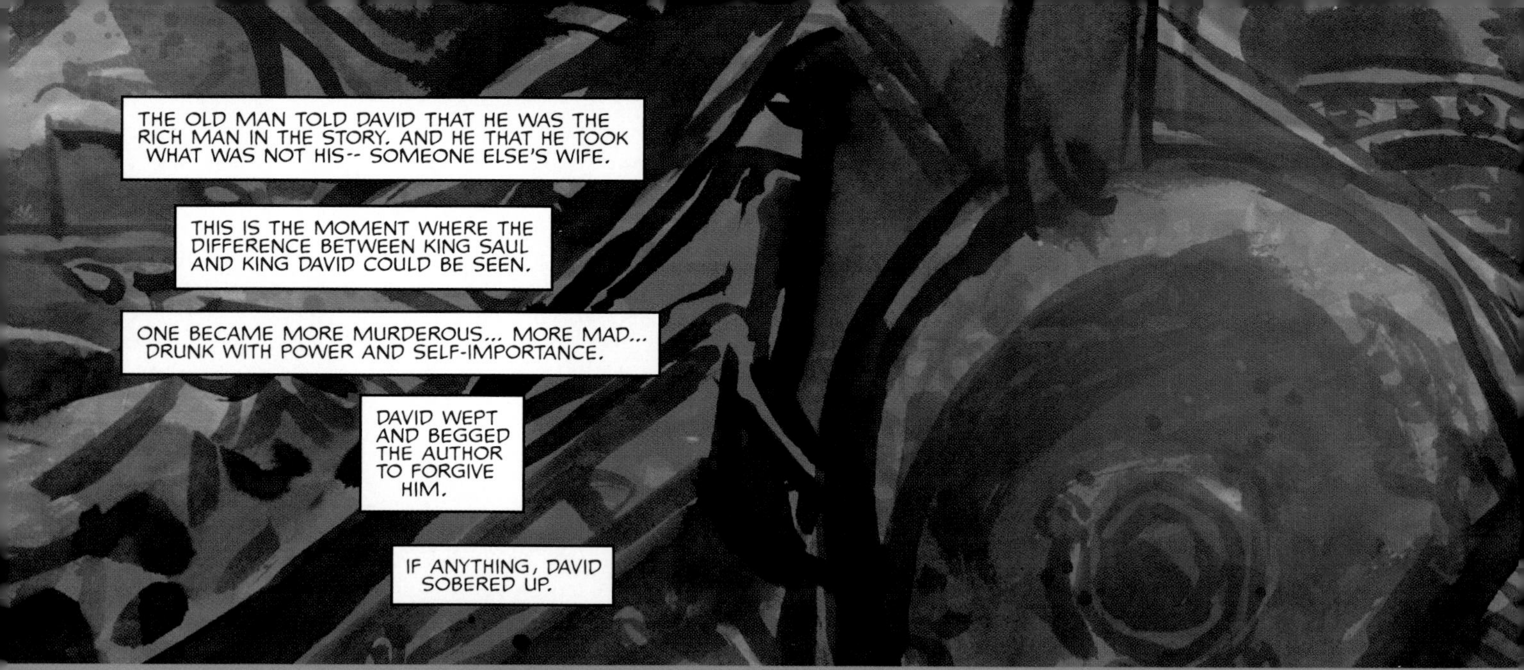
THE OLD MAN TOLD DAVID THAT HE WAS THE RICH MAN IN THE STORY, AND HE THAT HE TOOK WHAT WAS NOT HIS-- SOMEONE ELSE'S WIFE.
THIS IS THE MOMENT WHERE THE DIFFERENCE BETWEEN KING SAUL AND KING DAVID COULD BE SEEN.
ONE BECAME MORE MURDEROUS... MORE MAD... DRUNK WITH POWER AND SELF-IMPORTANCE.
DAVID WEPT AND BEGGED THE AUTHOR TO FORGIVE HIM.
IF ANYTHING, DAVID SOBERED UP.

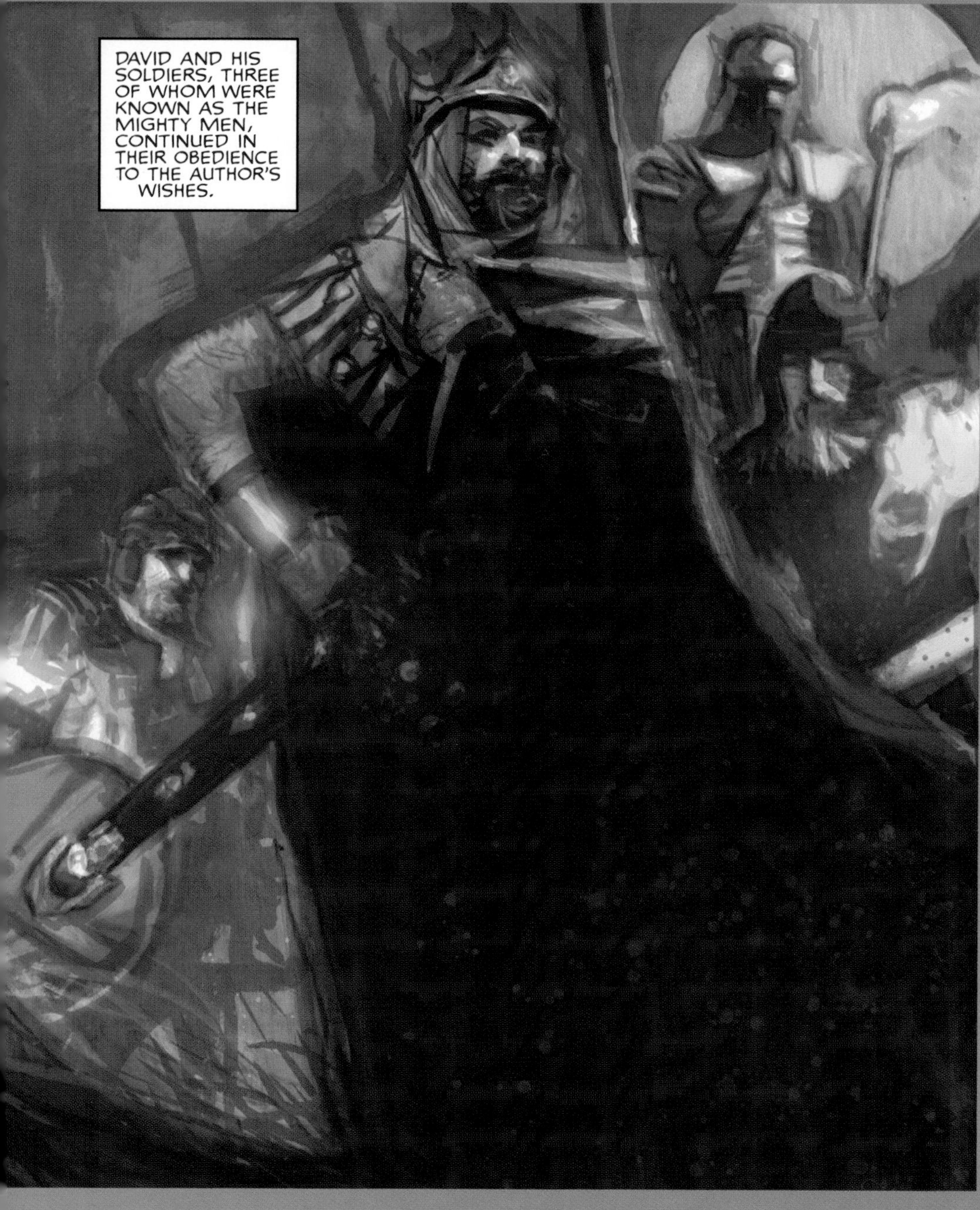
DAVID AND HIS SOLDIERS, THREE OF WHOM WERE KNOWN AS THE MIGHTY MEN, CONTINUED IN THEIR OBEDIENCE TO THE AUTHOR'S WISHES.

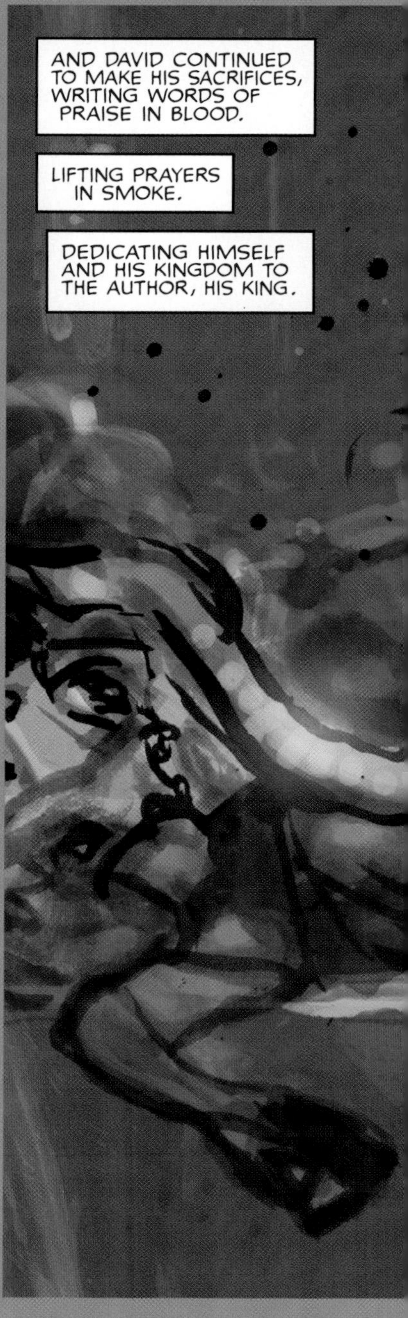
AND DAVID CONTINUED TO MAKE HIS SACRIFICES, WRITING WORDS OF PRAISE IN BLOOD.
LIFTING PRAYERS IN SMOKE.
DEDICATING HIMSELF AND HIS KINGDOM TO THE AUTHOR, HIS KING.

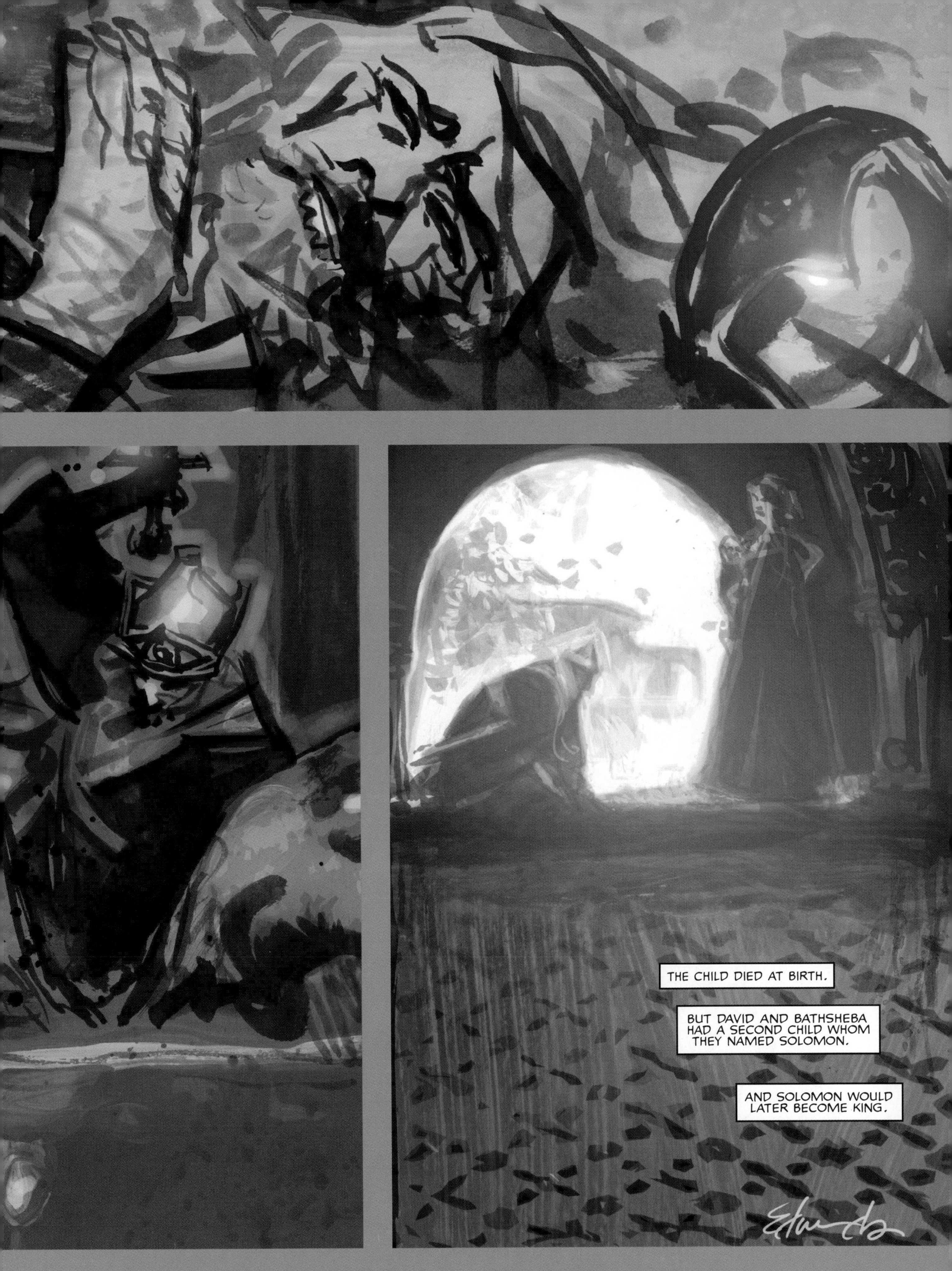
THE CHILD DIED AT BIRTH.
BUT DAVID AND BATHSHEBA HAD A SECOND CHILD WHOM THEY NAMED SOLOMON.
AND SOLOMON WOULD LATER BECOME KING.

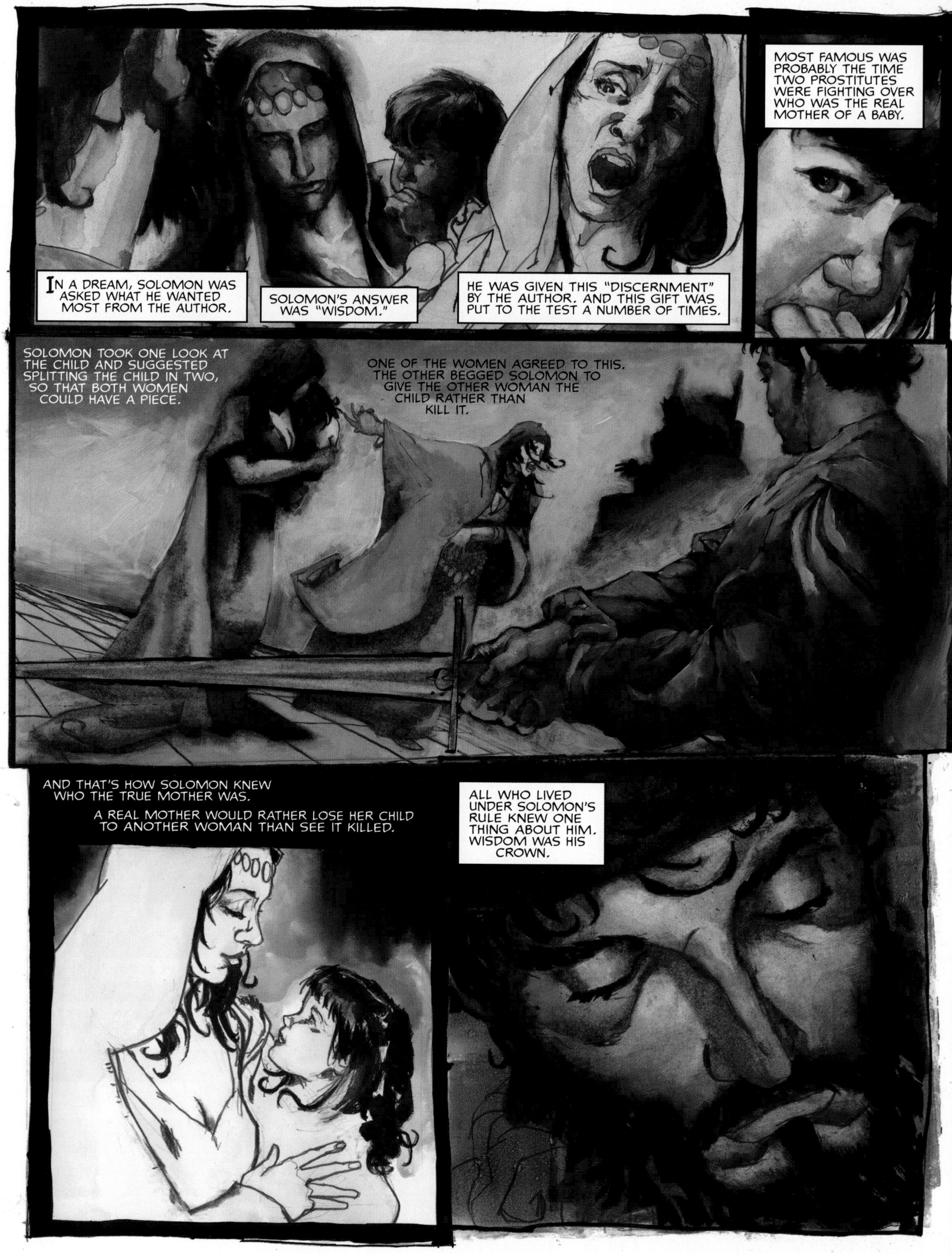
IN A DREAM, SOLOMON WAS ASKED WHAT HE WANTED MOST FROM THE AUTHOR.
SOLOMON'S ANSWER WAS "WISDOM."
HE WAS GIVEN THIS "DISCERNMENT" BY THE AUTHOR. AND THIS GIFT WAS PUT TO THE TEST A NUMBER OF TIMES.
MOST FAMOUS WAS PROBABLY THE TIME TWO PROSTITUTES WERE FIGHTING OVER WHO WAS THE REAL MOTHER OF A BABY.
SOLOMON TOOK ONE LOOK AT THE CHILD AND SUGGESTED SPLITTING THE CHILD IN TWO, SO THAT BOTH WOMEN COULD HAVE A PIECE.
ONE OF THE WOMEN AGREED TO THIS. THE OTHER BEGGED SOLOMON TO GIVE THE OTHER WOMAN THE CHILD RATHER THAN KILL IT.
AND THAT'S HOW SOLOMON KNEW WHO THE TRUE MOTHER WAS.
A REAL MOTHER WOULD RATHER LOSE HER CHILD TO ANOTHER WOMAN THAN SEE IT KILLED.
ALL WHO LIVED UNDER SOLOMON'S RULE KNEW ONE THING ABOUT HIM. WISDOM WAS HIS CROWN.

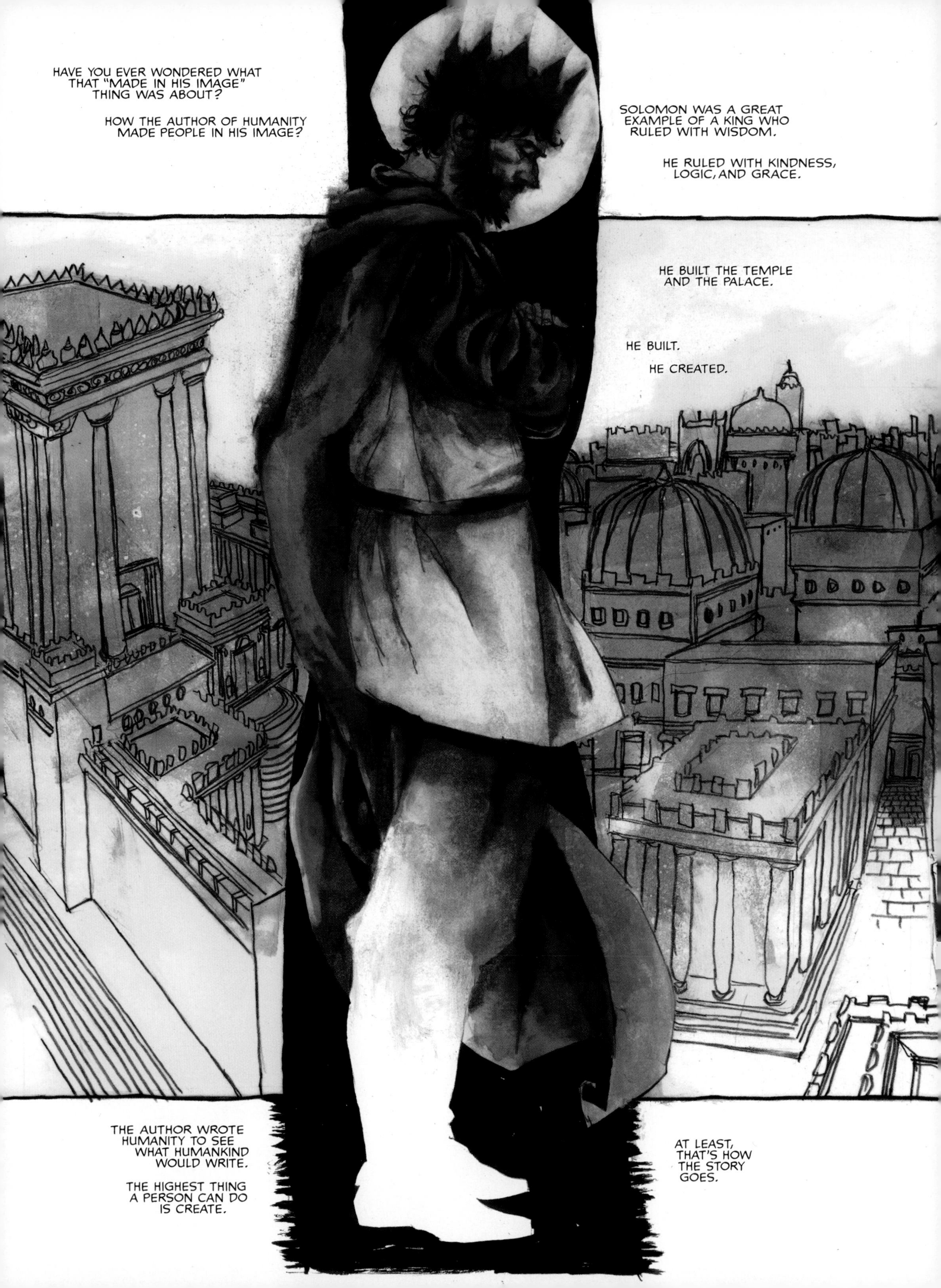
HAVE YOU EVER WONDERED WHAT THAT "MADE IN HIS IMAGE" THING WAS ABOUT?
HOW THE AUTHOR OF HUMANITY MADE PEOPLE IN HIS IMAGE?
SOLOMON WAS A GREAT EXAMPLE OF A KING WHO RULED WITH WISDOM.
HE RULED WITH KINDNESS, LOGIC, AND GRACE.
HE BUILT THE TEMPLE AND THE PALACE.
HE BUILT.
HE CREATED.
THE AUTHOR WROTE HUMANITY TO SEE WHAT HUMANKIND WOULD WRITE.
THE HIGHEST THING A PERSON CAN DO IS CREATE.
AT LEAST, THAT'S HOW THE STORY GOES.

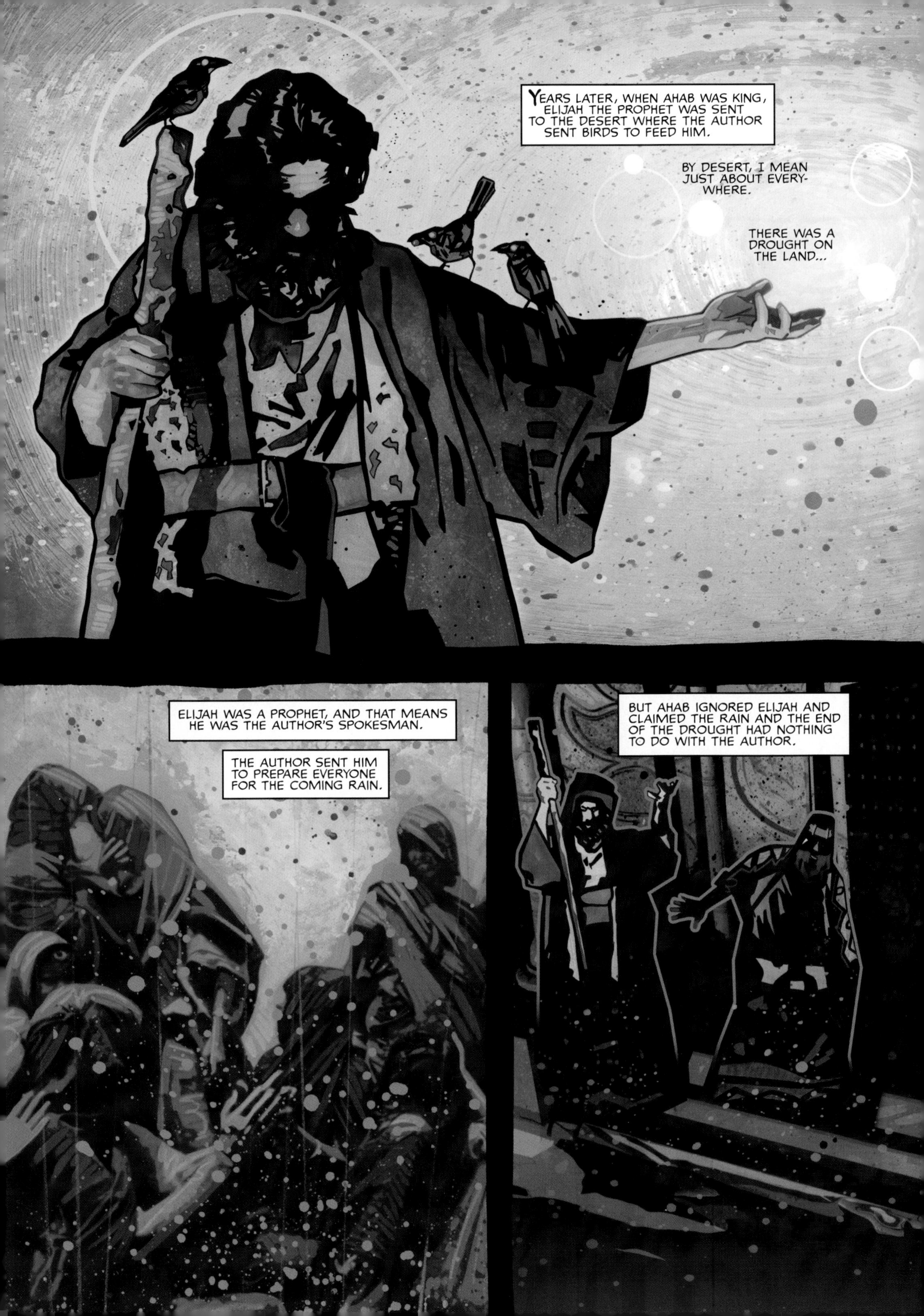
YEARS LATER, WHEN AHAB WAS KING, ELIJAH THE PROPHET WAS SENT TO THE DESERT WHERE THE AUTHOR SENT BIRDS TO FEED HIM.
BY DESERT, I MEAN JUST ABOUT EVERY-WHERE.
THERE WAS A DROUGHT ON THE LAND...
ELIJAH WAS A PROPHET, AND THAT MEANS HE WAS THE AUTHOR'S SPOKESMAN.
THE AUTHOR SENT HIM TO PREPARE EVERYONE FOR THE COMING RAIN.
BUT AHAB IGNORED ELIJAH AND CLAIMED THE RAIN AND THE END OF THE DROUGHT HAD NOTHING TO DO WITH THE AUTHOR.

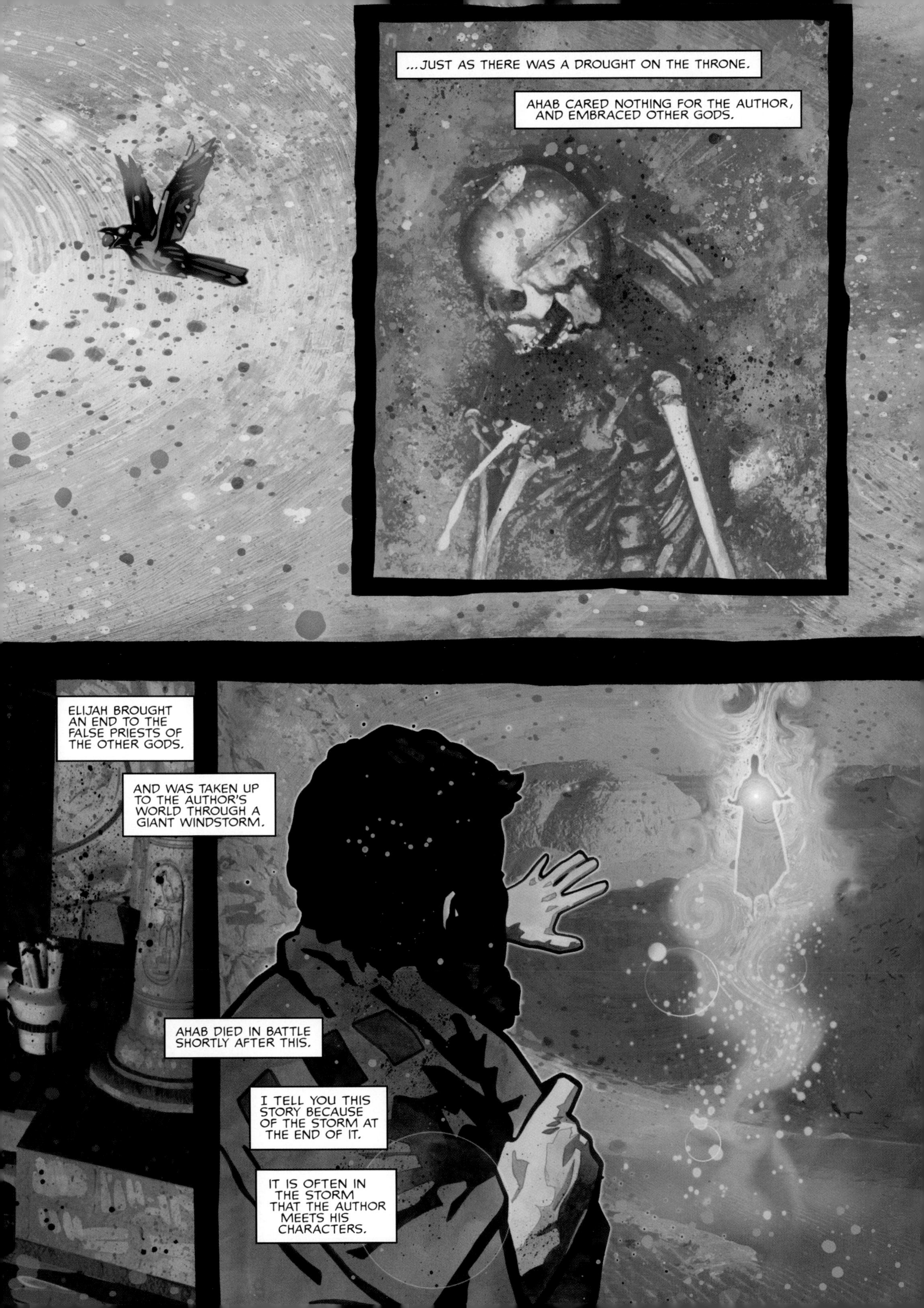
...JUST AS THERE WAS A DROUGHT ON THE THRONE.
AHAB CARED NOTHING FOR THE AUTHOR, AND EMBRACED OTHER GODS.
ELIJAH BROUGHT AN END TO THE FALSE PRIESTS OF THE OTHER GODS.
AND WAS TAKEN UP TO THE AUTHOR'S WORLD THROUGH A GIANT WINDSTORM.
AHAB DIED IN BATTLE SHORTLY AFTER THIS.
I TELL YOU THIS STORY BECAUSE OF THE STORM AT THE END OF IT.
IT IS OFTEN IN THE STORM THAT THE AUTHOR MEETS HIS CHARACTERS.

BUT PERHAPS THE WILDEST STORM IS THE ONE WITH THE CHARACTER KNOWN AS JOB.

THE STORY GOES LIKE THIS-- I KNOW YOU WON'T BE ABLE TO IMAGINE WHAT THIS LOOKS LIKE APART FROM THE IMAGERY THAT'S ALREADY IN YOUR MIND-- BUT IT'S LIKE THIS:

ONE DAY THE AUTHOR AND THE CHARACTER HE CURSED --LET'S CALL HIM THE DEVIL-- ARE HAVING A CONVERSATION.

THE DEVIL TOLD THE AUTHOR OF THE "WEAKNESS" AND "SELF-INTEREST" OF THE AUTHOR'S CHARACTERS.

BESIDES THE IRONY OF THE MOMENT-- THE FACT THAT THE AUTHOR HAD ALREADY CURSED THE CREATURE-- THE AUTHOR SUGGESTED THAT THE CREATURE CONSIDER THE MAN NAMED JOB.

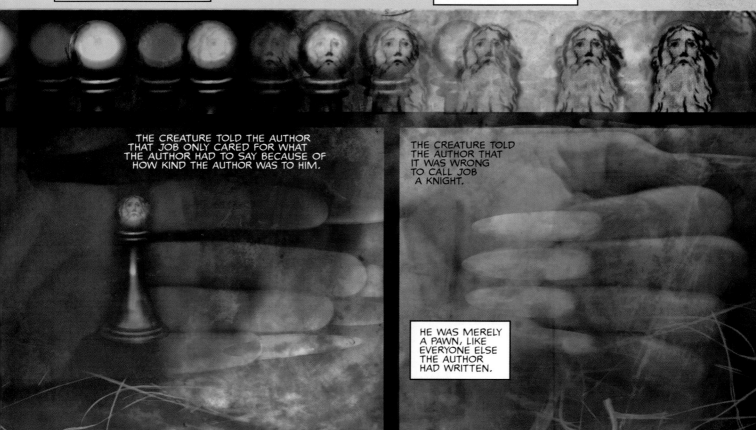

THE CREATURE TOLD THE AUTHOR THAT JOB ONLY CARED FOR WHAT THE AUTHOR HAD TO SAY BECAUSE OF HOW KIND THE AUTHOR WAS TO HIM.

THE CREATURE TOLD THE AUTHOR THAT IT WAS WRONG TO CALL JOB A KNIGHT.

HE WAS MERELY A PAWN, LIKE EVERYONE ELSE THE AUTHOR HAD WRITTEN.

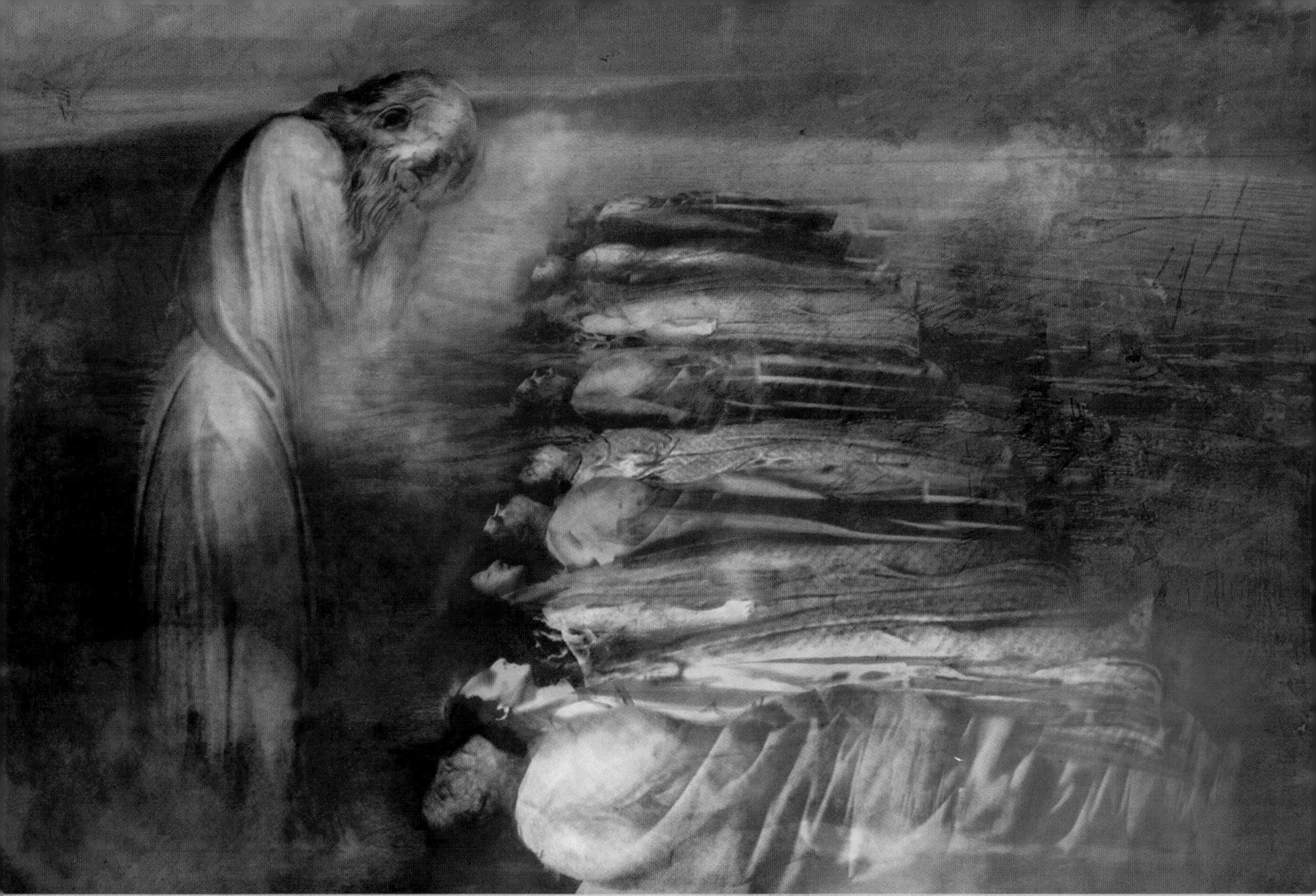

AND SO A DEAL WAS MADE.

THE CREATURE WAS GIVEN THE FREEDOM TO INFLICT PAIN AND CHAOS ON JOB, SHORT OF KILLING HIM.

THIS WAS TO PROVE TO THE DEVIL THAT NOT ALL OF HUMANITY WAS AS DECEITFUL AND REBELLIOUS AS THE CREATURE ITSELF.

TERRIBLE THINGS BEGAN TO HAPPEN TO JOB-- THE LOSS OF HIS PROFITS, THE DEATH OF HIS SONS, THE DESPAIR AND CONDEMNATION THAT CAME FROM HIS WIFE AND FRIENDS.

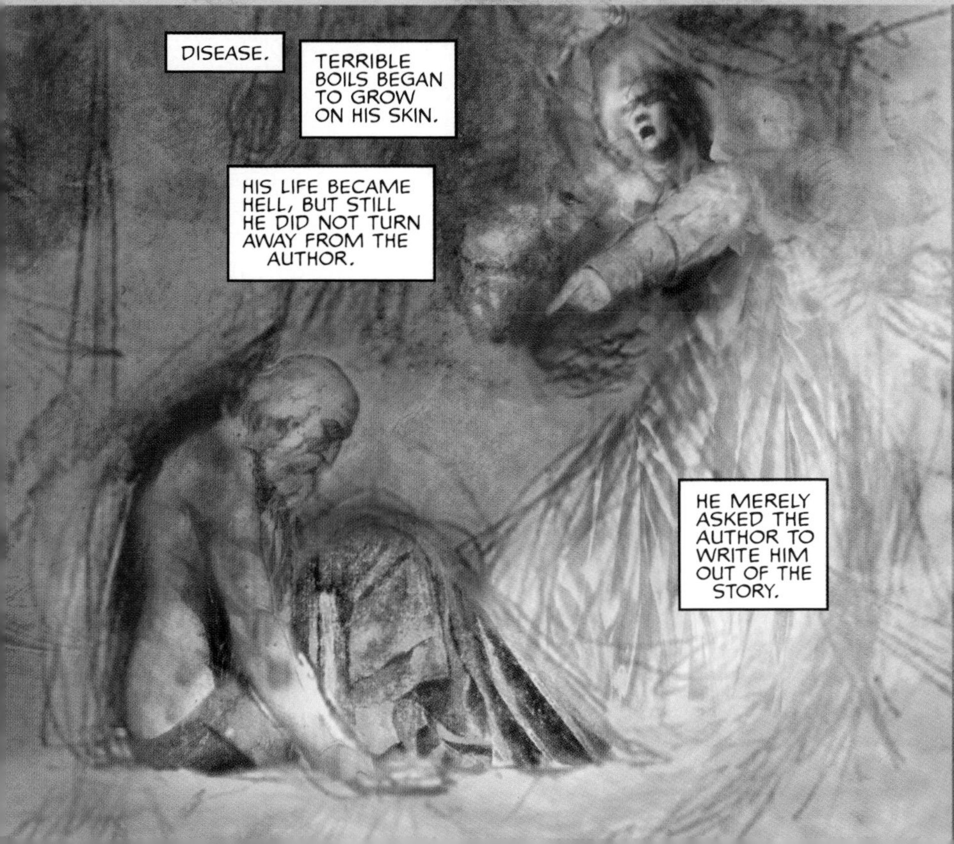
DISEASE.
TERRIBLE BOILS BEGAN TO GROW ON HIS SKIN.
HIS LIFE BECAME HELL, BUT STILL HE DID NOT TURN AWAY FROM THE AUTHOR.
HE MERELY ASKED THE AUTHOR TO WRITE HIM OUT OF THE STORY.

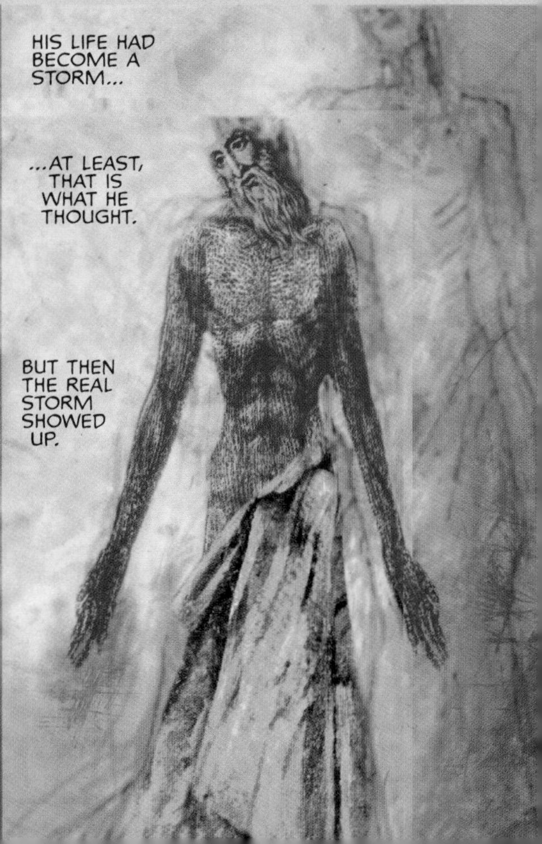
HIS LIFE HAD BECOME A STORM...
...AT LEAST, THAT IS WHAT HE THOUGHT.
BUT THEN THE REAL STORM SHOWED UP.

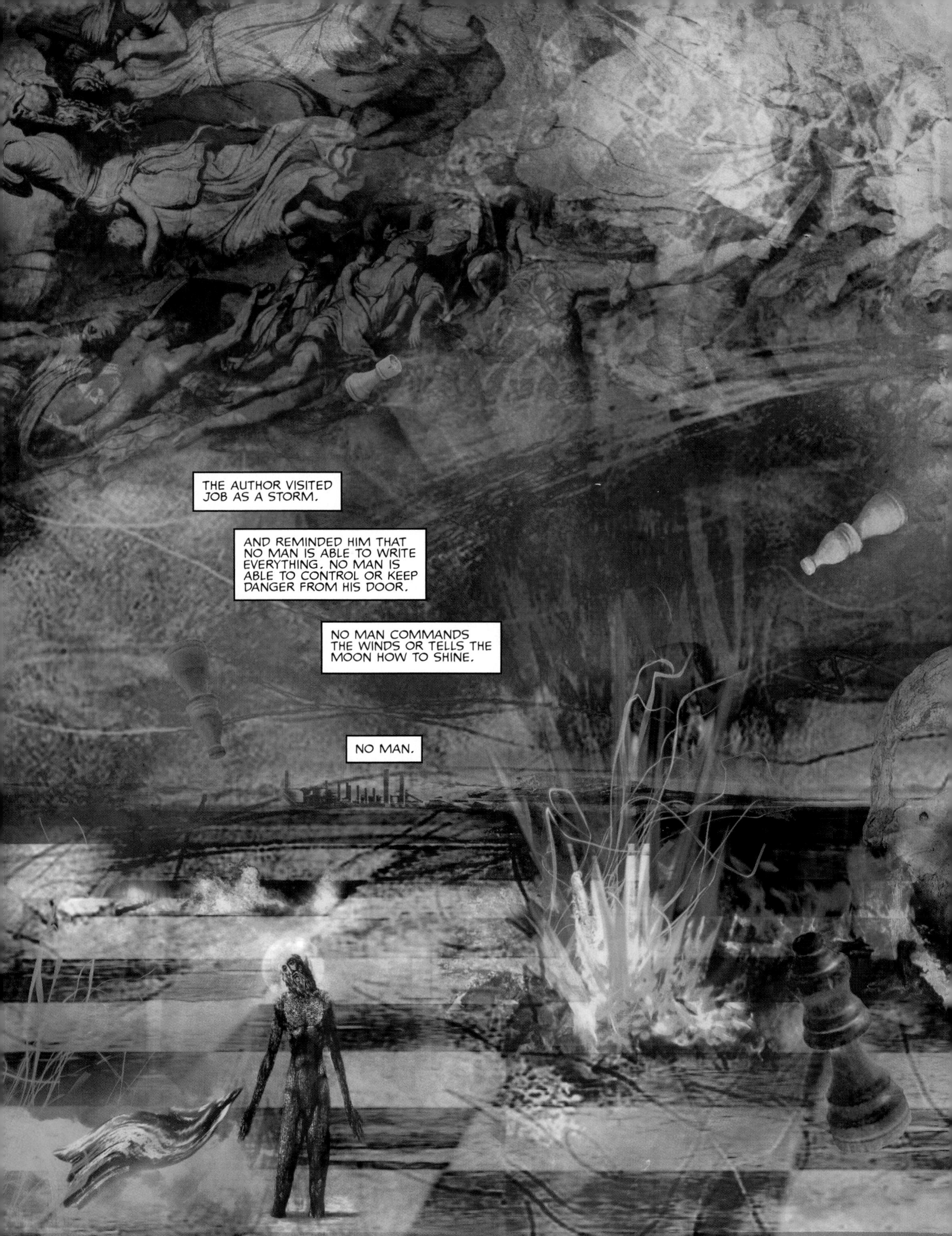
THE AUTHOR VISITED JOB AS A STORM.
AND REMINDED HIM THAT NO MAN IS ABLE TO WRITE EVERYTHING. NO MAN IS ABLE TO CONTROL OR KEEP DANGER FROM HIS DOOR.
NO MAN COMMANDS THE WINDS OR TELLS THE MOON HOW TO SHINE.
NO MAN.

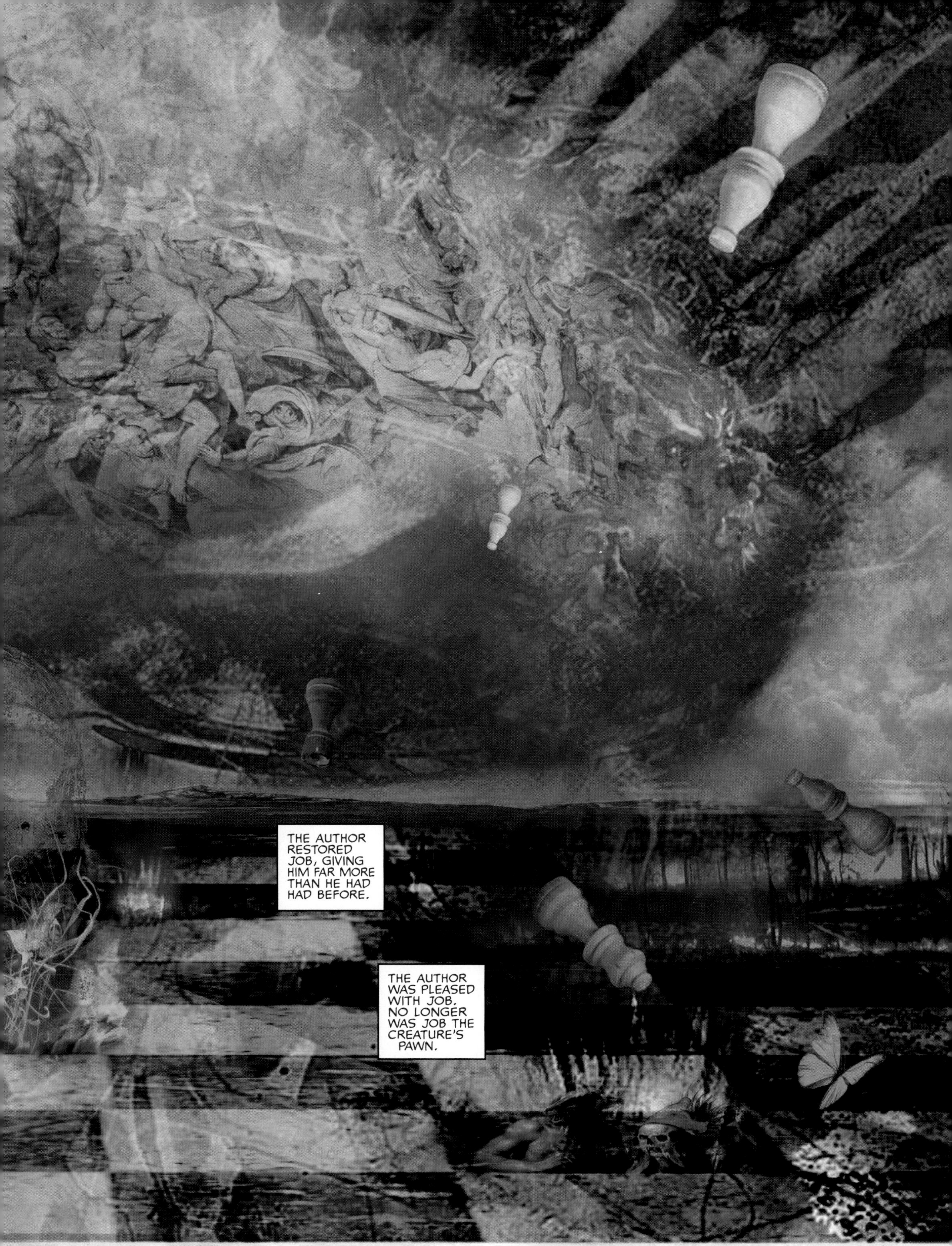
THE AUTHOR RESTORED JOB, GIVING HIM FAR MORE THAN HE HAD HAD BEFORE.
THE AUTHOR WAS PLEASED WITH JOB. NO LONGER WAS JOB THE CREATURE'S PAWN.

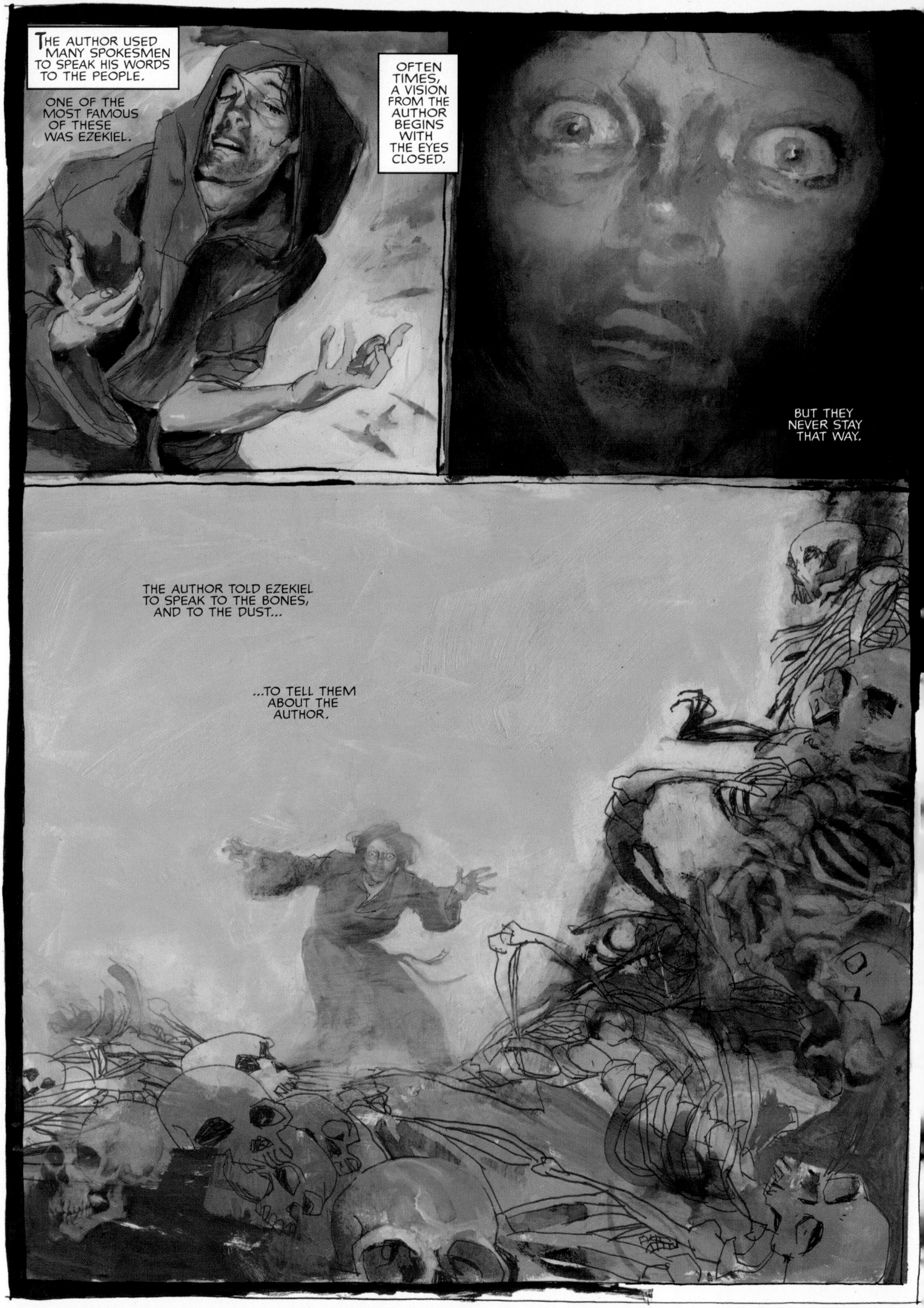
THE AUTHOR USED MANY SPOKESMEN TO SPEAK HIS WORDS TO THE PEOPLE.
ONE OF THE MOST FAMOUS OF THESE WAS EZEKIEL.
OFTEN TIMES, A VISION FROM THE AUTHOR BEGINS WITH THE EYES CLOSED.
BUT THEY NEVER STAY THAT WAY.
THE AUTHOR TOLD EZEKIEL TO SPEAK TO THE BONES, AND TO THE DUST...
...TO TELL THEM ABOUT THE AUTHOR.

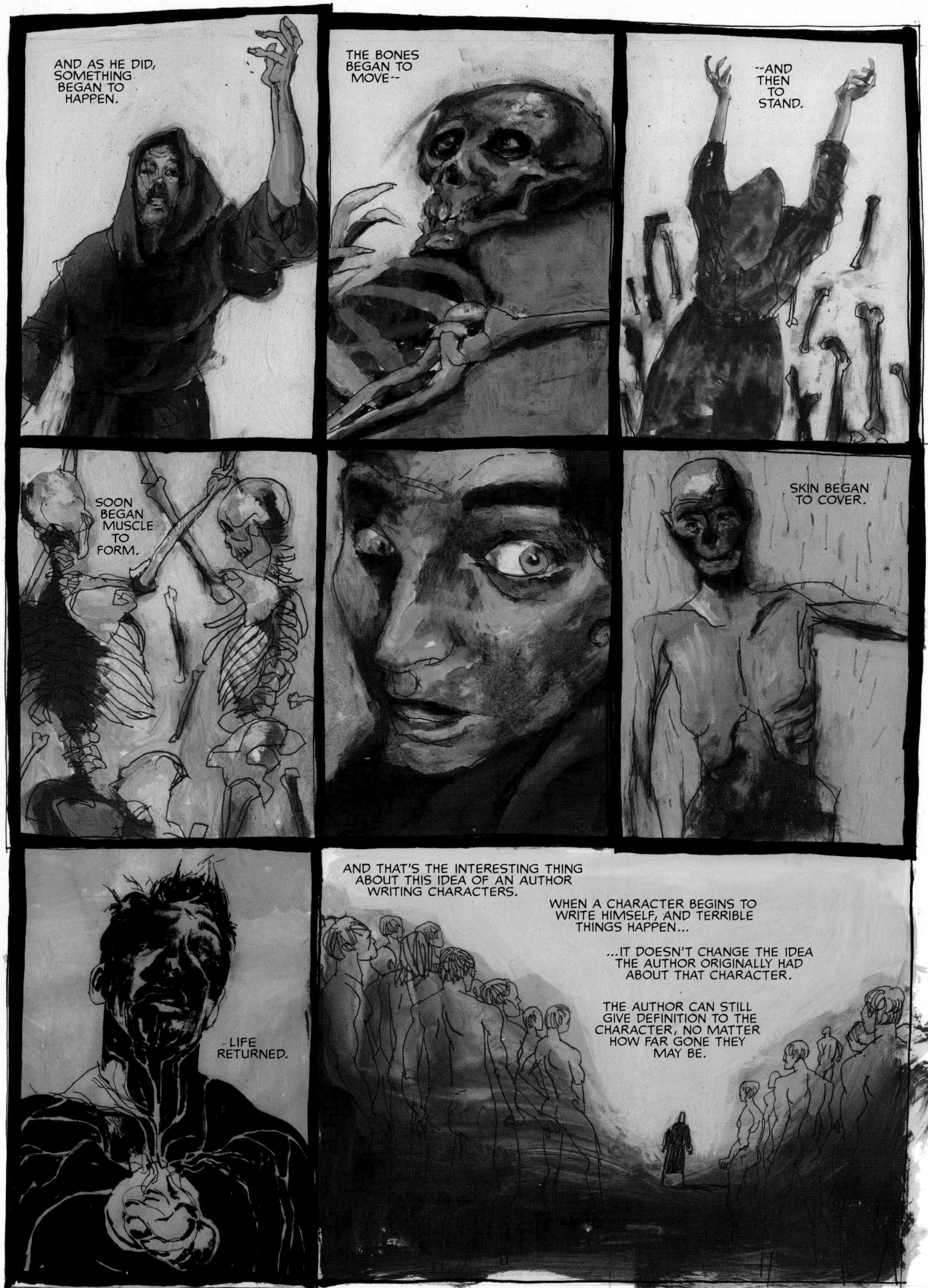
AND AS HE DID, SOMETHING BEGAN TO HAPPEN.
THE BONES BEGAN TO MOVE--
--AND THEN TO STAND.
SOON BEGAN MUSCLE TO FORM.
SKIN BEGAN TO COVER.
LIFE RETURNED.
AND THAT'S THE INTERESTING THING ABOUT THIS IDEA OF AN AUTHOR WRITING CHARACTERS.
WHEN A CHARACTER BEGINS TO WRITE HIMSELF, AND TERRIBLE THINGS HAPPEN...
...IT DOESN'T CHANGE THE IDEA THE AUTHOR ORIGINALLY HAD ABOUT THAT CHARACTER.
THE AUTHOR CAN STILL GIVE DEFINITION TO THE CHARACTER, NO MATTER HOW FAR GONE THEY MAY BE.

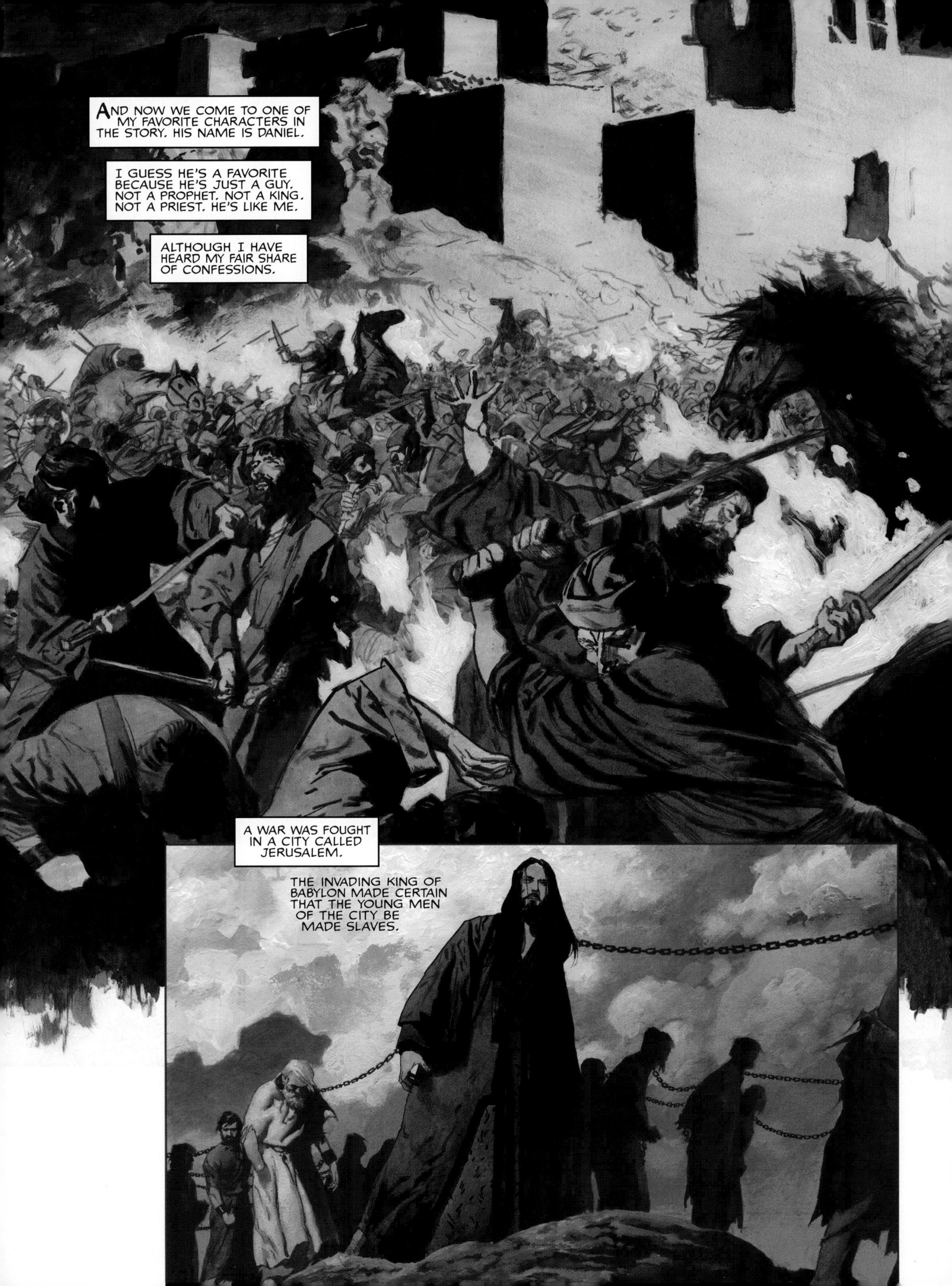
AND NOW WE COME TO ONE OF MY FAVORITE CHARACTERS IN THE STORY. HIS NAME IS DANIEL.
I GUESS HE'S A FAVORITE BECAUSE HE'S JUST A GUY. NOT A PROPHET. NOT A KING. NOT A PRIEST. HE'S LIKE ME.
ALTHOUGH I HAVE HEARD MY FAIR SHARE OF CONFESSIONS.
A WAR WAS FOUGHT IN A CITY CALLED JERUSALEM.
THE INVADING KING OF BABYLON MADE CERTAIN THAT THE YOUNG MEN OF THE CITY BE MADE SLAVES.

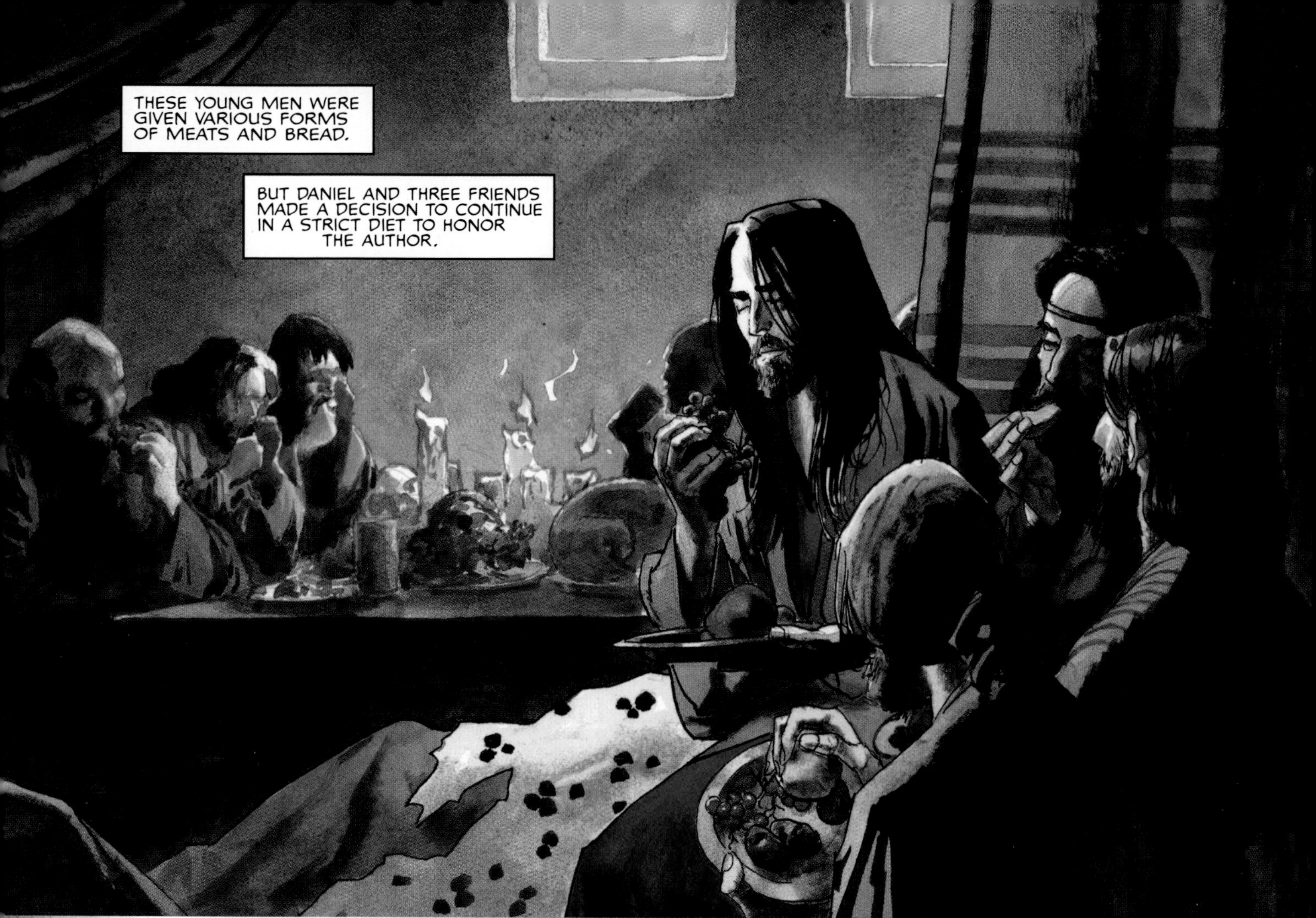
THESE YOUNG MEN WERE GIVEN VARIOUS FORMS OF MEATS AND BREAD.
BUT DANIEL AND THREE FRIENDS MADE A DECISION TO CONTINUE IN A STRICT DIET TO HONOR THE AUTHOR.

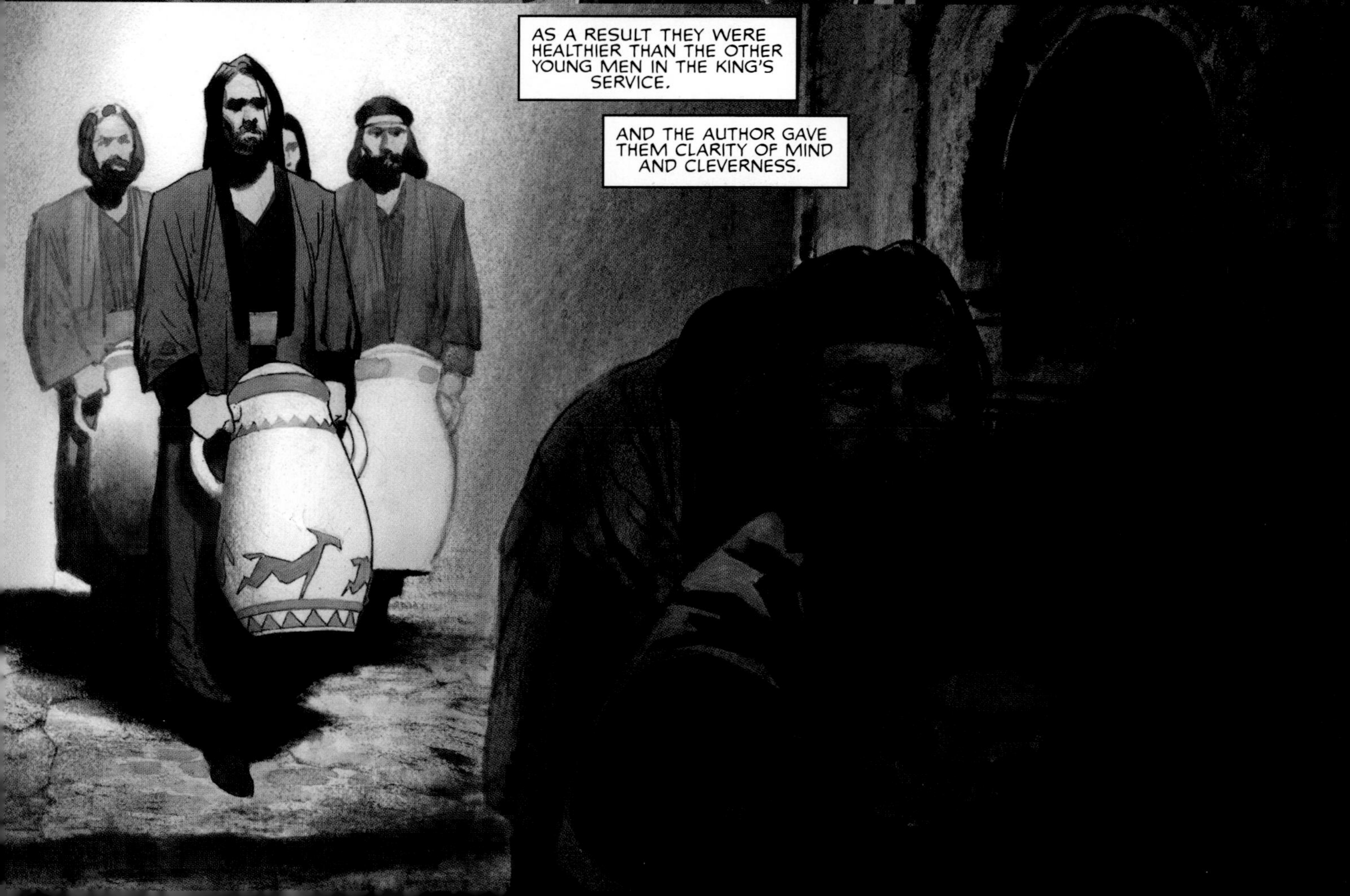
AS A RESULT THEY WERE HEALTHIER THAN THE OTHER YOUNG MEN IN THE KING'S SERVICE.
AND THE AUTHOR GAVE THEM CLARITY OF MIND AND CLEVERNESS.

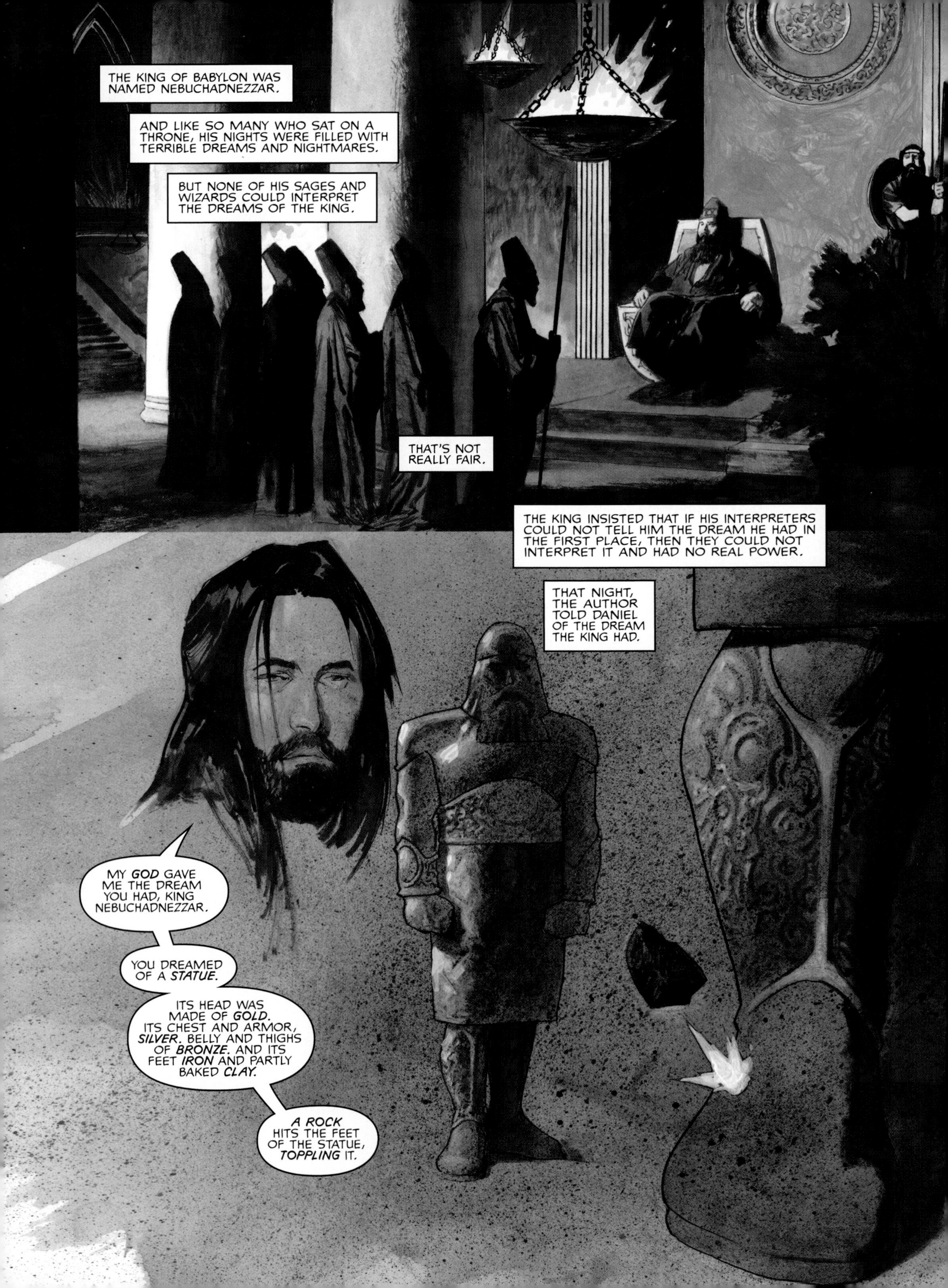
THE KING OF BABYLON WAS NAMED NEBUCHADNEZZAR.
AND LIKE SO MANY WHO SAT ON A THRONE, HIS NIGHTS WERE FILLED WITH TERRIBLE DREAMS AND NIGHTMARES.
BUT NONE OF HIS SAGES AND WIZARDS COULD INTERPRET THE DREAMS OF THE KING.
THAT'S NOT REALLY FAIR.
THE KING INSISTED THAT IF HIS INTERPRETERS COULD NOT TELL HIM THE DREAM HE HAD IN THE FIRST PLACE, THEN THEY COULD NOT INTERPRET IT AND HAD NO REAL POWER.
THAT NIGHT, THE AUTHOR TOLD DANIEL OF THE DREAM THE KING HAD.
MY **GOD** GAVE ME THE DREAM YOU HAD, KING NEBUCHADNEZZAR.
YOU DREAMED OF A ***STATUE***.
ITS HEAD WAS MADE OF **GOLD**. ITS CHEST AND ARMOR, ***SILVER***. BELLY AND THIGHS OF ***BRONZE***. AND ITS FEET ***IRON*** AND PARTLY BAKED ***CLAY***.
A ROCK HITS THE FEET OF THE STATUE, ***TOPPLING*** IT.

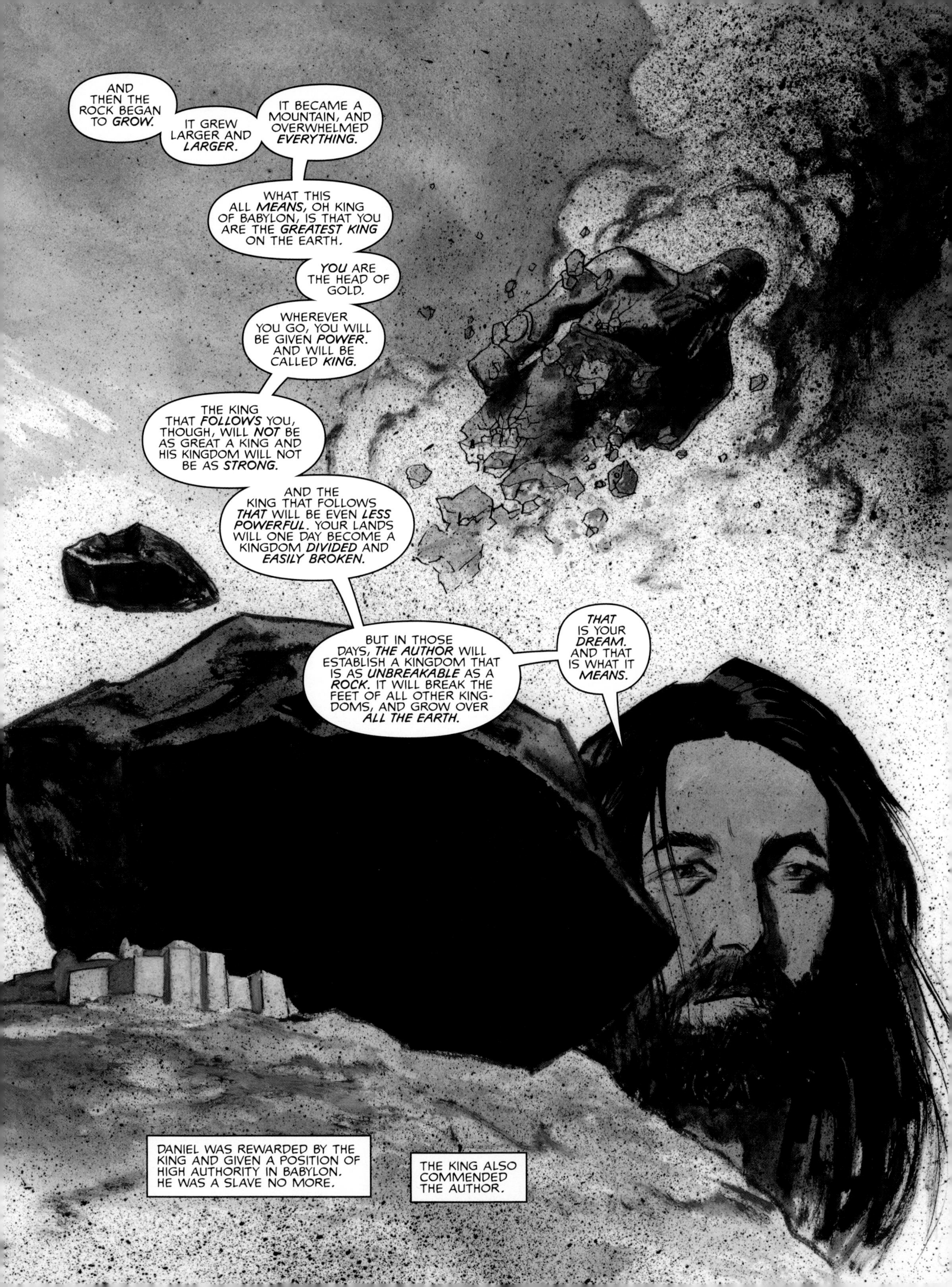
AND THEN THE ROCK BEGAN TO GROW.
IT GREW LARGER AND LARGER.
IT BECAME A MOUNTAIN, AND OVERWHELMED EVERYTHING.
WHAT THIS ALL MEANS, OH KING OF BABYLON, IS THAT YOU ARE THE GREATEST KING ON THE EARTH.
YOU ARE THE HEAD OF GOLD.
WHEREVER YOU GO, YOU WILL BE GIVEN POWER. AND WILL BE CALLED KING.
THE KING THAT FOLLOWS YOU, THOUGH, WILL NOT BE AS GREAT A KING AND HIS KINGDOM WILL NOT BE AS STRONG.
AND THE KING THAT FOLLOWS THAT WILL BE EVEN LESS POWERFUL. YOUR LANDS WILL ONE DAY BECOME A KINGDOM DIVIDED AND EASILY BROKEN.
BUT IN THOSE DAYS, THE AUTHOR WILL ESTABLISH A KINGDOM THAT IS AS UNBREAKABLE AS A ROCK. IT WILL BREAK THE FEET OF ALL OTHER KINGDOMS, AND GROW OVER ALL THE EARTH.
THAT IS YOUR DREAM. AND THAT IS WHAT IT MEANS.
DANIEL WAS REWARDED BY THE KING AND GIVEN A POSITION OF HIGH AUTHORITY IN BABYLON. HE WAS A SLAVE NO MORE.
THE KING ALSO COMMENDED THE AUTHOR.

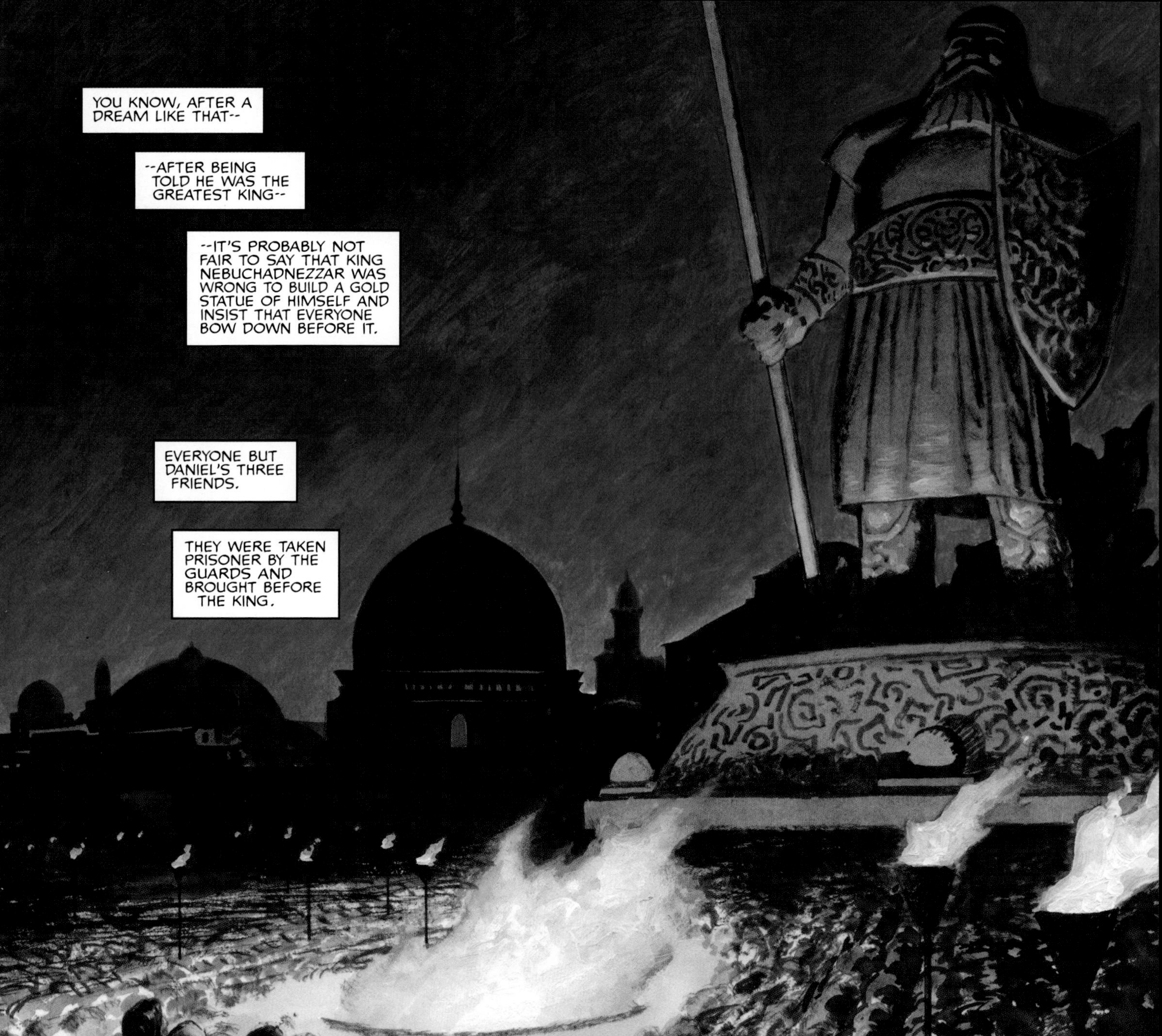
YOU KNOW, AFTER A DREAM LIKE THAT--
--AFTER BEING TOLD HE WAS THE GREATEST KING--
--IT'S PROBABLY NOT FAIR TO SAY THAT KING NEBUCHADNEZZAR WAS WRONG TO BUILD A GOLD STATUE OF HIMSELF AND INSIST THAT EVERYONE BOW DOWN BEFORE IT.
EVERYONE BUT DANIEL'S THREE FRIENDS.
THEY WERE TAKEN PRISONER BY THE GUARDS AND BROUGHT BEFORE THE KING.

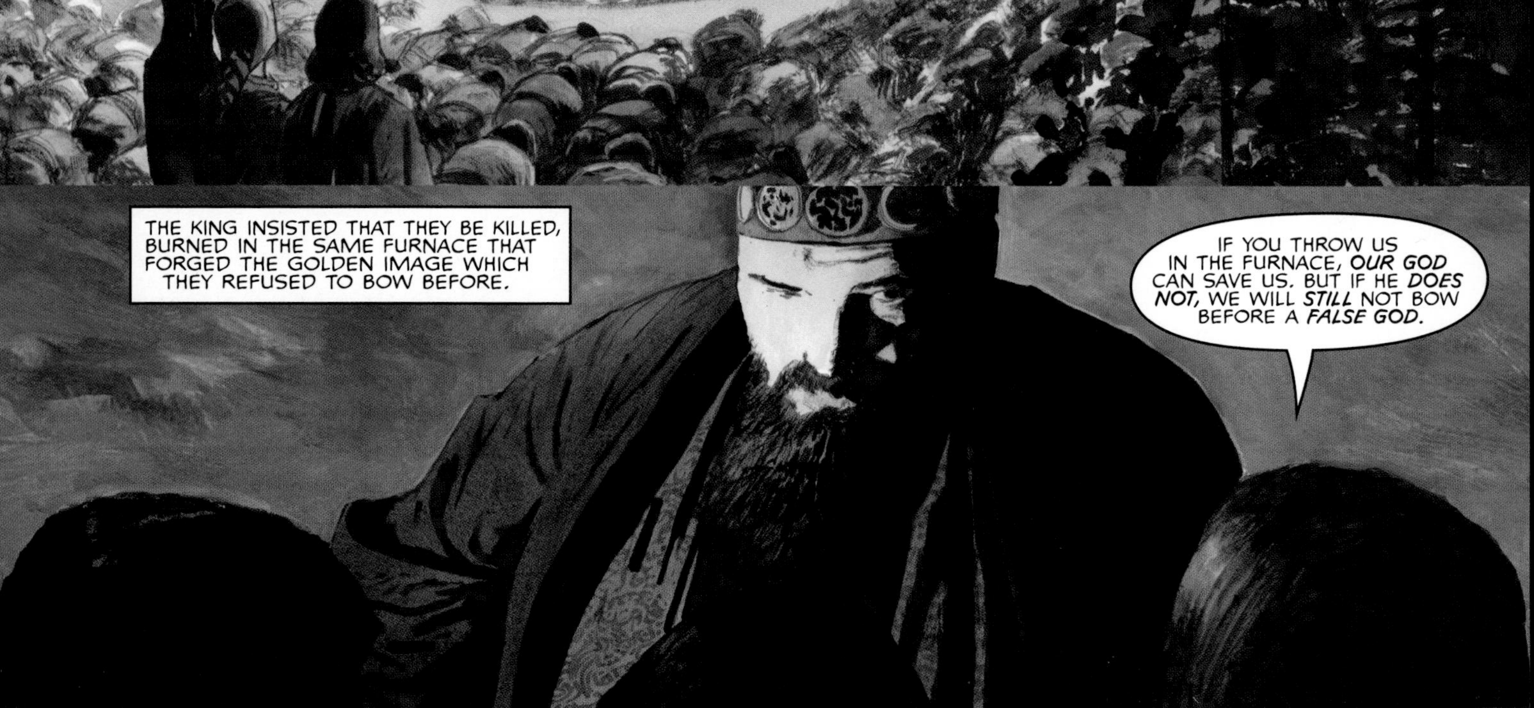
THE KING INSISTED THAT THEY BE KILLED, BURNED IN THE SAME FURNACE THAT FORGED THE GOLDEN IMAGE WHICH THEY REFUSED TO BOW BEFORE.
IF YOU THROW US IN THE FURNACE, OUR GOD CAN SAVE US. BUT IF HE DOES NOT, WE WILL STILL NOT BOW BEFORE A FALSE GOD.

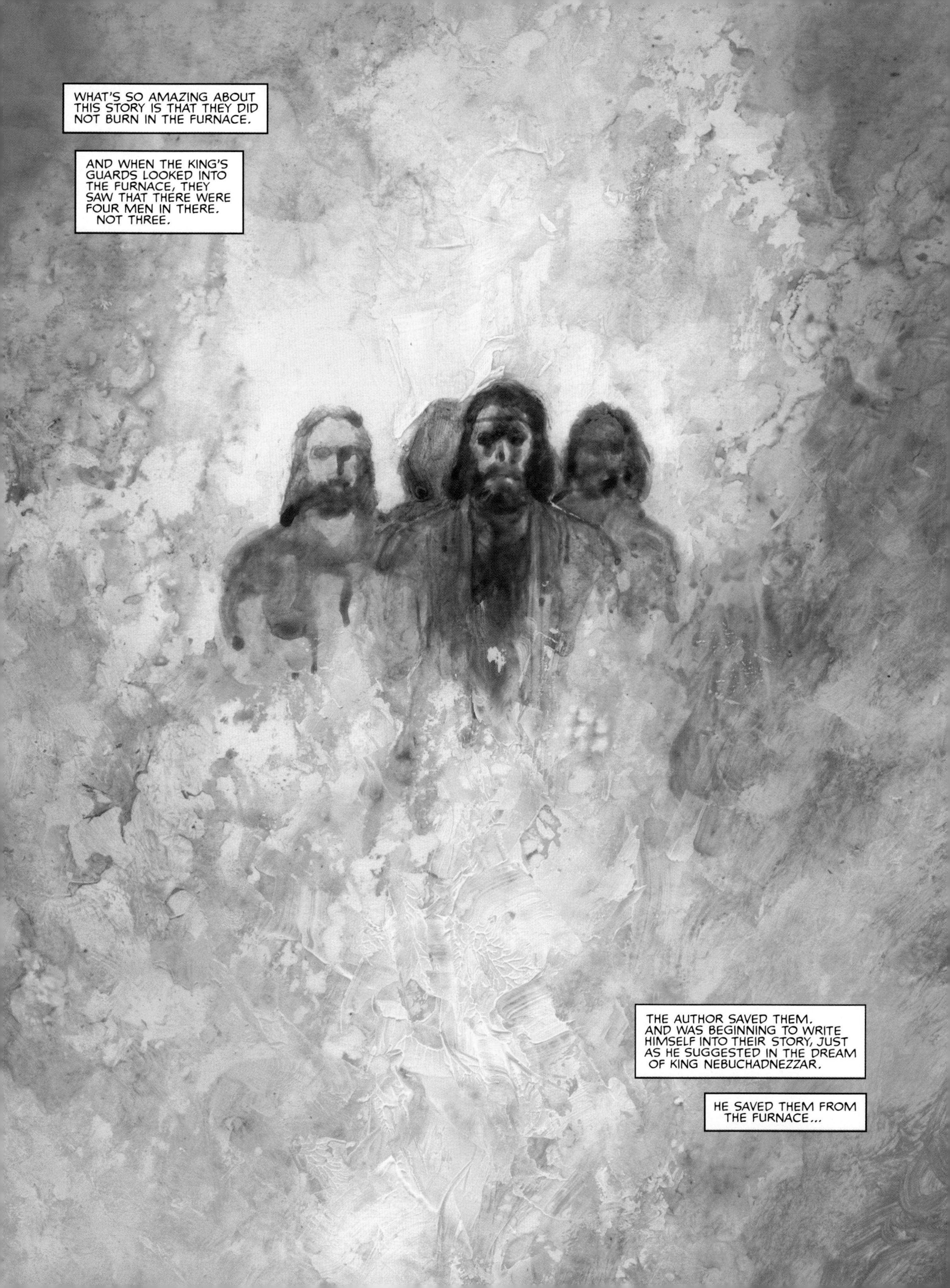
WHAT'S SO AMAZING ABOUT THIS STORY IS THAT THEY DID NOT BURN IN THE FURNACE.
AND WHEN THE KING'S GUARDS LOOKED INTO THE FURNACE, THEY SAW THAT THERE WERE FOUR MEN IN THERE. NOT THREE.
THE AUTHOR SAVED THEM. AND WAS BEGINNING TO WRITE HIMSELF INTO THEIR STORY, JUST AS HE SUGGESTED IN THE DREAM OF KING NEBUCHADNEZZAR.
HE SAVED THEM FROM THE FURNACE...

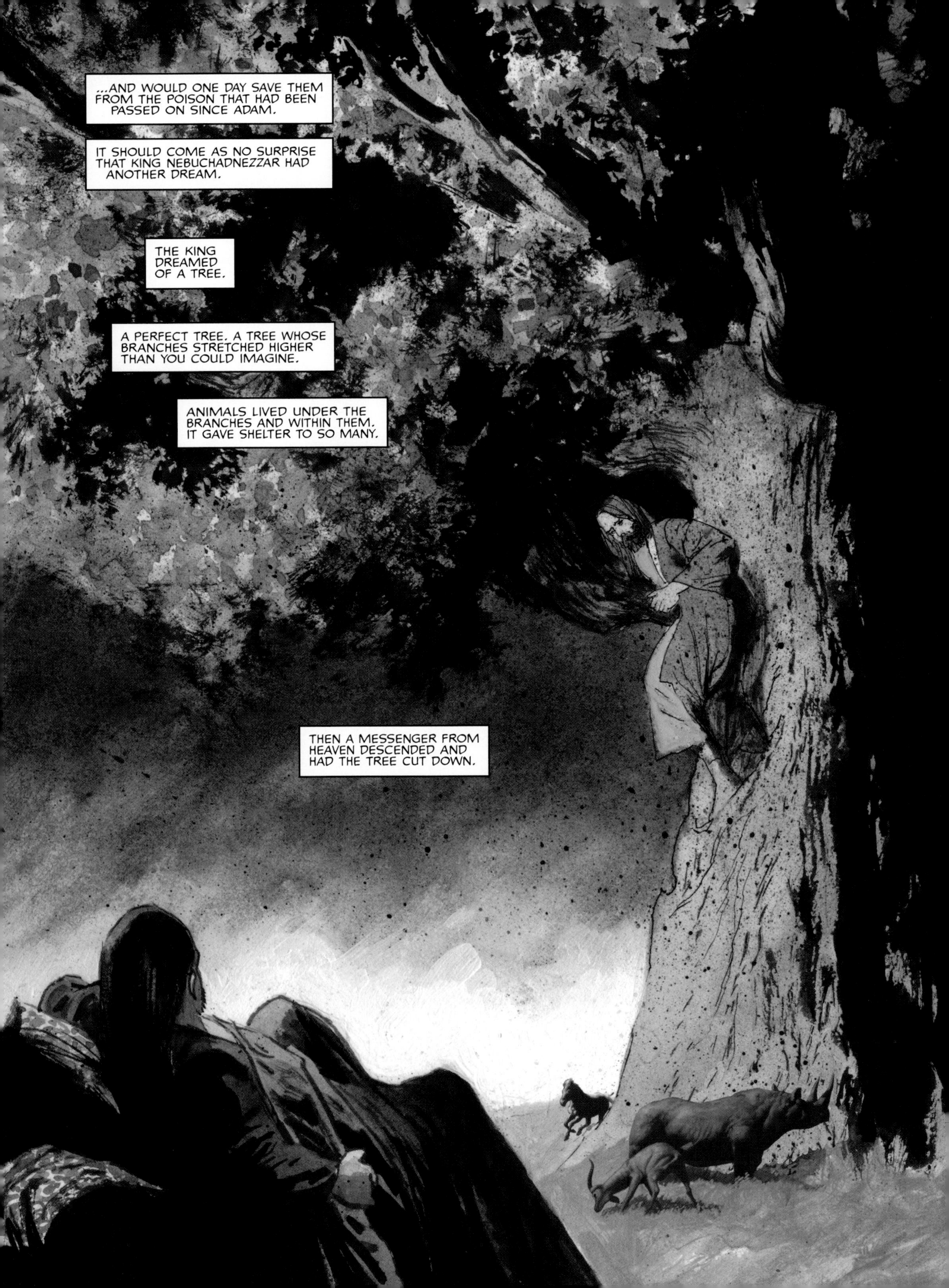
...AND WOULD ONE DAY SAVE THEM FROM THE POISON THAT HAD BEEN PASSED ON SINCE ADAM.
IT SHOULD COME AS NO SURPRISE THAT KING NEBUCHADNEZZAR HAD ANOTHER DREAM.
THE KING DREAMED OF A TREE.
A PERFECT TREE. A TREE WHOSE BRANCHES STRETCHED HIGHER THAN YOU COULD IMAGINE.
ANIMALS LIVED UNDER THE BRANCHES AND WITHIN THEM. IT GAVE SHELTER TO SO MANY.
THEN A MESSENGER FROM HEAVEN DESCENDED AND HAD THE TREE CUT DOWN.

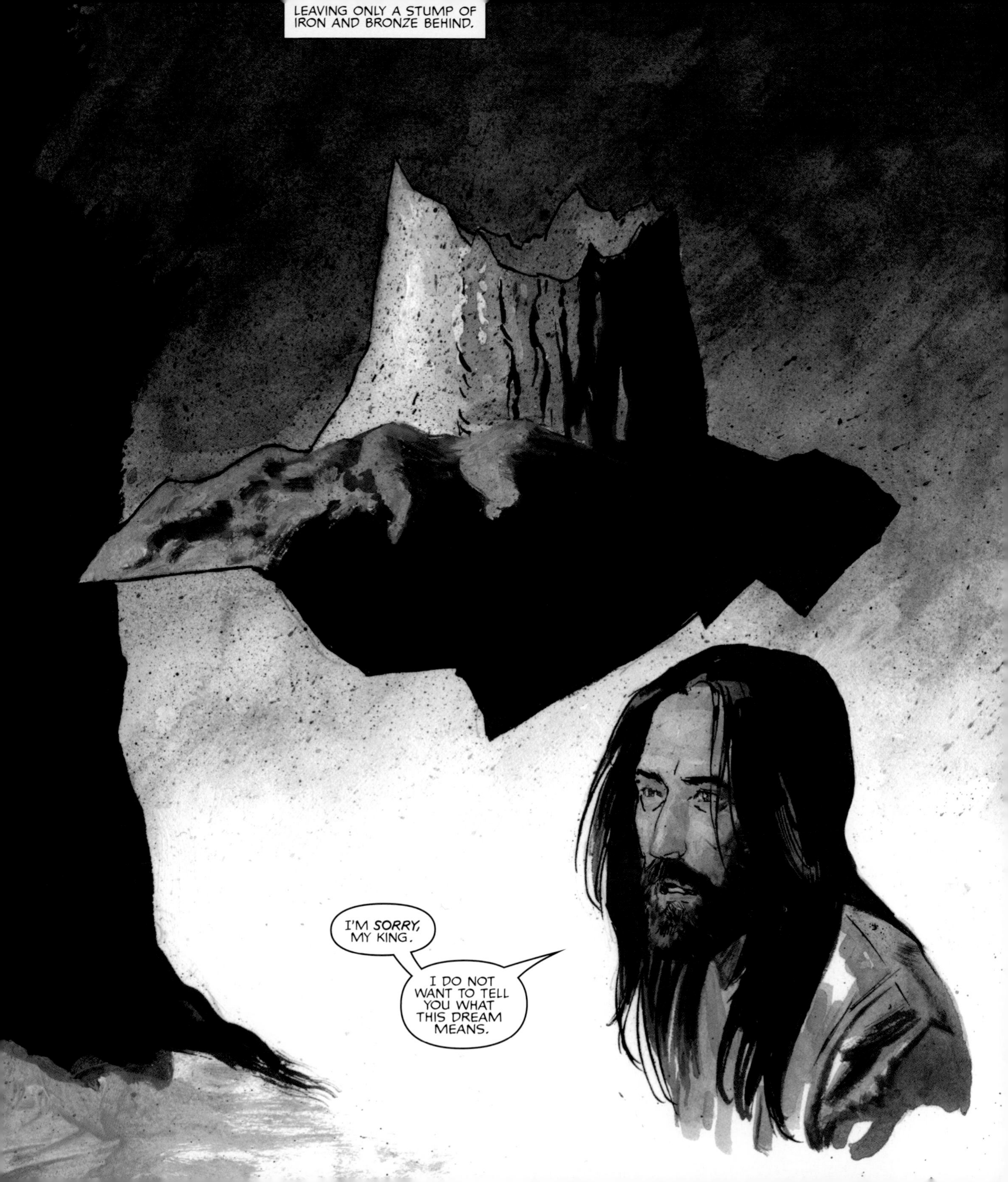
LEAVING ONLY A STUMP OF IRON AND BRONZE BEHIND.
I'M SORRY, MY KING.
I DO NOT WANT TO TELL YOU WHAT THIS DREAM MEANS.

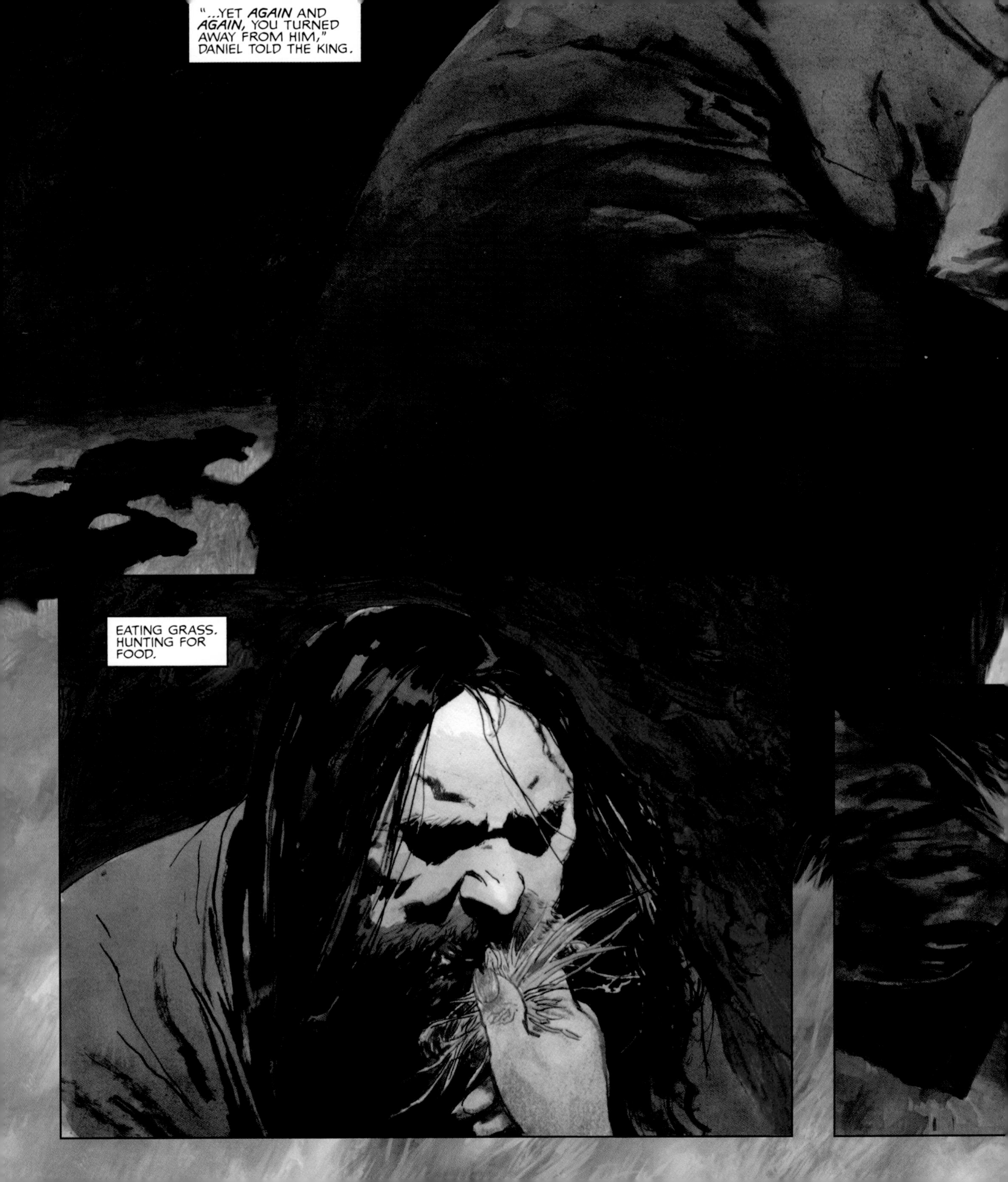
"...YET AGAIN AND AGAIN, YOU TURNED AWAY FROM HIM," DANIEL TOLD THE KING.
EATING GRASS. HUNTING FOR FOOD.

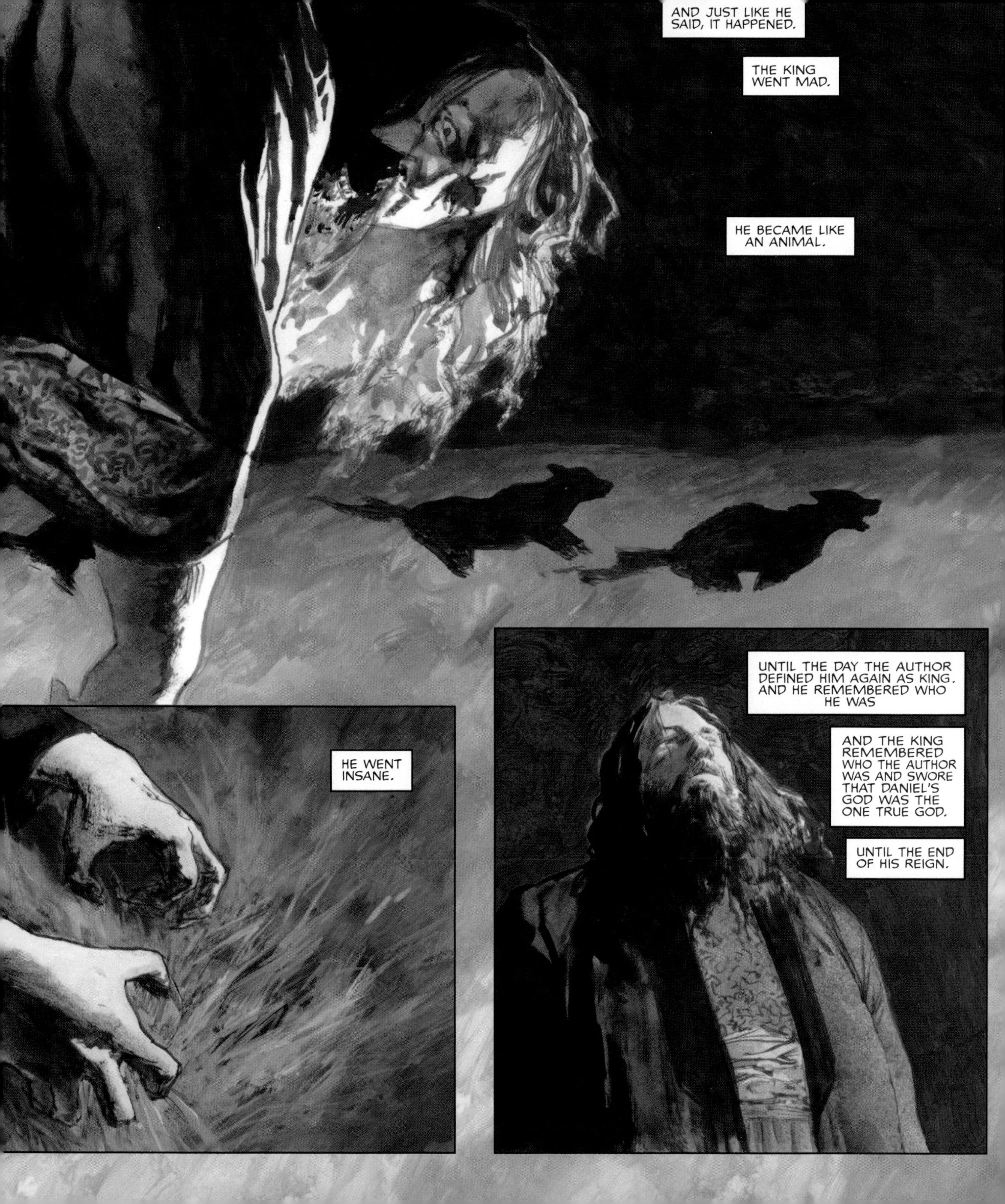
AND JUST LIKE HE SAID, IT HAPPENED.
THE KING WENT MAD.
HE BECAME LIKE AN ANIMAL.
HE WENT INSANE.
UNTIL THE DAY THE AUTHOR DEFINED HIM AGAIN AS KING. AND HE REMEMBERED WHO HE WAS
AND THE KING REMEMBERED WHO THE AUTHOR WAS AND SWORE THAT DANIEL'S GOD WAS THE ONE TRUE GOD.
UNTIL THE END OF HIS REIGN.

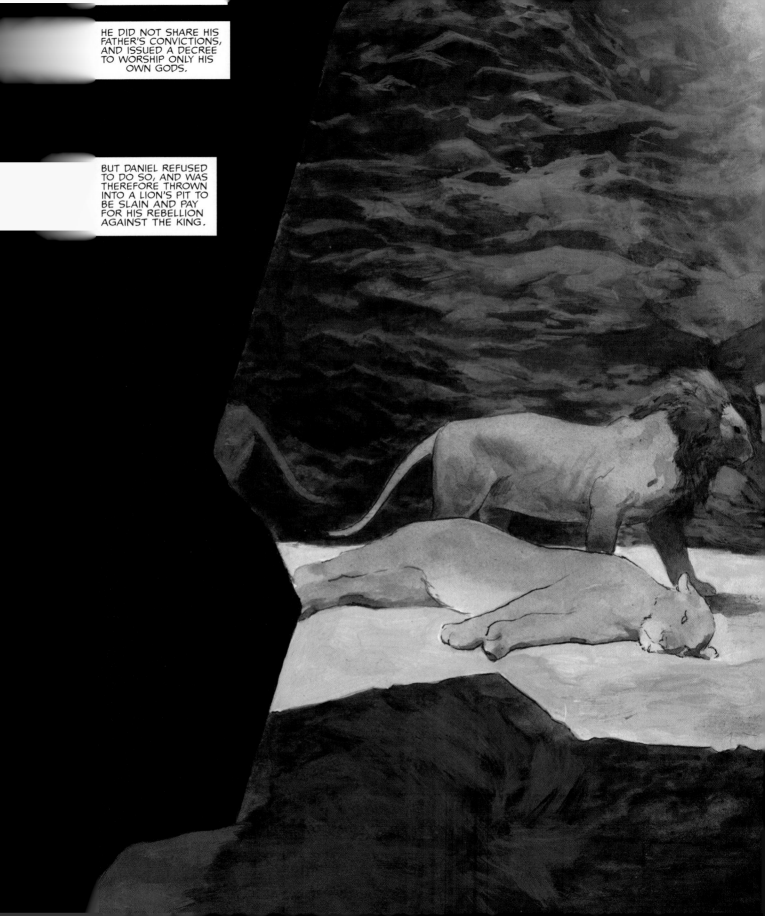

HE DID NOT SHARE HIS FATHER'S CONVICTIONS, AND ISSUED A DECREE TO WORSHIP ONLY HIS OWN GODS.

BUT DANIEL REFUSED TO DO SO, AND WAS THEREFORE THROWN INTO A LION'S PIT TO BE SLAIN AND PAY FOR HIS REBELLION AGAINST THE KING.

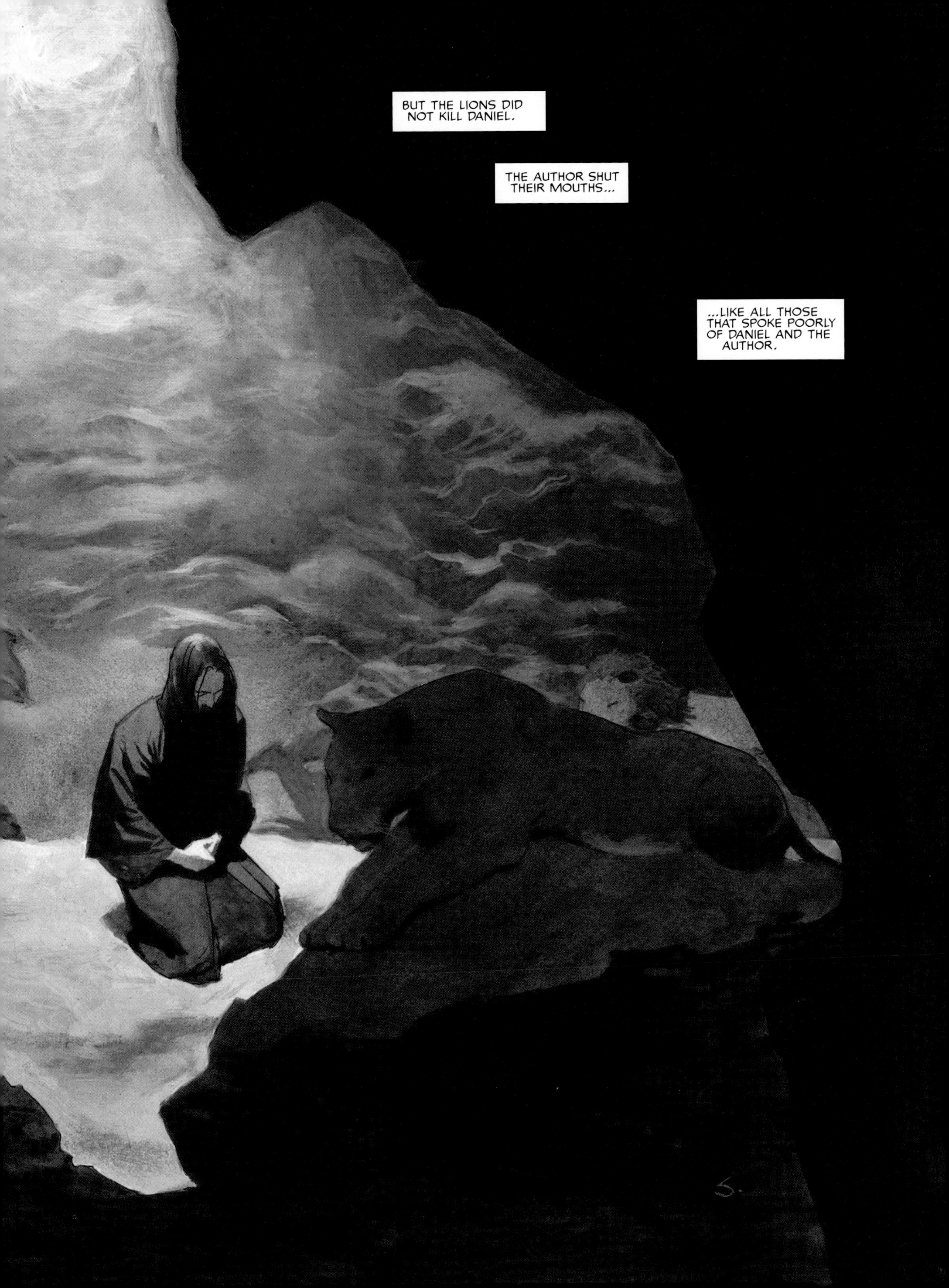
BUT THE LIONS DID NOT KILL DANIEL.
THE AUTHOR SHUT THEIR MOUTHS...
...LIKE ALL THOSE THAT SPOKE POORLY OF DANIEL AND THE AUTHOR.

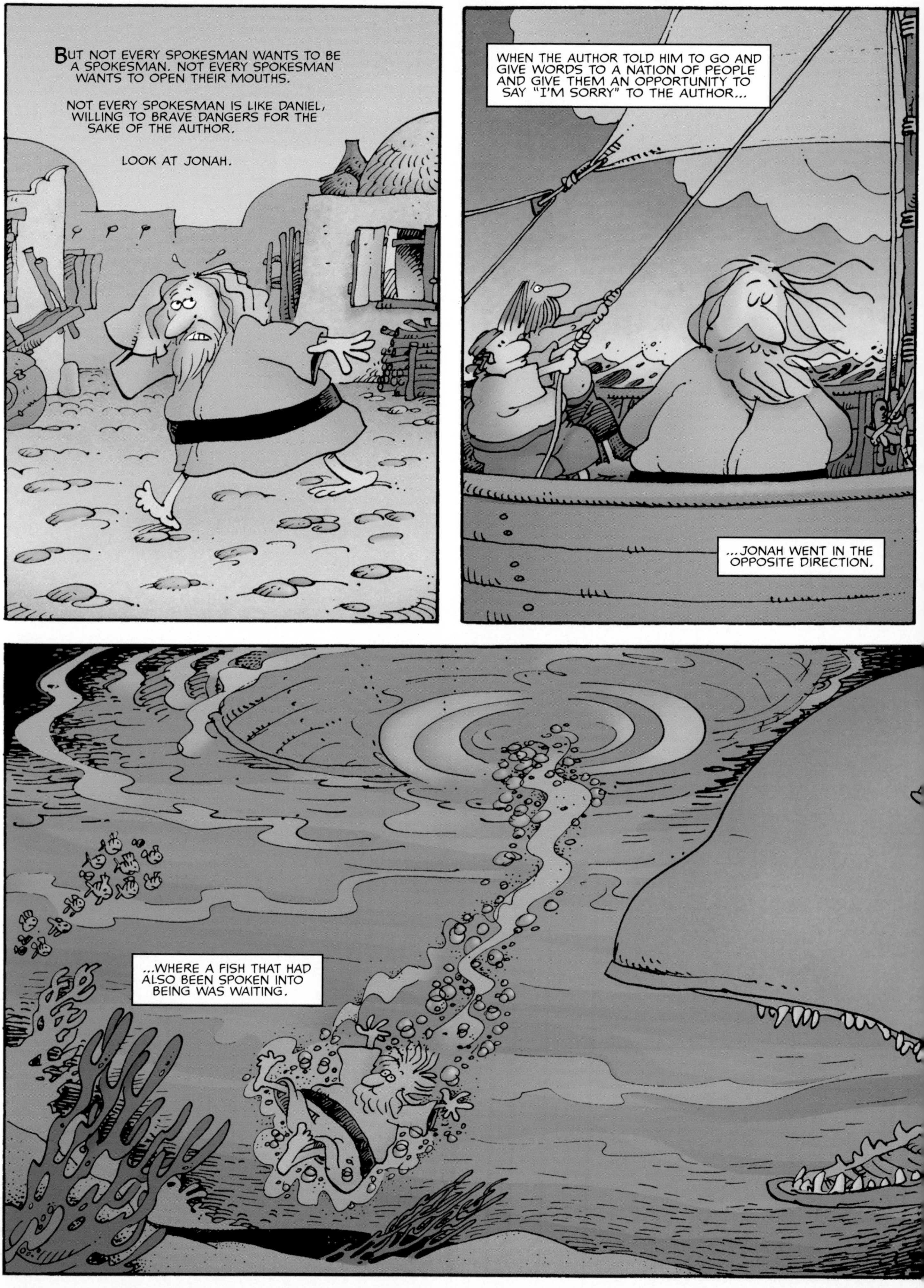
BUT NOT EVERY SPOKESMAN WANTS TO BE A SPOKESMAN. NOT EVERY SPOKESMAN WANTS TO OPEN THEIR MOUTHS.
NOT EVERY SPOKESMAN IS LIKE DANIEL, WILLING TO BRAVE DANGERS FOR THE SAKE OF THE AUTHOR.
LOOK AT JONAH.
WHEN THE AUTHOR TOLD HIM TO GO AND GIVE WORDS TO A NATION OF PEOPLE AND GIVE THEM AN OPPORTUNITY TO SAY "I'M SORRY" TO THE AUTHOR...
...JONAH WENT IN THE OPPOSITE DIRECTION.
...WHERE A FISH THAT HAD ALSO BEEN SPOKEN INTO BEING WAS WAITING.

BUT THE SEA THAT THE AUTHOR SPOKE INTO BEING WAS NOT A GOOD PLACE TO RUN TO.

JUST AS THERE WOULD BE NO PLACE ON THE LAND THE AUTHOR CALLED OUT OF THE SEA.

WHEN JONAH TOLD THE MEN ON THE BOAT THAT THE STORM WAS BECAUSE OF HIM, THAT THEY WOULD DIE BECAUSE OF HIM, THEY DID WHAT ANY PERSON INSANE WITH FEAR OF THE AUTHOR WOULD DO.

THEY DUMPED HIM OFF THE BOAT.

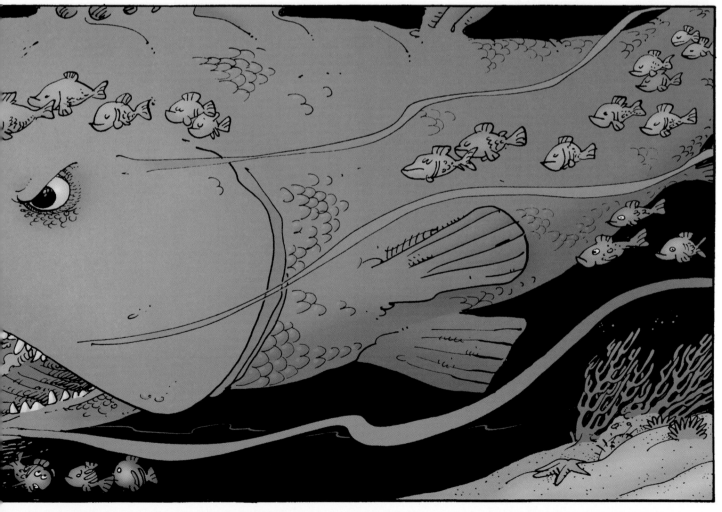

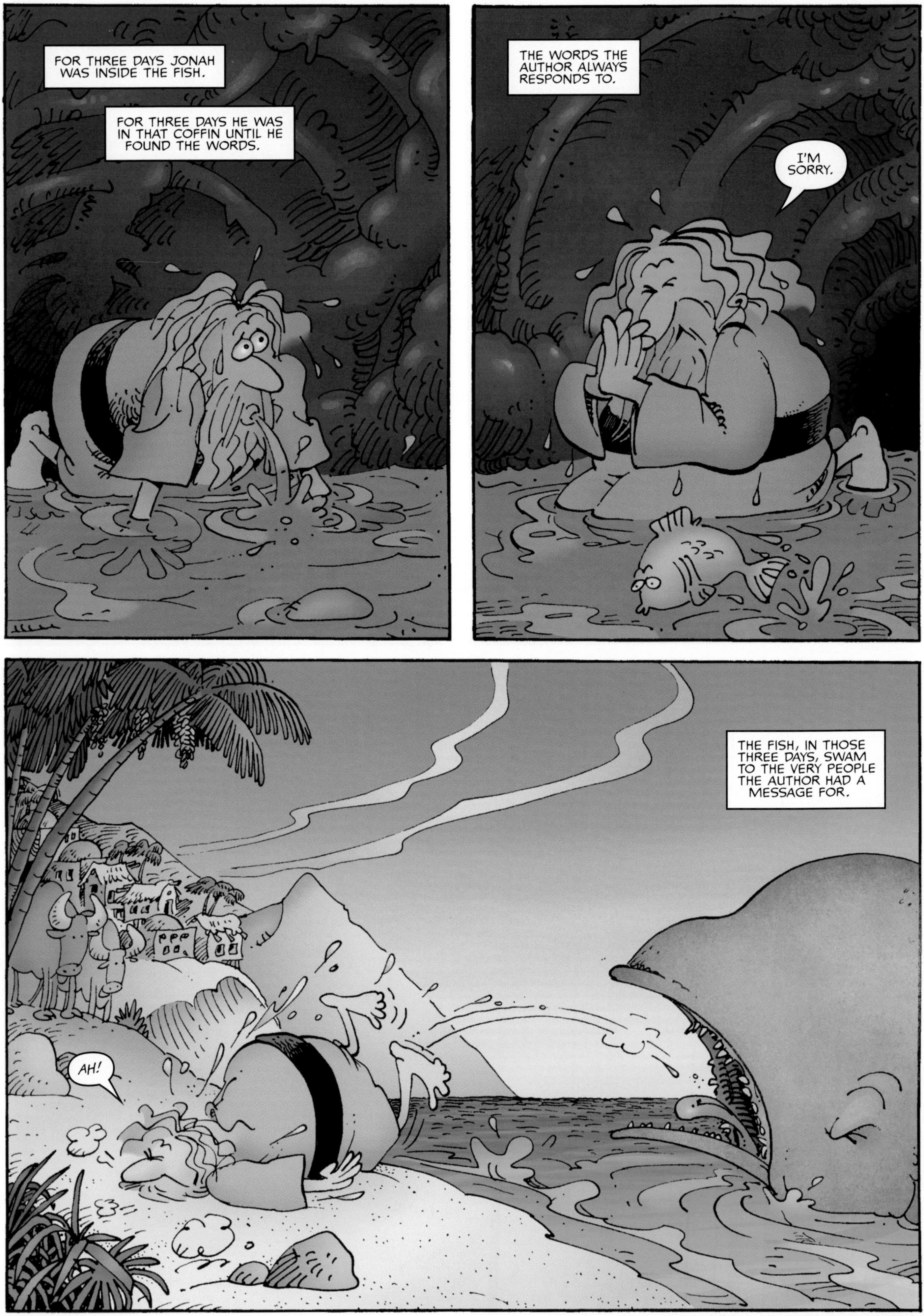
FOR THREE DAYS JONAH WAS INSIDE THE FISH.
FOR THREE DAYS HE WAS IN THAT COFFIN UNTIL HE FOUND THE WORDS.
THE WORDS THE AUTHOR ALWAYS RESPONDS TO.
I'M SORRY.
THE FISH, IN THOSE THREE DAYS, SWAM TO THE VERY PEOPLE THE AUTHOR HAD A MESSAGE FOR.
AH!

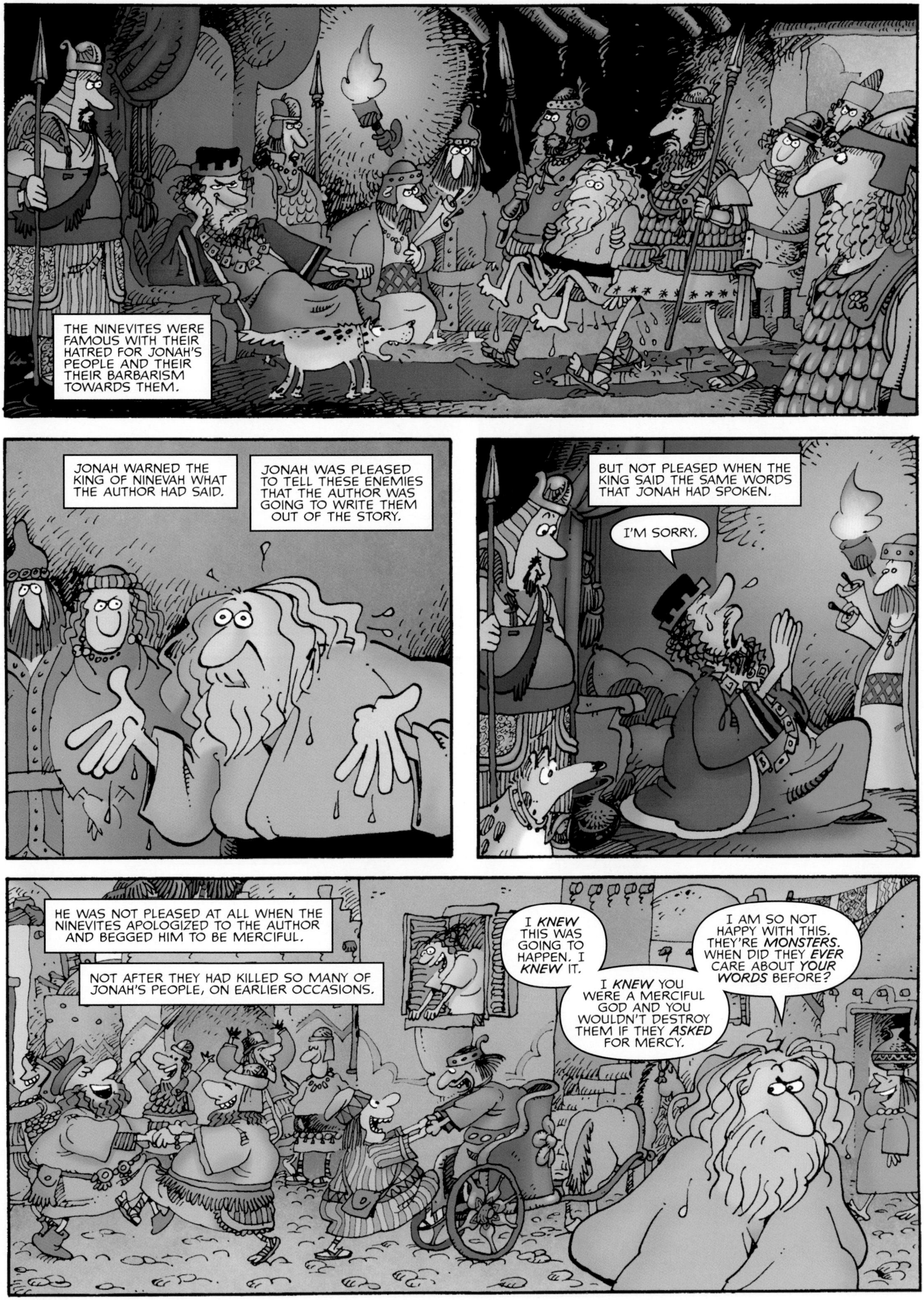
THE NINEVITES WERE FAMOUS WITH THEIR HATRED FOR JONAH'S PEOPLE AND THEIR THEIR BARBARISM TOWARDS THEM.
JONAH WARNED THE KING OF NINEVAH WHAT THE AUTHOR HAD SAID.
JONAH WAS PLEASED TO TELL THESE ENEMIES THAT THE AUTHOR WAS GOING TO WRITE THEM OUT OF THE STORY.
BUT NOT PLEASED WHEN THE KING SAID THE SAME WORDS THAT JONAH HAD SPOKEN.
I'M SORRY.
HE WAS NOT PLEASED AT ALL WHEN THE NINEVITES APOLOGIZED TO THE AUTHOR AND BEGGED HIM TO BE MERCIFUL.
NOT AFTER THEY HAD KILLED SO MANY OF JONAH'S PEOPLE, ON EARLIER OCCASIONS.
I *KNEW* THIS WAS GOING TO HAPPEN. I *KNEW* IT.
I *KNEW* YOU WERE A MERCIFUL GOD AND YOU WOULDN'T DESTROY THEM IF THEY *ASKED* FOR MERCY.
I AM SO NOT HAPPY WITH THIS. THEY'RE ***MONSTERS***. WHEN DID THEY ***EVER*** CARE ABOUT ***YOUR WORDS*** BEFORE?

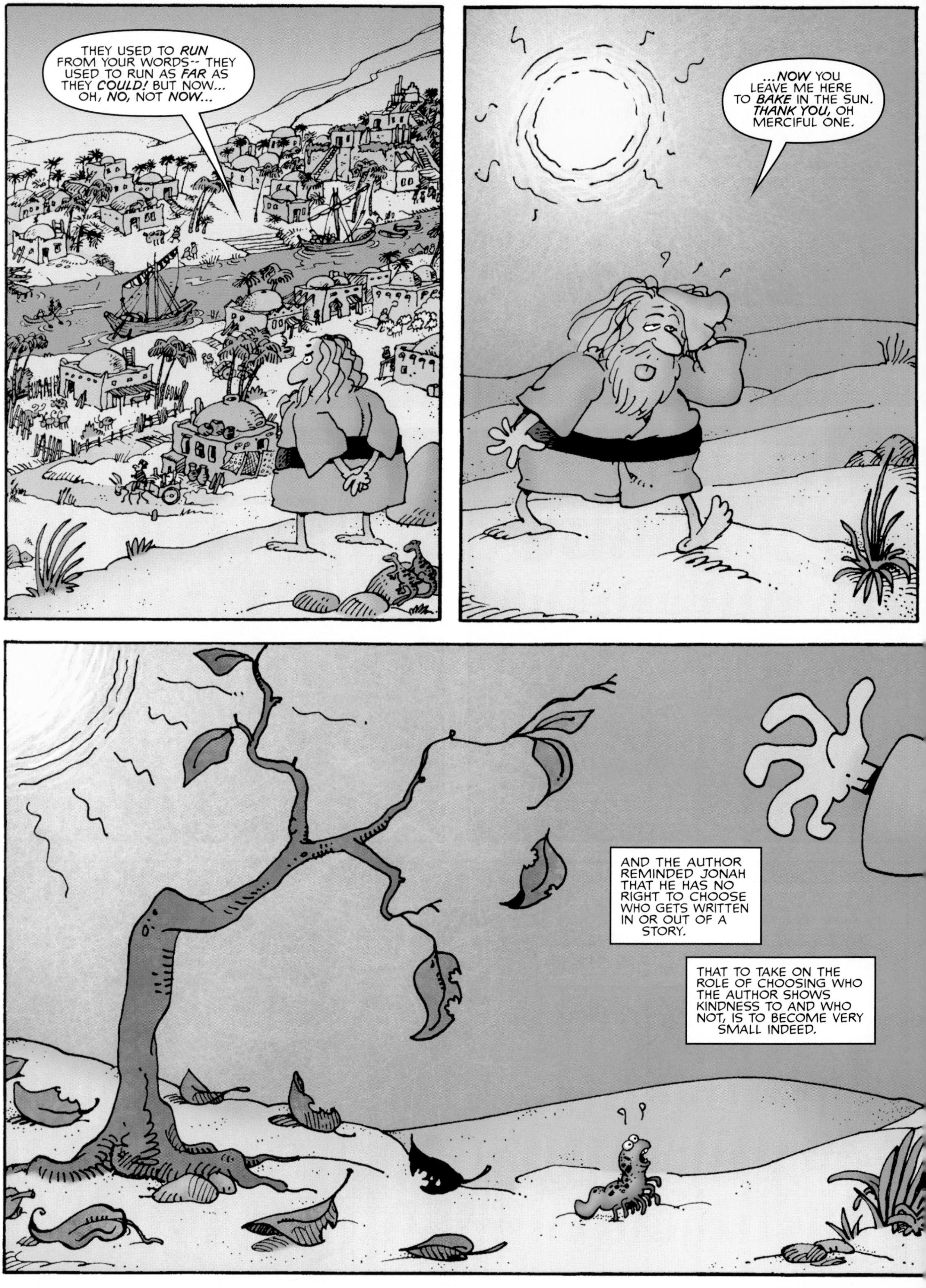
THEY USED TO RUN FROM YOUR WORDS-- THEY USED TO RUN AS FAR AS THEY COULD! BUT NOW... OH, NO, NOT NOW...
...NOW YOU LEAVE ME HERE TO BAKE IN THE SUN. THANK YOU, OH MERCIFUL ONE.
AND THE AUTHOR REMINDED JONAH THAT HE HAS NO RIGHT TO CHOOSE WHO GETS WRITTEN IN OR OUT OF A STORY.
THAT TO TAKE ON THE ROLE OF CHOOSING WHO THE AUTHOR SHOWS KINDNESS TO AND WHO NOT, IS TO BECOME VERY SMALL INDEED.

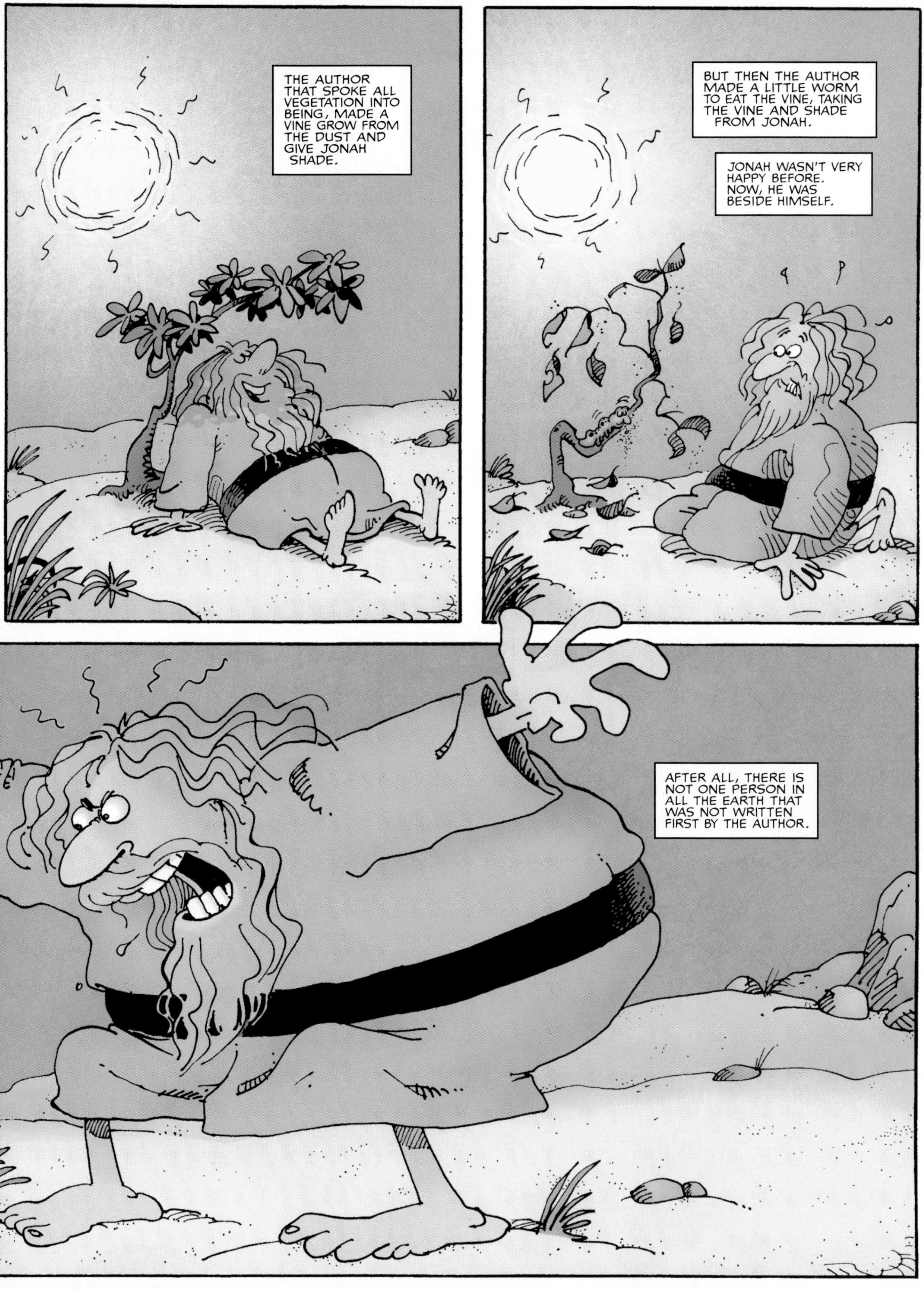
THE AUTHOR THAT SPOKE ALL VEGETATION INTO BEING, MADE A VINE GROW FROM THE DUST AND GIVE JONAH SHADE.
BUT THEN THE AUTHOR MADE A LITTLE WORM TO EAT THE VINE, TAKING THE VINE AND SHADE FROM JONAH.
JONAH WASN'T VERY HAPPY BEFORE. NOW, HE WAS BESIDE HIMSELF.
AFTER ALL, THERE IS NOT ONE PERSON IN ALL THE EARTH THAT WAS NOT WRITTEN FIRST BY THE AUTHOR.

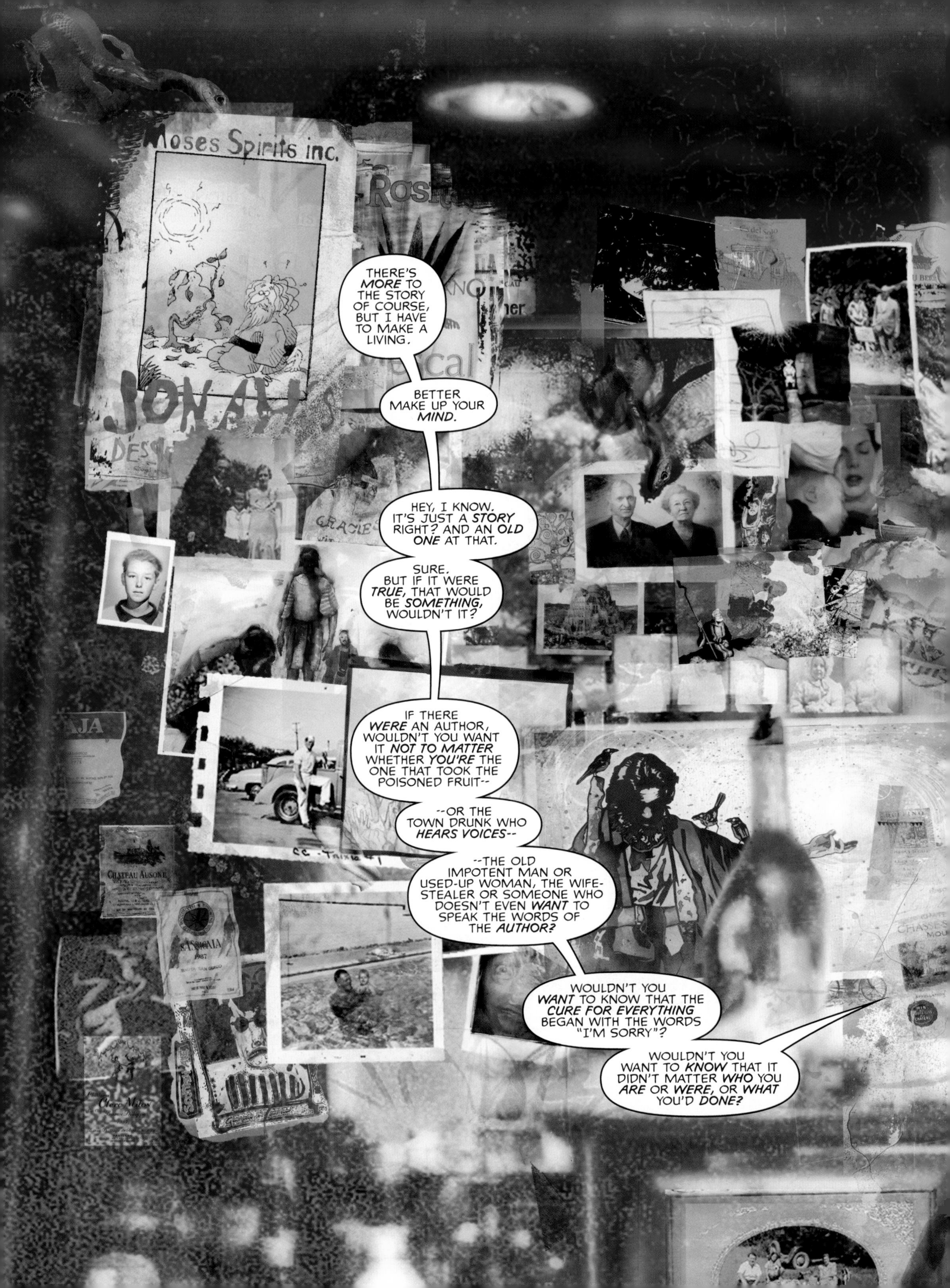
THERE'S MORE TO THE STORY OF COURSE, BUT I HAVE TO MAKE A LIVING.
BETTER MAKE UP YOUR MIND.
HEY, I KNOW. IT'S JUST A STORY RIGHT? AND AN OLD ONE AT THAT.
SURE. BUT IF IT WERE TRUE, THAT WOULD BE SOMETHING, WOULDN'T IT?
IF THERE WERE AN AUTHOR, WOULDN'T YOU WANT IT NOT TO MATTER WHETHER YOU'RE THE ONE THAT TOOK THE POISONED FRUIT--
--OR THE TOWN DRUNK WHO HEARS VOICES--
--THE OLD IMPOTENT MAN OR USED-UP WOMAN, THE WIFE-STEALER OR SOMEONE WHO DOESN'T EVEN WANT TO SPEAK THE WORDS OF THE AUTHOR?
WOULDN'T YOU WANT TO KNOW THAT THE CURE FOR EVERYTHING BEGAN WITH THE WORDS "I'M SORRY"?
WOULDN'T YOU WANT TO KNOW THAT IT DIDN'T MATTER WHO YOU ARE OR WERE, OR WHAT YOU'D DONE?
Moses Spirits inc.
JONAH'S
CHATEAU AUSONE
SASSICAIA
1987

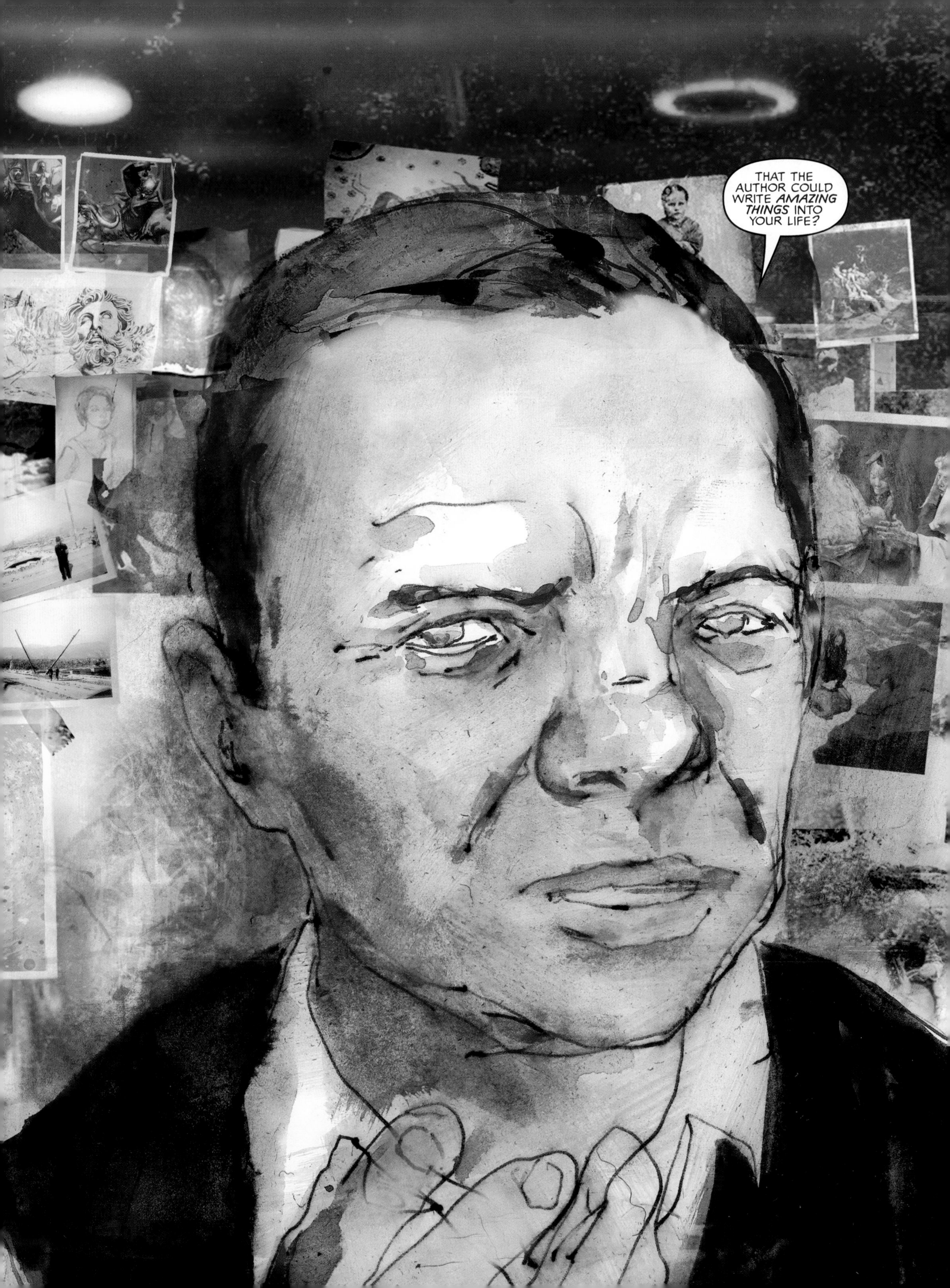
THAT THE AUTHOR COULD WRITE *AMAZING THINGS* INTO YOUR LIFE?

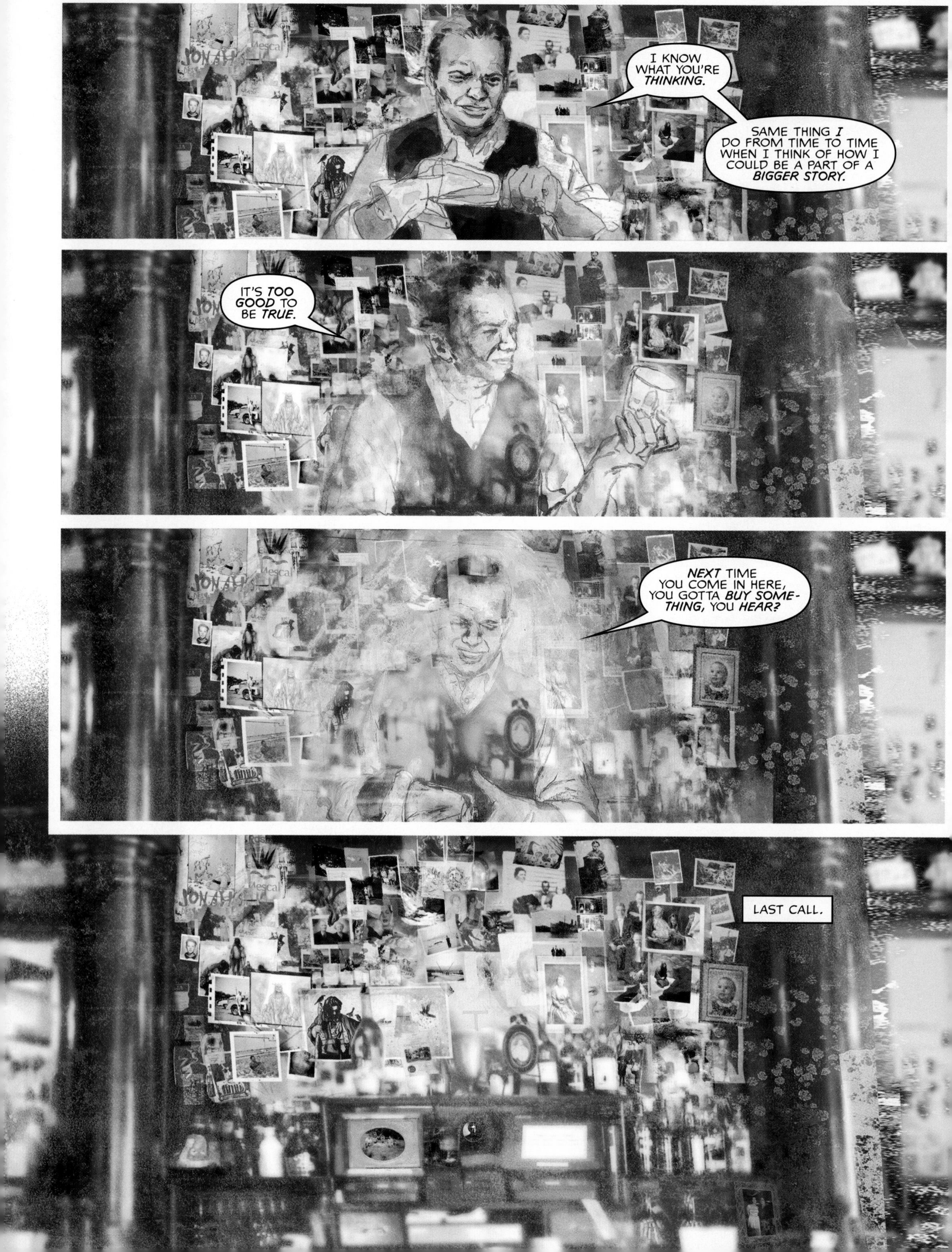
I KNOW WHAT YOU'RE *THINKING.*
SAME THING *I* DO FROM TIME TO TIME WHEN I THINK OF HOW I COULD BE A PART OF A *BIGGER STORY.*
IT'S *TOO GOOD* TO BE *TRUE.*
NEXT TIME YOU COME IN HERE, YOU GOTTA *BUY SOME-THING,* YOU *HEAR?*
LAST CALL.

ACKNOWLEDGMENTS

JASON ALEXANDER

JOHNATHAN BABCOCK

SANDY BISHOP

BARBARA BERNSTENGEL

DAVID BURKE

SCOTT CASE

DEREKH COHEN

DEBORAH COWELL

TREVÓN D. GROSS

RABBI BRADLEY HIRSCHFIELD

ZACH HOWARD

THOMPSON KNOX

KARINA LUCERO

ALYSIA McRAE

RUDY NEBRES

JERRY A. NOVICK

CHATMAN PAYNE

BEN PRENEVOST

LISSETTE PEREZ

MONIQUE RUBIO

JOSE R. RUIZ

LORENZO D. RUIZ

RAQUEL Y. RUIZ

DORETTE SAUNDERS

ANDREW SELTZ

ROBERT SCHWALB

GAIL WARREN

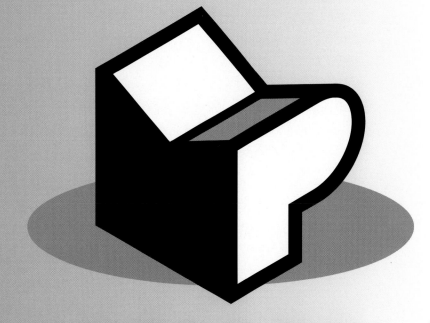

METRON PRESS™

JIM KRUEGER • *Writer*

Jim Krueger graduated Marquette University with a degree in Journalism. He won two Addy Awards during his first year as a copywriter. A year later he became a creative director at Marvel Comics and has since become a freelance comic book writer/property creator.

His original works include the *Foot Soldiers, Alphabet Supes, The Clock Maker* and the soon-to-be-released, *The Last Straw Man*. His first short film, *They Might Be Dragons*, which he wrote, directed, and produced won "Best In Class" at NYU and a "Best Short Film" award from The New York Independent Film Festival.

Other comic book writing includes the award-winning *Earth X trilogy* for Marvel Comics, as well as *Avengers, X-Men, Star Wars, Matrix and Batman,* and he has since introduced two new comic book formats.

On the drawing board are such projects as *Micronauts, Galactic* for Dark Horse Entertainment, *The Lion* (a C.S. Lewis-like fantasy), a new, short film called *"Looking Out For No. One (or is that No One?)"* and the *Justice League* for DC Comics.

Jim is also president and publisher of his own comic book entertainment company, 26 Soldiers, and was named as one of the top ten writers in comics and an innovator in the field by Wizard Magazine.

BILL KOEB • *JJ'S Bar*

Bill Koeb is an illustrator and painter who has exhibited in the New York and Los Angeles Societies of Illustrators Print magazine, and in group shows in New York and San Francisco. He has illustrated stories and articles for numerous publications including Washington City Paper, Ray-Gun, Stick, Atlanta, and The Village Voice. His work has appeared on book covers, CD's, and posters for concerts and plays.

Born in Los Angeles, CA in 1965, Bill grew up in Southern and Northern California, and discovered a love of drawing at an early age when he read comics. From 1985 to 1987, he studied painting and illustration at the Academy of Art, San Francisco with Barron Storey, Bill Shields, Tom Marsh, and Jim Sanford.

In 1989 Bill ventured into comics work, painting a story for *Clive Barker's Hellraiser* anthology. His other works in comics includes illustrating the short series *Faultlines* for Vertigo, Alan Moore's song, *The Hair of the Snake That Bit Me* for Caliber, and writing and drawing several short stories for Vanguard's *Tales From the Edge* anthology which include *Psychic Pedestrian* and *Time Stop*.

In 1995, Bill was commissioned to create original paintings for the movies *The Crow* and *City of Angels*, and from 1998 to 2001, he created over 40 illustrations for a Fireman's Fund print campaign that appeared in Fortune, Business Week, and the New York Times.

In May 2002, after living in San Francisco for 16 years, Bill, along with his wife, Julie, and their son, Gabriel, and two cats: Oliver and Rosie, relocated to North Carolina where they currently reside with a noisy dog named Gracie.

KENT WILLIAMS • *Ezekiel*

Draftsman and painter, illustrator and comics creator, Kent Williams is thirty-six years old. In 1980 he moved to New York to study at the Pratt Institute where he received his BFA in Drawing and Painting. His graphic novel/comics work includes *Tell Me, Dark* and *Blood: A Tale.* A selection of his works on paper, Kent Williams: Drawings & Monotypes, was published in 1991, and a catalogue of his paintings, Kent Williams: Selected Works, was published in 1995. His work has been printed in numerous national and international publications including Playboy, Omni, and The Learning Channel magazine. Williams is the recipient of a number of awards for his work, both for comics and illustration. They include The Yellow Kid Award, Lucca, Italy's prestigious comics award, three medals from the Society of Illustrators, New York, and The Joseph Henniger Award for Best of Show, from Illustration West 32.

Williams now lives in Chapel Hill, North Carolina with his wife, Sherilyn, and their two young sons, Kerig and Ian.

JASON ALEXANDER • *Jacob/Joseph* and *Solomon*

J. Alexander's credits include illustrator of adaptations of *Alice in Wonderland, Through the Looking Glass,* and *The Time Machine* for Dalmatian Press. He has completed numerous illustrations and cover paintings for Harris Comics, Image Comics, Wizards of the Coast, and White Wolf, Inc. He is the writer and artist on his comics series *Empty Zone– Starting on an Empty Pack* and *Conversations with the Dead.*

Jason's other credits include work on series such as *Queen and Country* for Oni Press and *Poison Elves* for Sirius Entertainment. He is currently working on a series of drawings and paintings for an art book and an upcoming graphic novel.

PHIL HESTER • *Cain & Abel*

Phil began working in comics while attending the University of Iowa. He graduated with a BFA in drawing with minors in Sculpture and Painting. Over the past 15 years, he has worked for nearly every comic book publisher and has had his work featured in over 300 published comics. Phil's credits include: *Swamp Thing, Detective, The Crow: Waking Nightmares, The Coffin* (writer), *The Wretch* ('96 Eisner Nominee), *The Creeper, Ultimate Marvel Team–Up, Brave Old World, Fringe, Rust, Namor, Taboo, The Picture Taker* (writer), *Attitude Lad, Deadline USA, Negative Burn, Clerks: The Lost Scene* and several others.

His current and upcoming work includes *Green Arrow, Deep Sleeper, Firebreather* and *The Operation.* Phil lives in rural Iowa with his wife and two children.

YVONNE GILBERT • *Samuel*

Yvonne was born and bred in Northumberland, England. She studied art at Newcastle College and Liverpool College of Art, where she earned her Diploma in Art and Design. A full-time lecturer for five years, Yvonne became a freelance illustrator in 1978 and has since worked for all the major British, and more recently U.S., publishers.

A talented artist, she is the sole illustrator of two books: *A Dictionary of Fairies* and *The Iron Wolf* by Richard Adams. In 1985, she won The Golden Stamp Award, and designed *"The World's Most Beautiful Stamp"* for the British Post Office.

Her work has been featured annually in the European Illustration Annual Exhibition and in many other exhibitions including those for the Scottish and Welsh Arts Council; the Bluecoat Gallery, Liverpool; Hamilton's Gallery, London; and the London Illustrators Art Gallery. Her solo exhibitions include shows at the Neville Gallery, Bath. In addition, her art is also part of the Private Collection of Mr. L.V. Seeborg of Maryland.

Yvonne works with a delicate pastel palette and she has that rare ability to capture the poignancy of childhood with a detail and charm unrivalled since the days of the early 20th century child artists. It is this unique quality that makes her art so truly outstanding.

RUDY NEBRES • *Samson*

Rudy Nebres was born in the Philippines. As a child his talent for drawing was evident and it quickly blossomed when he enrolled in a school for fine arts. Before graduation however, a local comic publication signed him on, and his artistic career was officially launched. In time, Rudy moved to ACE Publications, the largest publisher of comics in the Philippines.

In 1972, a talent scout and a lucky break helped land Rudy illustration work with DC Comics. Luck and talent continued to follow Rudy around and a year later, when Marvel came scouting they quickly put Rudy to work on their black and white line of magazines.

With his career solidly on the move, working for both Filipino and U.S. companies, Rudy immigrated to the U.S. in 1975. Soon he settled down to work on such titles as *Dr. Strange, the Incredible Hulk, King Conan,* and even *Spider-Man.* He has worked with John Buscema on *Warriors of the Shadow Realm* and *The Savage Sword of Conan.*

Rudy moved to Warren Publications during which time he received several awards for his work. Later he worked for Marvel Entertainment in Hollywood as a presentation artist on such projects as *Defenders of the Earth,* and for Continuity Studios where he penned such comics as *Armour, Samuree* and *ToyBoy.*

Rudy Nebres is currently a freelancer. He and his wife, Dolores, have two sons.

VINCE LOCKE • *Tower of Babel*

Vince Locke has worked on a wide variety of comics including *Deadworld, Sandman, A History of Violence* and *The Spectre.* He also does numerous illustrations and the occasional album cover. He lives in Michigan with his wife, Khrysta, and son, Ethan. Locke's work is prominently featured at vincelocke.com.

SERGIO ARAGONÉS • *Jonah*

Sergio Aragonés is said to be the fastest cartoonist in the world today. He is certainly the most honored, having won every major award in the field, including the National Cartoonists Society's Reuben Award and the Will Eisner Hall of Fame Award.

Born in 1937 in Castellon, Spain, Sergio and the Aragonés family relocated to Mexico during the Spanish Civil War. There, Sergio studied Architecture at the University of Mexico, and also learned pantomime under the direction of Alexandro Jodorowsky. His heart, however, was always in cartooning, a craft he discovered in the third grade, to the delight of his classmates and the annoyance of his instructors. He contributed to school newspapers and anywhere else he could get his sketches printed and, at age 17, began selling professionally to a wide array of Mexican publications. He maintained a weekly spot for over ten years in *Mañana Magazine*.

In 1962, he decided to try his luck in America, and arrived in New York with only twenty dollars and a folder bulging with his cartoon work. At first, work was slow in coming and what he did sell didn't pay very well, forcing him to work as a singer/poet in Greenwich Village restaurants and to pick up other odd jobs. Things changed when he mustered the courage to approach Mad Magazine. Embarrassed by his halting English, he went to their offices and asked for Antonio Prohias, the Cuban refugee who drew the popular *"Spy Vs. Spy"* feature. Sergio assumed that Prohias could translate for him, but he was wrong. Prohias, though thrilled to meet a fellow Hispanic cartoonist, spoke even less English than Sergio! He did, however, introduce his new "brother" about, and the Mad editors liked what they saw.

Sergio's first contribution — *"A Mad Look at the U.S. Space Effort"* — appeared in Mad #76, cover-dated January of 1963. For that same issue, he also contributed the cover gag (the first of many) and his first *"Marginal Thinking"* cartoons to be printed in the magazine's margins. He has since appeared in every issue of Mad except for one (blame the post office for the mix-up!) and has done thousands of his unique pantomime cartoons. He also produced 16 best-selling original Mad paperback books.

In the early eighties, Sergio teamed with wordsmith Mark Evanier to create the adventures of *Groo* the *Wanderer*. *Groo* quickly became one of the longest-running "creator-owned" comic book properties, outlasting many of the companies that published it. Together, Sergio and Mark have also produced other comics including *Fanboy, Boogeyman, Magnor, Blair Witch?*, and an acclaimed series in which together, they trash famous characters: *Sergio Aragonés Massacres Marvel, Sergio Aragonés Destroys DC*, and *Sergio Aragonés Stomps Star Wars*. For their comic book work, they have received multiple Eisner awards. Sergio has also "soloed" with two all-pantomime series, *Actions Speak* and *Louder Than Words*.

Sergio has also appeared as an actor-performer on television and motion pictures. His artwork has appeared on hundreds of advertisements and editorial features, and his animation has been featured on numerous TV shows, including *The Shirley MacLaine Special, The Cher Special, The Half–Hour Comedy Hour,* and *Dick Clark's TV Bloopers and Practical Jokes*.

He lives and works in Ojai, California.

SCOTT HAMPTON • *Daniel*

Scott has been working in comics since 1982. His first (and only) attempt at an ongoing series was *Silverheels* for Pacific Comics. Since then, he has contributed to many anthologies including *Epic Illustrated, Confessions of a Cereal Eater, Hellraiser, Tapping the Vein,* among others. He has painted graphic novels such as *Batman: Night Cries, The Upturned Stone,* and worked on mini-series including *Books of Magic* and *Black Widow.* He has most recently completed work on *Life Eaters,* a graphic novel for Wildstorm.

GREG SPALENKA • *Job*

Greg has been creating award-winning artwork for over twenty-one years. Since graduating with a BA from Art Center College of Design, his work has appeared in numerous publications around the world. Media such as Time, Rolling Stone, Playboy, The New Yorker, the New York Times, Washington Post, Harper Collins, Viking Putnam, PBS Television, and the San Francisco and Philadelphia Operas are a sampling of companies that have showcased his art.

Primarily a conceptual artist, Spalenka attempts to create imagery that is imbued with universal and metaphysical qualities. "I attempt to create art that affects the viewer on conceptual, visceral, and intuitive, or spiritual levels. All these qualities must be present in the art for it to feel complete or whole."

Greg teaches at several art colleges and has given workshops and lectures in the U.S. and Europe. In addition to illustration, Spalenka is involved in numerous personal book and music projects. An extensive array of his work can be viewed on spalenka.com

STEVE RUDE • *Cover Artist*

Steve, a lanky 6'5" Wisconsinite nicknamed "The Dude", considers Jack Kirby one of his biggest influences. To Kirby's streamlined dynamism, Steve has added his own style of polish and attention to detail that has made his work popular with fans. *Nexus,* an offbeat science fiction superhero, written and co-created with Mike Baron, remains his most sustained and best-known work to date.

Steve has won much industry recognition, including the Russ Manning Newcomer Award in 1983, and two Will Eisner Awards for artistic excellence. Rude is one of the hardest working artists in the field, constantly striving to improve his work. Much of his practice, model sketches, exercises, and experiments with new techniques can be found in his legendary sketchbooks. His work here often surpasses other artists' finished efforts.

Steve Rude's most recent works include *X–Men: Children of the Atom, Spiderman: Lifeline,* and *Thor: Godstorm.*

TOMMY LEE EDWARDS • *David*

Tommy Lee Edwards likes to jump around and have a hand in just about everything. He believes there is always something to learn at each place you visit--to take a piece of that place with you and carry it to the next. Tommy's goal has been to avoid being pigeonholed and he does so by adapting to the various environments in which he positions his art. A versatile artist, Tommy has tackled a myriad of genres including sci-fi, western, historical, fantasy, and horror.

Tommy's ability to generate exciting compositions while maintaining a consistency along the project's pre-existing design and actors' likenesses has launched him into licensing and has attracted such clients as Lucasfilm Ltd, Paramount Pictures, Sony, and Warner Bros. Some recent projects include artwork generated for *Star Wars, Men in Black 2,* and *Dinotopia.* Tommy's childhood passion for storytelling is being realized in his ability as a writer and illustrator of comics, a feature animation story artist, and as a visual development and character designer. The DreamWorks animated film *Sinbad* contains an eerie sequence that was storyboarded by Tommy. Books and magazines such as Star Wars Insider have showcased Tommy's art on their covers. His *Blair Witch Comic,* from Oni Press, was one of the biggest sellers the industry has seen in recent times.

After studying film and illustration at the Art Center College of Design, Tommy moved from Los Angeles to Chapel Hill, NC with his wife, Melissa, and their two children. Comic collectors may recall Melissa's work as a colorist on books like *Earth-X, Disavowed, Static Shock,* and *Zombie World.* Numerous trips between California and New York, along with Fed Ex and high-speed e-mail prove that Tommy can deliver to any client virtually anywhere in the world.

JOHN VAN FLEET • *Elijah*

Born near the Delaware Water Gap in New Jersey, John Van Fleet attended Pratt Institute of Art and Design with best friends George Pratt and Mark Chiarello. After graduation, John returned to Pratt to accept the position of Assistant Chairman of the Art and Design department where he also taught classes in illustration. John's work in comics came at the encouragement of his good friends and he has never looked back.

His accomplishments include being 2002 Will Eisner Nominee for Best Painter/Multimedia Artist. Some of John's clients include MGM Studios, Sony Pictures, Random House, Harper Press, White Wolf Publishing, Wizards of the Coast, Topps Publishing, D.C., Marvel, Wild Storm, Dark Horse Comics, Warner Brothers, Mammoth Records, Atari Games, and TDK Games. His association with these cinematography and publishing giants has led to art projects which include *Men in Black 2, The X-Files, W.B.'s Smallville, Vampire: the Masquerade, Star Wars, The Ray Bradbury Chronicles, Batman, Star Trek,* and *The Matrix.* And graphic novels such as *Shadows Fall* for Vertigo Comics, *Typhoid* for Marvel Comics, *Batman: The Chalice, The Ankh, Cast Shadows* for D.C. comics, *The X-files Movie* for Topps Publishing.

THOMPSON KNOX • *Colorist, Moses*

Although this is only his second published work in this industry, Thompson Knox has been a computer artist for almost as long as he has been reading comics. Having purchased his first Macintosh nearly ten years ago (with profits from Marvel Comics stock), he began experimenting with digital image manipulation immediately and quickly learned the tools of the design trade. Thompson's knowledge of those tools landed him in the web development business where he has worked professionally since 1996. Perhaps his grandma, an artist herself, was right about him having "a sense" when choosing a crayon with which to color...just watch him now...he's coloring Moses.

TEDDY KRISTIANSEN • *Noah, Saul*

Teddy H. Kristiansen lives and works in Denmark where he reads and draws, and draws and reads, and eats and digs in the garden. He doesn't drive a car. But his wife, Hope, can drive a car and together they sometimes drive their car with their daughters Emily, Sophia, and Lulu.

ZACH HOWARD • *Moses*

Zach Howard's first break in the graphic arts business was a backup story in *SugarBuzz #8*. His next notable job was working on a *Hellboy* short story. He has since penciled four fantastic issues of *The Clockmaker*, written by Jim Krueger. With that completed, he began work on a four-issue mini-series titled *Heaven's Devils* that will be out in the fall of 2003. He believes that his work on *Testament* is by far the best job he's ever had. Zach currently lives somewhere that he doesn't want to live and is never happy unless he is surfing. He can be reached at *www.zachhoward.com*

BEN PRENEVOST • *Colorist, Joshua, Samson, Ruth*

Ben admits that becoming a computer colorist stemmed from his love of computer graphics and comic books. Having always been strongly interested in art since he was a child, Ben one day discovered he could combine the two. For years he practiced with everything— from pencil drawings to painting to sculpture. In high school an art teacher mentored him, and helped him develop his skills as an artist. At the young age of 15, Ben was convinced that he was destined to have an art-related occupation. In his third year of high school, he was accepted into the Minnesota Center for Arts Education from which he graduated in 1995.

By the time he became interested in working in digital coloring, he already had a fairly good understanding of form, light, and color. After learning the software and techniques, Ben practiced coloring over his own drawings, and later moved on to practicing over professional art. In January 1998 he landed his first professional coloring job with Lightning Comics. Since then, Ben has been working professionally in the field.

MARIO RUIZ • *Ruth*

Mario Ruiz has spent more than 16 years in the field of graphic arts and design. His first published work, *Samson: Judge of Israel,* has garnered critical acclaim and acceptance in the comic book community. *Testament* will mark his second published work. Mario has done work in the past for Marvel Comics, 20th Century Fox, and several advertising agencies throughout New York City. He is currently active as editorial and creative director (and 400 lb gorilla) for Metron Press.

GEORGE PRATT • *Abraham*

George Pratt, a native of Beaumont, Texas, moved to New York City in 1980 to study drawing and painting at Pratt Institute, where, in later years, he taught Methods and Media, as well as Storytelling. He also taught at the Joe Kubert School in Dover, NJ, at the School for Visual Arts in the Master Illustration program, and did a stint as Visiting Professor at Savannah College of Art and Design. A successful painter, his work graces private collections throughout the world, and has been exhibited in the Houston Museum of Fine Art.

George's first novel, *Enemy Ace: War Idyll* (DC Comics/Warner Books), is in its fourth printing in the U.S., has been translated into nine languages, and was on the required reading list at West Point Military Academy. The book was nominated for both the Eisner and Harvey Awards for Best Graphic Novel. In Europe, it won the prestigious France Info Award for Best Foreign Graphic Novel, and it captured the Speakeasy Award for Best Foreign Graphic Novel in England.

George's credits lists numerous accomplishments such as *No Man's Land*, another retrospective on war, published by Tundra, which highlights sketches, monotypes and paintings. The work has been on exhibition throughout the U.S., Canada, and Europe. He has also written and fully painted *Harvest Breed*, a Batman graphic novel for DC Comics/Warner Brothers. The book was nominated for two Eisner Awards: Best Graphic Novel and Best Painter. In addition, George has written and painted *Wolverine: Netsuke*, a four-issue mini-series for Marvel Comics that was nominated for the Best Mini-Series Award by Wizard Magazine.

He has collaborated with Steven Budlong and James McGillion to complete *See You In Hell, Blind Boy*, a documentary film about his travels through the Mississippi Delta researching his blues novel of the same name. The film won Best Feature Documentary at the New York International Independent Film Festival, and was accepted and shown at the Santa Barbara, Nashville, and Hot Springs Film Festivals.

George continues to illustrate and design books and book jackets for various publishers, including Random House, Henry Holt, Inc., Warner Books, Clarion Books, and Columbia Studios.